THE UNITED STATES AND LATIN AMERICA

Providing a concise, balanced and incisive analysis of US diplomatic relations with Latin America from 1776 to the end of the twentieth century, this timely work explores central themes such as the structure of diplomatic relations in the western hemisphere, and the pursuit of American national interest by the use of diplomacy, cultural imperialism and economic and military power.

Joseph Smith examines the rise of the US as an independent power and its policy towards Latin American movements for independence. In addition, issues such as the evolution of the Monroe Doctrine, Pan-Americanism, dollar diplomacy and the challenge of communism are explored. Highlighting Latin American responses to US policy over a significant time span, this study documents the development of a complex historical relationship in which the United States has claimed a pre-eminent role, arousing as much resentment as acquiescence from its southern neighbours.

Including a discussion of the current issues of debt, trade and narcotics control, this unique and valuable study will be of significance to all those with an interest in US and Latin American international relations.

Joseph Smith is Reader in American Diplomatic History at the University of Exeter and has previously taught at the College of William and Mary and the University of Colorado at Denver. He is the author of *A History of Brazil, 1500–2000* (2002).

INTERNATIONAL RELATIONS AND HISTORY
Series Editor Jeremy Black
Professor of History, University of Exeter

THE EMERGENCE OF THE GLOBAL POLITICAL ECONOMY
William Thompson

DEMOCRACY AND PEACE MAKING
Philip Towle

THE UNITED STATES AND LATIN AMERICA
Joseph Smith

To Michael [illegible]
with best wishes
Joe

THE UNITED STATES AND LATIN AMERICA

A history of American diplomacy, 1776–2000

Joseph Smith

LONDON AND NEW YORK

First published 2005
by Routledge
2 Park Square, Milton Park, Abingdon, Oxon OX14 4RN

Simultaneously published in the USA and Canada
by Routledge
270 Madison Ave, New York, NY 10016

Routledge is an imprint of the Taylor & Francis Group

Typeset in Galliard by Florence Production Ltd, Stoodleigh, Devon
Printed and bound in Great Britain by
The Cromwell Press, Trowbridge, Wiltshire

British Library Cataloguing in Publication Data
A catalogue record for this book is available from the British Library

Library of Congress Cataloging in Publication Data
A catalogue record for this title has been requested

ISBN 0–415–35834–5 (hbk)
ISBN 0–415–35835–3 (pbk)

CONTENTS

ACKNOWLEDGEMENTS

I wish to thank Tom Leonard and Kyle Longley for inviting me to participate in a series of conferences on inter-American diplomatic relations that were held during the 1990s. These very pleasant and informative occasions reaffirmed for me the importance of studying and writing about this topic. I was therefore delighted when my colleague, Jeremy Black, gave me the opportunity to prepare both an interpretive study and also what I hope will be an accessible text for students. The completion of the writing owes much to a Research Leave Award from the Arts and Humanities Research Board that gave me a vital period of release from teaching duties at Exeter. As always, however, my greatest personal debt is to Rachael for her encouragement and support without which I would never have successfully finished the project.

Exeter, November 2004.

CANADA
UNITED STATES
MEXICO
CUBA
DOM. REP.
JAMAICA
PUERTO RICO
HAITI
BELIZE
HONDURAS
GUATEMALA
EL SALVADOR
NICARAGUA
GRENADA
COSTA RICA
PANAMA
VENEZUELA
GUYANA
SURINAME
FRENCH GUIANA
COLOMBIA
ECUADOR
PERU
BRAZIL
BOLIVIA
PARAGUAY
CHILE
ARGENTINA
URUGUAY
FALKLAND ISLANDS

1

INDEPENDENCE (1776–1830)

Distant colonial neighbours

After the celebrated voyage of discovery by Christopher Columbus in 1492 European monarchs proceeded to conquer and exploit the territory, resources and native peoples of the 'New World' that made up the Western Hemisphere or Americas. In the process colonial empires were established characterized by hierarchical systems in which Europeans and 'creoles' (white Europeans born in the New World) exercised political, economic, social and cultural authority over the native peoples and Africans who were imported as slave labour. The largest empire belonged to the king of Spain and was initially divided into two separate viceroyalties. Its local centres of administrative power and wealth lay in Mexico City, capital of the Viceroyalty of New Spain, and Lima, capital of the Viceroyalty of Peru. The borders of the Spanish-American empire were extensive and ultimately reached as far north as the Pacific Northwest and as far south as Cape Horn. Possession of the vast territory of Brazil that lay in South America was claimed by the king of Portugal. The main settlement of the English (British) was the relatively smaller but much more compact geographical area that eventually developed into the Thirteen North American Colonies stretching from New England in the north to Georgia in the south. In contrast to the Spanish-American empire, the British colonies notably lacked large populations of native peoples.[1]

While geography gave the various British, Spanish and Portuguese colonial possessions a common location in the Western Hemisphere, a sense of unity and common history was lacking because geographical factors also meant that relations were not close during the colonial period that lasted from the sixteenth century to the close of the eighteenth century. With the exception of the islands of the Caribbean, the respective colonial empires were separated both by large distances and very poor communications by sea and overland. An additional barrier was the influence of the dynastic rivalries of Europe, which meant that political and commercial relations – especially between the North American colonies and the Spanish and

Portuguese empires – were generally marked by hostility rather than by friendship and cooperation. Furthermore, the North American colonists mainly came from the countries of Western and Northern Europe and regarded themselves as very different from the people of the Mediterranean countries in terms of race, culture and history. They inherited and shared the traditional attitudes of Great Britain, their principal country of origin, in being particularly suspicious and contemptuous of people of Latin descent in general and Spaniards in particular. The Spanish crown was especially reviled as a degenerate institution and inveterate enemy of political freedom and humanitarian values.[2]

Spanish colonists reciprocated by showing dislike and distrust of the Anglo-Saxon and 'Yankee' (Yanqui) settlers in the North American colonies. They were similarly strongly influenced by stereotypical views that linked the North Americans with the infamous exploits of John Hawkins, Francis Drake and Henry Morgan, ruthless English pirates and buccaneers who had plundered merchant shipping and terrorized peaceful communities. In addition, antagonism was fuelled by religious differences because many of the North American colonists were zealous Protestants who had been imbued with the memory of the notorious 'Spanish fury' or 'Black Legend' in which Spaniards were held responsible for the vicious persecution and death of thousands of civilians, including women and children, in the Netherlands in the sixteenth century. In the Spanish and Portuguese empires Catholicism was the official religion, and there was little sympathy or toleration for Protestants who were condemned as heretics.

Mutual distrust and negative images were further reinforced by lack of travel and physical contact. Moreover, there was the barrier of different languages. Few works written in English were translated into Spanish and vice versa so that even the educated elites were remarkably ill informed about each other.[3] Social contact and collaboration were promoted to an extent by mutual economic interests, which were reflected in the development of trade between North American merchants who catered to the needs of the Spanish settlers in the Caribbean islands for such items as fish, grain, tobacco, slaves and the re-export of British goods. During the colonial period, however, trade was adversely affected by the restrictive policy of mercantilism pursued by all the European powers. This policy sought to establish a closed market in which complete control would be exercised over colonial commerce, both imports and exports, with the aim of enriching and achieving economic self-sufficiency for the imperial metropolis located in Europe. However, the enforcement of mercantilism was often lax in the Spanish and Portuguese empires. Consequently, smuggling was widespread and often condoned by local customs officials because Spain and Portugal were unable to provide many of the goods that the colonists both wanted and needed. By default, they turned to British and North American suppliers.[4]

Formation of the United States

From 1774 to 1783 the American Revolution occurred, in which the North American colonies successfully fought for and won their independence from Great Britain. Not only was rebellion justified but the basis of what would become the American democratic mission was affirmed in the Declaration of Independence on 4 July 1776: 'We hold these truths to be self-evident, that all men are created equal, that they are endowed by their Creator with certain unalienable Rights, that among these are Life, Liberty and the pursuit of Happiness.'[5] The result was the creation of the United States (US) of America that formally came into existence in 1787 as the first sovereign independent state in the Western Hemisphere. The emergence of the new nation was not an isolated incident, but was a direct consequence of the prevailing system of international relations based on European great power politics. In fact, both France and Spain gave significant military, financial and diplomatic support to the American colonists in their struggle for independence. The principal motive of those governments was not to promote American political freedom but the selfish one of undermining Britain, their great European rival, and to regain colonial territory lost during the Seven Years' War (1756–63). 'Spain has no other objective than to recover the shameful usurpations of Gibraltar and Minorca', commented the Spanish minister of state, the count of Floridablanca.[6] In the view of the French foreign minister, the count of Vergennes, the tempting opportunity to swing the balance of power in France's favour could not be ignored. While Vergennes believed that 'the American insurgents are friends for years to come',[7] he was aware of the danger that American revolutionary ideas of republicanism and anti-colonialism posed to the existing monarchical systems of Europe. In effect, they were a direct challenge to the claim of European kings to exercise the right of imperial rule over overseas territories. Nevertheless, France and Spain readily acquiesced in granting diplomatic recognition to the new republic of the United States of America. The rivalries of the 'Old World' as expressed in the selfish calculations of Europe's statesmen therefore directly assisted and facilitated the creation of the United States. While they looked askance at a political system that, in their opinion, would lead inevitably to anarchy and mob rule, the crowned heads of Europe recognized the new republic as a sovereign nation that merited the establishment of formal diplomatic relations.

The diplomatic activity of the new American republic was concentrated upon the Atlantic world whose centre of power lay in Western Europe. Its political leaders wanted friendly relations with the European powers, but they were determined to be seen to be acting differently from Europeans in their conduct of foreign policy. This was based upon a distinctive revolutionary ideology that stressed inherent American virtue and moral superiority and equated European diplomatic practice with the elitist and repressive political systems of the Old World. In addition, the new nation consciously sought to preserve its independence of action and to distance itself from what was feared would be damaging entanglements with the European powers. 'Our detached and distant situation invites and enables us to pursue a different course', remarked President George Washington in his celebrated 'Farewell Address' in September 1796.[8] But avoidance of possible entanglements did not mean complete isolation from foreign affairs. On the one hand, there was the constant requirement to consider the question of national security that was expressed in the concern to provide for defence against possible European encroachment. Fortunately, a major British military effort to regain its former colonial possessions was not considered likely. A more tangible threat was associated with Spain whose own imperial possessions bordered the new republic to the south and west. American national security policy, however, was as much offensive as defensive. Contrary to fashionable European ideas that a 'true' republic should be limited in its geographical area, a rationale for territorial expansionism was put forward by James Madison of Virginia which argued that republican government would best survive and thrive in large rather than small areas. The intention was not only to maintain existing national borders but to look for opportunities to enlarge them by expanding into Canada in the north and by seizing control of the important port of New Orleans and the region bordering the Gulf of Mexico to the south. Noting with dismay the rapidly growing American population and its hunger for acquiring land, the Spanish minister, Carlos Martínez de Irujo, warned his government in 1802 of 'the ominous movement of the people of the United States'.[9] In this sense, the new American republic sought to continue the imperialistic policy of Great Britain in pursuing territorial expansion by means of securing access to land, natural resources and, where necessary, the absorption without their consent, removal or even elimination of native peoples who resided in these areas. Right from the beginning of its national history, the United States, therefore, chose to become an active participant in the long-standing battle among the great European powers to acquire territory with the aim of gaining a pre-eminent political, commercial and military influence in the Western Hemisphere.

A propensity for expansion was also expressed in the American desire to trade overseas and to spread liberal commercial ideas. This brought increased contact with the Spanish-American colonies and especially the Caribbean islands because they were the closest market in geographical terms. Even during the period of the struggle to win independence from Great Britain, the Continental Congress in 1781 had sent Robert Smith as a special agent to Havana, Cuba, with the purpose of promoting trade. The attempt to expand commerce, however, was hampered by the determination of Spain to maintain the policy of mercantilism that traditionally sought to prevent foreigners from trading with its American empire. In this respect, control over the Mississippi River and its tributaries was a crucial consideration. Spain had reasserted its administrative authority in the Mississippi region during the American Revolution and in 1784 closed the river to free navigation by American ships. In 1797, however, financial costs arising from the French Revolutionary Wars, the difficulty of sending merchant ships across the Atlantic in time of war and the consequent increase in smuggling activities resulted in Spain relaxing its commercial restrictions and opening its colonial ports to neutral shipping. American merchants were well placed to take advantage. The US government also responded by establishing consular agencies in New Orleans and Havana. Additional agencies followed in Santiago de Cuba in 1798 and La Guaira, Venezuela, in 1800. Although American agents were not given official diplomatic recognition by the Spanish government, their presence and commercial activities were tolerated, if not encouraged, by local officials.

The success of the American Revolution and the subsequent creation of the American republic was a development of enormous significance for the history of the Western Hemisphere, but its impact on contemporary Latin Americans was muted because popular awareness of the event was extremely limited. The mass of people in both the Spanish-American and Portuguese empires were illiterate and ignorant of political developments beyond their immediate locality. The educated elites who dominated the government and economy had access to foreign news, but they were generally unsympathetic to ideas of political freedom and republicanism that were invariably associated with social disorder and the dreaded contingency of slave uprising. As a result they were loyal to the crown and regarded royal authority as a necessary if not essential bastion of order and privilege. On the other hand, the success of the North American colonists in winning independence and, especially, the fact that the United States subsequently remained in existence as a living example of freedom and republicanism were noted in Latin America as achievements that could not be ignored. The texts of the 1776 Declaration of Independence and the American Constitution were translated and appeared in Spanish newspapers that were later brought to Latin America. The works of Thomas Paine were also published in Spanish and particular attention was paid to his justification of colonial insurgency in *Common Sense*. Some Latin American liberals such as the Venezuelan revolutionary, Francisco de Miranda, actually visited the United States. Miranda travelled extensively from Boston to Charleston and met with several prominent revolutionary leaders, including George Washington and Alexander Hamilton. But his stay in 1783–4 was only temporary because he was en route to London. Indeed, the culture and politics of Europe continued to dominate the Latin American educated elite. For those liberals who embraced the new radical political ideas, it was the Enlightenment, especially the writings of the French *philosophes* such as Voltaire and Montesquieu and British political theorists such as John Locke and Jeremy

Bentham, and also the course of the French Revolution that were regarded as more fascinating and relevant than developments in the United States.

Outbreak of the Wars for Latin American Independence

From its inception the government of the new United States found itself constrained in its efforts to make diplomatic and commercial contact with neighbouring countries in the Western Hemisphere. A few unofficial commercial agents were appointed to serve overseas, but in dealing with affairs affecting the colonies, diplomatic relations were properly directed via the respective European capitals in Madrid, Lisbon or London, where American diplomats were in official residence. In fact, as Washington had indicated in his 'Farewell Address', the people of the new American republic were preoccupied with their own domestic affairs. When it came to diplomacy their attention was mostly directed to developments in Europe arising from the French Revolution in 1789 and the subsequent wars that visibly affected their own territorial boundaries and commercial prosperity. Prominent American politicians such as Thomas Jefferson and James Monroe had personal experience of living in France. By contrast, very little was known about Spanish America and Brazil. Events taking place in those distant countries were of marginal importance. However, the outbreak of the Wars for Independence from 1808 onwards brought Latin American affairs to the notice of the people of the United States. In effect, this represented a virtual 'discovery' by Americans of their southern neighbours.

In 1808 the French emperor, Napoleon Bonaparte, compelled the abdication of the Spanish ruling family and unilaterally declared his brother, Joseph, as the new king of Spain. The action provoked protest and insurgency in Spain that spread to the empire where the resulting questioning of Spanish local authority stimulated movements led by creoles for outright economic and political independence. The outbreak of insurgency in Spanish America occurred at a time when, following the precepts of George Washington and Thomas Jefferson, the United States was in the process of establishing the diplomatic tradition of 'no entangling alliances' and avoidance of involvement in the dynastic affairs of the Old World. At first sight, however, the revolutionary developments to the south appeared to justify a policy of active and supportive diplomatic intervention. American political leaders harboured a traditional dislike of Spain. Moreover, the insurgents were fighting to secure political freedom from oppressive European monarchical rule and were evidently pursuing the same struggle that the American colonists had conducted only a few decades earlier. Indeed, the mutual bonds of geographical proximity and the promotion of republican ideology were apparent to President Thomas Jefferson as soon as he heard of the rumours of political revolt in Mexico and Cuba in 1808. In a private letter written in October 1808 he described the insurgents as 'patriots' and added: 'We consider their interests and ours as the same, and that the object of both must be to exclude all European influence from this hemisphere.'[10] In December 1811 the US Congress passed a 'public declaration' supportive of the insurgents stating 'that they behold with friendly interest the establishment of independence by the Spanish-American provinces; that, as neighbors and inhabitants of the same hemisphere, the United States feel great solicitude for their welfare'.[11] After being kept so far apart during the colonial period, the congressional declaration was significant in expressing the view of American political leaders that the United States definitely shared a common hemispheric political interest and affinity with the people of Spanish America.

American sympathies were reflected in practical terms by agents of the Spanish-American insurgents being allowed to purchase ships and supplies, including munitions, in the United States and to have access to American ports such as Baltimore and New Orleans for use as bases for privateering operations against Spanish shipping. A few Americans even volunteered for service in the insurgent armies and navies. But these were actions sponsored and undertaken by private individuals and companies. The United States was not at war with Spain so the official policy of the federal government was neutrality. Consequently, the presidential administrations of Thomas Jefferson (1801–9), James Madison (1809–17) and James Monroe (1817–25) all stressed their desire to maintain peaceful and friendly relations with Spain. In 1823 Monroe's secretary of state, John Quincy Adams, summed up the position by saying that the United States had 'considered the struggle of the colonies for independence as a case of civil war, to which their national obligations prescribed to them to remain neutral'.[12] Although the United States intended to observe rather than make events, neutrality did not mean absolute impartiality. Indeed, Adams claimed that the United States significantly differed from the European powers in this respect. As he explained in June 1819: 'The course of policy pursued by the European Governments and by the United States on this subject has been that of neutrality. But Europe has been neutral with a leaning of inclination on the side of authority and Spain, while the United States have been neutral, with a leaning of inclination on the side of liberty and South America.'[13]

Considerations of European power politics were uppermost in the minds of American diplomats in formulating policy towards the Latin American movements for independence. Neutrality was not only regarded as the correct legal policy for the United States to adopt but it was also sensible on account of the risk that any overt intervention on the side of the insurgents could be interpreted by Spain as a deliberate challenge to its authority and, therefore, grounds for war. Such a conflict could be very much to America's military disadvantage because European powers might be provoked into helping Spain. In this respect, the intentions of Great Britain were a particular concern. The United States had been at war with Great Britain from 1812 to 1814 and resentment still lingered. While serving as American minister to Great Britain, John Quincy Adams wrote from London in 1816: 'If the United States were openly to join the cause of South America, and consequently be engaged in a war with Spain the British people would immediately consider [the United States] as the principals in the contest, all their jealousies and national antipathies would be enlisted against the common American cause' and Great Britain would join war on the side of Spain 'merely because the United States would be on the other side'.[14] In addition, a war with Spain also posed the likely prospect of America being confronted by a combined European military threat without allies. Despite these considerations, however, the United States did not remain completely detached from events. This was reflected in the 1811 No-Transfer Resolution that clearly indicated American ambitions to expand territorially and also provided a precursor to the Monroe Doctrine. Fearing that Britain might exploit Spain's weakness and opportunistically gain possession of Spanish Florida, Secretary of State James Monroe requested Congress to pass a secret resolution in January 1811 stating that 'the United States . . . cannot, without serious inquietude, see any part of the said territory [Florida] pass into the hands of any foreign power'.[15] The executive was authorized to use military force, if necessary, to prevent such a transfer from taking place.

The policy of neutrality was also justified so long as America's national security was not directly affected by the fighting taking place in Mexico or South America. In fact, the actual hostilities did not directly impinge upon the United States so that there was neither need nor requirement to build up land defences or mount naval patrols to defend the coastline against external attack. Nor was there a compelling economic reason to go to war. Indeed, entering into hostilities with Spain would immediately curtail American trade with the colonies that were still under Spanish control. Moreover, American merchants were also able to trade with those countries where the insurgents had established governments. In 1811 Joel Roberts Poinsett of South Carolina was appointed as special agent of the United States to South America. Poinsett was to proceed to Buenos Aires and was given instructions by the state department 'to diffuse the impression that the United States cherish the sincerest good will towards the people of Spanish America as neighbors, as belonging to the same portion of the globe, and as having a mutual interest in cultivating friendly intercourse'. Secretary of State Robert Smith was more specific in his statement that: 'The real as well as ostensible object of your mission is to explain the mutual advantages of commerce with the United States, to promote liberal and stable relations, and to transmit seasonable information on the subject.'[16]

A definite desire existed to seize commercial opportunities and win markets in Latin America, but it was moderated by the fact that American merchants were historically more accustomed and predisposed to trading with Europe. During the first two decades of the nineteenth century trade with the Spanish-American colonies was never more than 10 to 12 per cent of total American trade. Europe and not Spanish America continued to provide the main market for American agricultural exports. Particularly important was the grain trade with Spain, which increased six-fold from 1807 to 1811. Indeed, American commercial policy was closely linked to political developments in Europe as exemplified by the decisions to introduce the 1807 Embargo on external trade and to go to war against Britain in 1812. In fact, these events highlighted the importance accorded to trade with Europe and shifted American attention away from Latin American affairs. This was evident to the agent of Buenos Aires, Manuel H. de Aguirre, who visited the United States in July 1817. He believed that the Monroe Administration was more interested in its commercial relations with Europe than with Spanish America. American officials showed little sympathy for or desire to aid the Latin American movements for independence. 'I believe', he reported, 'that if they do anything in our favor even indirectly it will be for the purpose of enriching their merchants.'[17]

An element of diplomatic caution was also necessary on account of the lack of accurate information in the United States about what exactly was happening in distant Latin America. The nature and course of rebellion varied greatly in a vast region extending from Mexico to the River Plate. Furthermore, news was frequently ambiguous, contradictory and out of date. The regular and principal source of information came in the form of newspapers and journals from Madrid and was heavily influenced by Spanish censorship, which invariably led to reports that elevated the successes of the Spanish army and belittled the activities of the insurgents. In fact, from 1814 to 1818 it appeared that the insurgents had lost the military battle and were in a state of desperation. Furthermore, despite allusions to hemispheric mutual interest and affinity, historically entrenched attitudes continued to play their part so that American sympathy for the insurgents was frequently tempered with cynicism and prejudice. The rise of political revolt in the colonies merely confirmed the traditional perception of the inherent instability and backwardness of those people and places. Jefferson believed that the insurgents were motivated by patriotism and would win independence, but he despaired about the likely results. 'History, I believe,' he noted in 1813, 'furnishes no example of a priest-ridden people maintaining a free civil government.'[18] Congressman John Randolph of Virginia drew parallels with the violence and political excesses of the French Revolution when he stated in 1816: 'The struggle for liberty in South America will turn out in the end something like the French liberty, a detestable despotism.'[19] The editor of the influential *North American Review*, Edward Everett, highlighted the acute and long-standing differences between the two societies when he argued against American diplomatic recognition of the insurgents in 1821:

> We have no concern with South America; we have no sympathy with them. We are sprung from different stocks, we speak different languages, we have been brought up in different social and moral schools, we have been governed by different codes of law, we profess radically different codes of religion. . . . Not all the treaties we could make, nor the commissioners we could send out, nor the money we could lend them, would transform their Pueyrredons and their Artigases into Adamses or Franklins, or their Bolivars into Washingtons.[20]

In fact, the policy of neutrality advanced American national self-interest because it brought a number of material benefits. Just as in the American Revolution, the United States once again benefited from European rivalry and the great powers fighting among themselves. For example, Spain relaxed the policy of mercantilism in 1797 and by opening colonial ports to trade with neutrals thereby provided increased commercial opportunities for American merchants. The desperate need of the European powers for money to finance the war persuaded the French ruler, Napoleon Bonaparte, to sell the Louisiana Territory to the United States in 1803. The territory, consisting of 827,000 acres, cost $15 million or 3.5 cents per acre and, notably, included the important and strategically located port of New Orleans. The same financial necessity also prompted Spain to consider the sale of Spanish Florida and consequently to offer an opportunity for the United States to acquire long disputed borderland territory. The upsurge in the movements for independence further weakened Spain's bargaining position during the complex negotiations that started in 1817 and eventually resulted in the conclusion of the Adams–Onís Treaty or Transcontinental Treaty on 22 February 1819. The implementation of the treaty was delayed by Spanish failure to ratify. This ratification was finally secured on 14 February 1821. The treaty represented a great personal success for Adams, whose diplomacy was instrumental in gaining half a continent for his nation. In the treaty Spain ceded Florida to the United States and also recognized the 42nd parallel (the border between Oregon and California) as dividing the two countries in the west. The drawing of the boundary on the Pacific coast was significant in indicating that the United States was for the first time officially recognized as a transcontinental nation.[21]

The negotiation and protracted ratification of the Adams–Onís Treaty occurred at a time when the insurgent armies commanded by the two 'Liberators', Simón Bolívar from Venezuela and José de San Martín from Argentina, were making significant military progress in South America, and the case for diplomatic recognition of the insurgent governments was becoming more substantial. The desire to conclude the Adams–Onís Treaty, however, was an influential reason for a continuation of the policy of American neutrality in that, until formal ratification was finally secured in 1821, the United States delayed recognizing the independence of the new republics. This apparently self-serving approach was noticed and caused resentment in South America. After 'ten years of struggle and travail that beggar description', Bolívar complained in December 1819 that Americans had been just like Europeans in showing 'indifference' and remaining 'but passive spectators of our anguish'.[22] It was even suspected that the policy of American neutrality was tinged with bias in favour of Spain. On news of the signing of the Adams–Onís Treaty in 1819, Consul William G. Miller wrote from Buenos Aires:

> We are no longer looked up to [by the people of Buenos Aires] as Americans, the protectors of liberty and the supporters of the independence and of the cause of our South American brothers, but rather as neutrals determined to assist Spain in the reconquest of the country.[23]

Latin American attitudes towards the United States were greatly influenced by the fact that, in terms of their educational and cultural background, the creoles who led the Spanish-American movements for independence were mostly concerned with events occurring in France and Spain. When they sought external support, they looked not to the United States but primarily to Great Britain, the world's leading financial, commercial and maritime power. While many of the insurgent leaders wanted to overthrow Spanish monarchical rule, they were also politically conservative and were concerned over the influence of revolutionary ideas on the masses. A particular cause of anxiety for landowners and slave-holders was the prospect of social upheaval and racial violence as exemplified by the revolts of free blacks and slaves that had occurred in the French colony of Haiti during the 1790s. Led and inspired by Toussaint Louverture and Jean-Jacques Dessalines, the Haitian Revolution had resulted in the creation of an independent republic in 1804, the second independent state to be established in the New World. Notably, the 1804 Haitian Constitution gave citizenship and freedom to black men. In imitation of Napoleon, Dessalines declared himself emperor of Haiti. The United States, however, joined with the European powers in refusing to grant recognition to a nation ruled by a race of people that were regarded as inferior. Their perception of Haiti as barbarous and violent appeared to be confirmed by the assassination of Dessalines in 1806.

The innate conservatism of the Spanish-American creoles was also reflected in the fact that they did not automatically share either the American aversion to the principle of monarchy or the commitment to promote republicanism. 'The idea that all America must be republican, since all

Europe is royalist, has taken root [in the United States]', warned the Brazilian diplomat José Silvestre Rebello in June 1824.[24] By contrast, the Latin American elites possessed a predisposition to favour centralized authority and showed ambivalence to the concept of American federalism. The political achievements of the United States were admired, but they were regarded as unique if not alien. For example, Bolívar told the British minister that he regarded the United States and its people as very different from those of South America:

> The United States, therefore, formed a solitary instance in the page of history of a nation uniting and establishing at once, without anarchy and on a just and solid basis, a Federative League and Government. In South America, on the other hand, the inhabitants had [. . .] but just emerged out of a state of slavery; to expect wisdom, good order and honesty from such materials was an absurdity, and power consequently too suddenly placed in such hands would probably be abused.[25]

The question of ending the period of neutrality and switching to a policy of selective diplomatic recognition became more pressing for the United States after the United Provinces of the Rio de La Plata declared their independence in December 1816, an action that was followed by San Martín's military victories over loyalist forces in 1817 in Chile. President Monroe responded by suggesting the possibility of granting recognition to the United Provinces of the Rio de la Plata. It was decided, however, to wait and seek more definite information about the stability of the insurgent governments. In July 1817 a special commission consisting of Caesar Rodney, John Graham and Judge Theodorick Bland, was appointed 'to obtain, in a manner more comprehensive than has heretofore been done, correct information of the actual state of affairs in those colonies'.[26] The commissioners left Hampton Roads on 4 December 1817 and proceeded to visit Rio de Janeiro, Montevideo and Buenos Aires. Bland went on to Chile. The commission reported to the president in November 1818.

Monroe's policy was influenced by domestic political factors because the appointment of the commissioners was also a response to the lobbying activities in the US Congress by supporters of the insurgents. Congress exerted further political pressure on the Monroe Administration when the Speaker of the House, Henry Clay of Kentucky, advocated diplomatic recognition as a way of confirming the existence of an 'American system' based upon republicanism and clearly separate both politically and geographically from that of Europe. In 1818 Clay said:

> There can not be a doubt that Spanish America, once independent, whatever may be the form of the governments established

> in its several parts, these governments will be animated by an American feeling, and guided by an American policy. They will obey the laws of the system of the New World, of which they will compose a part, in contradistinction to that of Europe.[27]

Unfortunately for Clay, his eloquent advocacy of an all embracing 'Pan American' political system was too ambitious and visionary. Moreover, it received little support from the reports of the commissioners that were used by the Monroe Administration to deny recognition on the grounds that such action was premature. In his report on the Rio de la Plata, Bland ruled out the chances of any Spanish reconquest, but the rise of local military chiefs to prominent political positions made him pessimistic about the future:

> unless the present civil dissensions are healed, and the warring provinces are pacified and reconciled with each other, a very great proportion, if not all, the benefits and advantages of the revolution . . . will be totally destroyed, or, at least, very much diminished and delayed.[28]

A similar example of ethnocentric thinking was revealed by Secretary of State John Quincy Adams who rejected popular analogies linking the achievements in Spanish America with those of the American Revolution. He commented scathingly on the character of the new governments in March 1821:

> They are not likely to promote the spirit of freedom or order by their example. They have not the first elements of good or free government. Arbitrary power, military and ecclesiastical, was stamped upon their education, upon their habits, and upon all their institutions . . . I had little expectation of any beneficial result to this country from any future connection with them, political or commercial.[29]

Recognition of Latin American independence by the United States

In 1821 the Adams–Onís Treaty was finally ratified by the Spanish government. In that year it also became evident that the momentum of military success was definitely in favour of the Spanish-American insurgents. Reports of a decisive military victory by Bolívar over Spanish forces at Carabobo in Venezuela and San Martín's unopposed entry into Lima, the crucial Spanish centre of power in South America, provided the impetus for the House of Representatives to pass a resolution proposed by Henry Clay which declared that 'it was ready to support the President whenever he should think it expedient to recognize their governments'.[30] Shortly afterwards, news was received that Mexico and Central America had effectively become independent nations. In 1822 they were joined by Brazil and Gran Colombia, the new state created by Bolívar that comprised Venezuela, Colombia and Ecuador. Events had finally taken their course and Spain's control over its colonies appeared to be definitely at an end. 'It is manifest', Monroe told the House of Representatives on 8 March 1822, 'that all those provinces are not only in the full enjoyment of their independence, but, considering the state of the war and other circumstances, that there is not the most remote prospect of their being deprived of it.'[31] The president requested that Congress vote an appropriation to pay for the expenses involved in a policy of formal diplomatic recognition. An affirmative vote was soon forthcoming from the House of Representatives.

Despite Monroe's resounding rhetoric, the policy of establishing diplomatic relations was implemented cautiously in piecemeal fashion. The first official act in which the United States conferred diplomatic recognition on the new governments took place on 19 June 1822 when John Quincy Adams presented Manuel Torres to President Monroe as chargé d'affaires from the Republic of Colombia. Torres was chosen because he had been resident in the United States since 1797 and was the only accredited Latin American diplomat currently in Washington. On 12 December 1822, shortly after his arrival in the United States, José Manuel Zozaya was received by Monroe as minister of the Mexican Empire. On 26 May 1824 José Silvestre Rebello was similarly received as representing the Empire of Brazil. By the end of his administration in 1825, President Monroe had recognized the independence of Mexico, the Federation of the Provinces of Central America, Gran Colombia (comprising Venezuela, Colombia and Ecuador), Chile, the United Provinces of the River Plate (Argentina) and Brazil.

An interesting feature of Monroe's decision to grant diplomatic recognition was its unilateral aspect. Despite the fact that it was a relatively 'new' nation, the US government acted confidently and showed that it did feel the need to have close consultation or prior discussion with the great European powers. Furthermore, the United States was, notably, the first outside power to accord official diplomatic recognition to the Latin American states in 1822. It was not until 1825 that Great Britain signed treaties with the United Provinces of the River Plate and Gran Colombia. Indeed, the timing of American action ahead of that by the British was both politically and commercially motivated in that the United States hoped to gain special advantages in the new states. In addition, there was a desire to support and promote the spread of liberty and republicanism even though both Mexico and Brazil were still monarchies when recognition was first conferred. No doubt the move to recognize also reflected a realistic if belated confirmation of insurgent military victories. On the other hand, caution combined with consideration of American national self-interest remained in evidence in the decision not to recognize any change in the governments of Peru or Cuba so long as Spanish forces in those colonies remained undefeated.

The acts of recognition were phased over several months and illustrated an overly proper if somewhat dilatory diplomatic approach on both sides. While the leaders of the new Latin American states were pleased to receive American recognition, they were slow to send ministers to represent their interests in the United States. The appointment by the US government of diplomatic officials to serve overseas was similarly dragged out. Indeed, the first American ministers were not formally appointed until January 1823. Eventually Richard Anderson was sent to Colombia, Caesar Rodney to Buenos Aires and Heman Allen to Chile. Joel Poinsett was later appointed to Mexico. The delay was due to the fact that the Monroe Administration was preoccupied with more urgent domestic political issues relating to the 1824 presidential election. There was also a desire to proceed with caution so as not to provoke the hostility of the European powers, because the sending of American ministers to the new governments also represented a decision to withdraw recognition of Spain's claim that it continued to exercise legitimate authority over its colonial possessions.

Monroe Doctrine

By 1823 Spanish control over its American empire appeared to be on the brink of dissolution, but assistance for Spain suddenly appeared in the form of the Holy Alliance of Russia, France, Austria and Prussia, an organization of European rulers whose declared aim was to reverse the damage inflicted by the French Revolution and restore legitimate monarchs to their rightful positions of authority. French troops had already achieved this for King Ferdinand VII in Spain in 1822–3 and were judged capable of performing a similar task in Latin America where it was believed that the new states were politically unstable and militarily weak. However, the Holy Alliance faced the opposition of Great Britain whose government was especially alarmed at the prospect of an increase in French political and commercial influence and, most of all, the possible establishment of a French colony in the Americas. The British foreign minister, George Canning, proposed a joint Anglo-American protest to prevent military intervention by France.

The prospect of military interference by the Holy Alliance in the New World was indeed regarded as a threat to American national security. The Monroe Administration wished to act in support of Latin American independence, but was suspicious of Canning's motives and characteristically wary of entering into entanglements with European powers. The Anglophobic secretary of state, John Quincy Adams, was particularly influential in arguing that the United States should not be seen to be acting as a junior partner to Great Britain. 'It would be more candid, as well as more dignified', stated Adams, 'to avow our principles explicitly to Russia and France, than to come in as a cock-boat in the wake of the British man-of-war.'[32] Canning's proposal was, therefore, carefully considered but eventually rejected.

Instead of diplomatic cooperation with Great Britain, Monroe preferred to adopt an independent course of action and prepared a statement of policy that was delivered in a Special Message to Congress on 2 December 1823. Though it had little historical validity, the message put great emphasis on the idea of the separation of the New World from the Old World. It was also claimed that the people of Latin America had joined the United States in rejecting the monarchical political system of Europe. According to Monroe, that particular form of government was 'essentially different', and he declared that plans to extend it to the Western Hemisphere would be regarded as 'dangerous to our peace and safety'. The president went on to warn that any attempt by European powers to oppress the new independent governments of Latin America would be regarded as 'the manifestation of an unfriendly disposition to the United States'.[33] The admonition was clearly directed at the members of the Holy Alliance and their scheme to restore the authority of the Spanish king,[34] but it also posed a challenge to Great Britain. Monroe was conscious that the latter power was the great rival of the United States in the evolving battle for pre-eminent political and commercial influence in the new Latin American states. Consequently, the message in part represented an American determination not to allow Latin America to become a British protectorate by default.[35]

Although Monroe's message was directed at the European heads of state, it also had specific relevance to the countries of Latin America. In fact, it presumed a leadership role that claimed to speak on their behalf even though there was no prior consultation with Latin American leaders or governments. The new countries were simply declared to be under the protection of the United States, a presumption that implied unilateral and not collective action and also American superiority in an asymmetrical relationship of unequals. Moreover, the exact form that this protection would take was not explained. Despite the critical words aimed at Europe, the statement was not a declaration of war; instead, it referred in vague terms to opposing attempts at making future territorial acquisitions. 'With the existing colonies or dependencies of any European power', Monroe stressed, 'we have not interfered and shall not interfere.'[36] On the other hand, the idea of the political separation of the 'New World' from the 'Old World' was used to justify the prohibitions placed on European policy in acquiring new territory in the Americas although no such restriction was put on the United States. While the tone of the message implied that the United States saw itself as a world power, Monroe's words represented only a presidential statement of policy that had no force in international law. Their effect would depend upon the reaction of other nations and whether the United States would have the will and the capability to enforce them if challenged. This proved to be unnecessary, primarily because Great Britain did not publicly oppose the statement. Moreover, preparations for a French military expedition to the New World were never actually implemented. In fact, it was arguably the deterrent of the British navy, the world's most powerful naval force, and Canning's diplomatic skill in securing an understanding with the French government in October 1823 rather than Monroe's message to Congress that deterred the Holy Alliance from undertaking military intervention in Latin America.

Aftermath of the Monroe Doctrine

At one level Monroe's message was simply a defensive response to a specific threat of military intervention posed by the Holy Alliance. However, the principles that he enunciated in 1823 also raised the wider issue of American national security and in doing so had significant foreign policy implications for the future. In addition, the idea of a separate and distinctive western hemispheric political system in which the United States assumed a pre-eminent and protective role reflected the rhetoric of the American Revolution and developed into a national symbol around which Americans could readily identify. Indeed, Monroe's statement not only provided a rationale for diplomatic action but also eventually acquired the status of a 'doctrine' and in the process became a venerated American political tradition.

The initial reaction of the governments of Europe and Latin America, however, did not indicate the degree of international importance that the message was to gain in the future. King Ferdinand of Spain evidently never bothered to read it and no formal protest was ever forthcoming from his government. 'The document in question enunciates the views and pretensions so exaggerated, it establishes principles so contrary to the rights of the European powers', declared the Imperial Russian government, 'that it merits only the most profound contempt.'[37] Despite the challenging and offensive tone of the message, the Russian minister in Washington, Baron Tuyll van Serooskerken, was instructed to adopt a passive attitude and maintain silence. The speech generally received only passing mention in the Latin American press. Nevertheless, some political leaders welcomed the involvement and assistance of the United States in hemispheric affairs. They perceived the contents of the message, especially the principle of non-colonization, as offering a useful means of helping Latin America to resist the aggressive threats of European nations. For example, the Brazilian minister referred to Monroe's 'effective declaration' when sounding out the US government about the prospect of concluding either a formal or informal military alliance.[38] The Argentine president, Bernardino Rivadavia, publicly praised the message and ordered translations to be made and sent to the neighbouring governments of Chile, Peru and Colombia. The American minister at Buenos Aires, Caesar A. Rodney, confirmed that 'this masterly State Paper had inspired us here', and he predicted that it 'will have a most extensive influence'.[39]

The fear of becoming ensnared in future overseas entanglements or commitments meant that suggestions of an alliance with Brazil were discouraged. Indeed, Monroe and Adams displayed a basic reluctance to act in concert with the Latin Americans and essentially showed no desire to follow up the message in a practical or systematic way. In fact, there was no need to do so because the threat of European military intervention never actually materialized. George Canning effectively marginalized the public relations impact of the message by stating, with some justification, that his own diplomatic skill combined with the threat to use British naval power had been the decisive factors in defeating the threat of the Holy Alliance. He claimed that Great Britain wished to be the foremost friend, protector and example for the new countries. As part of his strategy to counter the effect of Monroe's 1823 statement, Canning boasted that he personally had 'called the New World into existence to redress the balance of the Old'. Moreover, the British diplomat predicted that 'if we do not throw it away, [it is] ours'.[40] Indeed, Great Britain was the most powerful foreign influence upon the newly independent states of Latin America, the majority of which were eager to conclude commercial treaties with the world's leading industrial and commercial nation. Moreover, Latin Americans appreciated the importance of military power and judged Great Britain to be much stronger in this particular respect than the United States. In fact, Monroe's professed desire to protect Latin America contrasted with his studied reluctance over several years, both as secretary of state and president, to abandon his government's policy of neutrality. Accordingly, Canning's views were given more credence, especially in South America where the British were regarded as the real friends of Latin American independence, while the Americans were generally considered presumptuous if not hypocritical.

Panama Congress

The awkward relationship between the United States and its southern neighbours was illustrated by the saga of the 1826 Panama Congress. The meeting was the idea of Simón Bolívar and was intended to encourage steps to provide for the common defence of the former Spanish-American colonies in preparation against an expected Spanish attempt at military reconquest of its empire. Though he was addressing the same issue that had confronted Monroe in 1823, Bolívar made no direct mention of the president's message. In contrast to Monroe, he notably preferred consultation leading to multilateral rather than unilateral action. His ultimate aim was the formation of a federation of Latin American states to replace the unity of the Spanish-American empire. Initially, the United States was not included in the original invitations sent out in 1824. This was justified by Bolívar on the grounds that the United States was officially neutral in the current war against Spain.[41] The exclusion also indicated the continued existence of a deep political and cultural division between the United States and the Spanish-American countries.

When an invitation was eventually extended to the United States in 1825, it coincided with a period of political dissension resulting from the controversial presidential election of 1824 in which the House of Representatives had chosen John Quincy Adams as president. In return, Adams appointed Henry Clay as his secretary of state. Domestic political factors, therefore, intruded into the debate as those American politicians in the US Congress who were opponents of Clay and his 'American system' showed no inclination for their country to assume a leading role in hemispheric affairs. Furthermore, there was evident displeasure that their government had not been initially consulted about the preparations for the meeting. Some anxiety was also expressed that acceptance of the invitation might result in undesirable and restrictive diplomatic entanglements. Mindful that Bolívar was known to favour the abolition of slavery, Southern congressmen were particularly concerned that the congress might adopt anti-slavery measures that would disturb the institution of slavery within the United States. In line with the Pan-American ideas of his secretary of state, President Adams pointed out, however, that the meeting would be purely consultative and advocated American attendance. He was especially keen to cultivate good relations with the new nations. 'Having been the first to recognize their independence,' Adams informed Congress, 'we have laid the foundation of our future intercourse with them in the broadest principles of reciprocity and the most cordial feelings of fraternal friendship.'[42] The matter was debated in Congress over a period of four months and eventually two delegates, Richard Anderson of Kentucky and John Sergeant of Pennsylvania, were appointed, though not without some opposition being expressed. The traditional ethnocentric viewpoint was exemplified by Senator John Berrien of Georgia in March 1826 in his desire not to involve 'the interests of this Union in a foreign association, composed of States with whom we have no natural connection'.[43]

After requiring such contentious congressional debates to produce an affirmative decision it was ironic that the American delegates never actually attended the Panama Congress in person. Anderson duly left his post in Colombia but died en route to Panama. Sergeant was informed before he departed from the United States that the Panama Congress had already adjourned and would reconvene in Mexico. The congress had met in Panama from 22 June to 15 July 1826, but was attended by delegates from only four Latin American states. Notable absentees included Argentina, Brazil and Chile. Peru participated in the Panama meeting, but refused to send a delegate to Mexico. The delegates discussed a range of issues, including the establishment of arbitration procedures to resolve disputes, the abolition of the slave trade and even the formation of a multinational army and navy to deter the Holy Alliance. With the exception of Gran Colombia, however, no state ever ratified any of the agreements concluded at the meetings in Panama and later at Tacubaya, Mexico. The failure to agree to some form of defensive alliance was explicable in that Spain no longer posed the serious military threat that Bolívar had originally envisaged when he had first proposed the idea of the meeting in 1824. The fact that the Panama Congress had actually taken place would have considerable symbolic value in the future for advocates of hemispheric unity. Nevertheless, in 1826 the evident disunion among the new Latin American states was a blow to Bolívar's idea of forming a federation based upon a common language, religion and historical traditions. In addition, the congress also demonstrated that the United States and the countries of Latin America were still distant neighbours. The government and the people of the United States were clearly unwilling to join Pan-American schemes and attached little importance to the concept even when advocated by such a prominent figure as Bolívar. The ambivalent state of American policy towards Latin America was noted by the British minister at Washington, Charles Vaughan, who concluded:

> The dilatory manner in which the resolution to send Representatives has been adopted, and the adherence of a large party in Congress to the legacy, which they say was left them by Washington never to engage the country in 'entangling alliances', does not betray so much as might have been expected the anxiety said to pervade this Government of obtaining at any cost a paramount influence over the new Governments of South America.[44]

2

TERRITORIAL EXPANSIONISM (1830–79)

Diplomatic and economic neglect

Although President Monroe's 1823 message expressed his country's concern to protect the newly independent nations of Latin America from European aggression, this did not result in the United States adopting a policy of close interest or direct involvement in hemispheric affairs.[1] In fact, the detached and, at times, uneasy diplomatic relationship between the United States and its southern neighbours that had been a characteristic feature of the colonial period persisted into the nineteenth century. This was illustrated by Bolívar's initial decision not to invite a delegate from the United States to the 1826 Panama Congress and the ensuing reluctance of many members of the US Congress to agree to send a representative to the meeting. Furthermore, the seemingly wayward and disturbing course of political events in the newly independent states of Latin America accentuated the differences between the societies. They also promoted and strengthened American attitudes of superiority bordering on disdain for the character and competence of their southern neighbours.

American politicians were particularly dismayed as it became apparent that the achievement of independence had not resulted in the establishment of viable democratic systems of government. Instead of enjoying the blessings of peace and civilization, most of the new republics were soon rent by civil unrest and political disorder. Their fabled wealth, in terms of available silver and gold, was either non-existent or rapidly depleted and, in a number of cases, their military capacity was turned upon themselves. 'America is ungovernable', lamented the disillusioned Liberator, Simón Bolívar, only a month before his death in 1830.[2] Reports of frequent changes of governments and the collapse of attempted political unions such as Bolívar's Gran Colombia in 1830 and the Federation of the United Provinces of Central America in 1838 merely served to confirm the pessimistic predictions of Thomas Jefferson and John Quincy Adams that the new nations would not be able to break away from their repressive Spanish heritage and would soon fall into political instability. The occurrence of violent coups and the rise to power of military rulers were especially deplored. The American chargé in Lima, James Pickett, summed up the bleak political prospects for the people of Peru in 1845:

> I doubt too their fitness, in general, for a democratic form of government and for democratic institutions; but still they ought to have and might have, something better than the despicable and detestable military despotisms by which they have been so long dishonored and oppressed.[3]

In marked contrast to the North American colonies, the fragmentation of the Spanish-American empire into a number of separate states, each often experiencing major political and economic difficulties, meant that a new Latin American power bloc, either individually or collectively, did not come into existence to become a force either in world or hemispheric affairs. The new nations did not, therefore, pose a serious strategic or military threat to the national security of the United States. Valued mainly for their economic potential, they assumed a place on the periphery of the existing international system that revolved around the great European powers. While the US government was keen to conclude bilateral treaties of friendship, navigation and commerce with all its new neighbours, it showed no desire to intervene or to become actively involved in their domestic political affairs. Though somewhat fitfully and usually with inadequate funding, American diplomatic and consular representation was established and maintained in all the new countries. Relations were mostly concerned with transacting the daily routine of commercial and consular business. Where major disputes arose between Latin American states, the US government deliberately chose to adopt a cautious and mainly reactive policy. For example, when war broke out in 1825 between Argentina and Brazil over control of the Banda Oriental, an area that would become modern Uruguay, the United States responded negatively to the Argentine request that the Monroe Doctrine be invoked against Brazil. Determined to avoid foreign entanglements and to be seen to be acting even-handedly, President John Quincy Adams explained in July 1828:

> The war cannot be conceived as presenting a state of things bearing the remotest analogy to the case which President Monroe's message deprecates. It is a war strictly American in origin and its object. It is a war in which the Allies of Europe have taken no part.[4]

Moreover, Monroe's 1823 message initially appeared to have little significance or even relevance because it had never become a matter of public diplomatic correspondence between the United States and other governments. Moreover, its broader implications, warning against European interference in

Latin American political affairs, were simply ignored by European powers. A new European colony was formally established in the Western Hemisphere when Great Britain assumed sovereign control over the Falkland Islands (Islas Malvinas) in 1833. In a few cases, the use of coercive military force in the form of 'gunboat diplomacy' was openly employed by European governments to seek redress of grievances allegedly suffered by their nationals. For example, French troops briefly occupied the Mexican port of Veracruz in 1838. Great Britain and France used their naval forces to mount an economic blockade of Buenos Aires in 1845 in order to put pressure on the government of Juan Manuel Rosas in Argentina to change its policies. Neither European power saw any need either to consult with or to seek the approval of the United States before embarking on military action.

The response of the US government was muted in both instances. But inaction possessed important implications for the future because American diplomatic passivity over the colonization of the Falkland Islands signified an acknowledgment that British claims to possession predated President Monroe's 1823 statement. Failure to gain support from Washington in this instance contributed to the development of a legacy of Argentine distrust of the United States. Argentina was also displeased in the case of the Anglo-French blockade in 1845, when Secretary of State James Buchanan offered 'the whole moral influence of this Republic' to help resolve the dispute, but stressed that 'existing circumstances render it impossible for the United States to enter this war'.[5] Buchanan's tactful language disguised the fact that no formal diplomatic protest against the Anglo-French action would be forthcoming from the United States. In fact, the extent of the European danger had been greatly exaggerated because it was evident that, like many similar attempts at gunboat diplomacy in Latin America, the British and the French had militarily over-reached themselves and that their naval force was clearly inadequate and unable to achieve its assigned mission. This was recognized by the British minister in Buenos Aires when he summed up in 1847 that 'there is not a country in the universe where European diplomacy will always find itself so helpless, and indeed hopeless, as here'.[6]

The geopolitical reality was that these European incursions were perceived in Washington as remote and infrequent events involving distant places that did not directly threaten the security of the United States or result in the formal acquisition of new colonial territory.[7] Moreover, they also occurred at a time when the United States and its people were preoccupied with their own internal development and territorial expansion in the North American continent. This negative American attitude meant that the most powerful foreign influence upon the new independent states of Latin America was exerted by the European powers and especially Great Britain. It was that country which was the leading source of foreign trade and investment and which was also perceived by the Latin American elite as a foremost example of superior political and social culture. As the 1845 blockade of the

River Plate demonstrated, however, British influence did not extend to the ability to control Latin American political affairs. Like the United States, the British government chose to avoid becoming entangled in Latin American political and military affairs. *Laissez-faire* was the preferred approach. In 1830 the British political leader, Robert Peel, expressed 'a deep interest in the welfare and prosperity of these infant states', but believed that progress would be best achieved not by foreign diplomatic intervention but by those countries settling their internal conflicts in their own way.[8]

The detached diplomatic attitude shown towards Latin America by foreign powers was also explained by the failure of the region to live up to its 'eldorado' image. American politicians and merchants had joined with their European counterparts in believing that the achievement of Latin American independence would lead to lucrative financial benefits. However, these expectations were disappointed because the resulting trade produced only modest returns. The protracted length of the Wars for Independence had resulted in severe local economic damage and destruction. After an initial boom in trade immediately following the achievement of independence, subsequent commercial growth was severely constrained by the fact that the consumer market in Latin America was much smaller and poorer than anticipated and could not afford to purchase large quantities of foreign imports. Trade was also frequently disrupted by political disorder and civil unrest. Furthermore, the new governments faced considerable economic problems arising from a general shortage of revenue, and they often sought to resolve these by increasing tariff schedules, especially on imports, even though this aroused the opposition of foreign merchants. They also resorted to borrowing large loans, mainly from private investors in Great Britain. This created a massive economic bubble that quickly burst and destroyed many national finances during the 1820s, while also giving Latin American governments an enduring reputation for financial recklessness and profligacy. American investment was minimal. Apart from Mexico, Cuba and Brazil, there was only modest growth in commercial contact between the United States and the new independent nations of Latin America. While the people of the United States did not live at the same low subsistence level as those in Latin America, the economic reality was that for much of the nineteenth century the United States was primarily an agrarian economy concentrating on the export of foodstuffs and raw materials just like the countries of Latin America. 'They want none of our production,' remarked John Quincy Adams in March 1821, 'and we could afford to purchase very few of theirs.'[9] In similar vein a Chilean diplomat reported the comments of Secretary of State Henry Clay: 'Chile has nothing to give us, nor have we anything to give her.'[10]

American merchants were particularly envious and critical of the powerful influence exercised by Great Britain in all aspects of commercial activity in Latin America. For most of the nineteenth century, however, they could do little to upset British economic pre-eminence. The latter rested not so much on Great Britain's diplomatic skills and assumed capacity to extract unfair commercial advantages for its own merchants but the ability of 'the workshop of the world' to supply and transport and also to provide credit facilities for the purchase of the manufactured goods that the Latin Americans wanted. John Quincy Adams accurately predicted in June 1822:

> Do what we can, the commerce with South America will be much more important and useful to Great Britain than to us, and Great Britain will be a power vastly more important to them [the new states] than we, for the simple reason that she has the power of supplying their want by her manufacture. We have few such supplies to furnish them.[11]

By contrast, American politicians, merchants and bankers were notoriously deficient in breaking down commercial barriers by providing their own shipping services and capital to finance trade. The famous sailing ships known as 'Yankee clippers' gradually became uncompetitive and redundant as American shipping interests proved to be curiously reluctant to adapt to the introduction of steam power from the 1840s onwards. The resulting lack of direct steamship lines between the United States and Latin America meant that both passengers and freight usually had to travel on British or French ships via a compulsory stop at a European port. The Protestant clergymen, Daniel Kidder and James Fletcher, who travelled to Brazil during the 1850s described sea communications between the United States and Brazil as 'exceedingly difficult' and pointed out that Great Britain 'is reaping golden harvests' while 'our Government and our merchants, notwithstanding their boasted enterprise, have done next to nothing to foster trade with Brazil'.[12] The Brazilian minister in London, Sérgio Teixeira de Macedo, confirmed in 1854 that the commerce between Great Britain and Brazil 'is carried on with English capital, on English ships, by English companies' and that 'the profits . . . the interest on capital . . . the payments for insurance, the commissions, and the dividends from the business, everything goes into the pockets of Englishmen'.[13]

The lack of success in penetrating Latin American markets was often attributed by contemporaries to the uneven quality of the American foreign and consular service. One reason for this criticism was that American diplomats and consuls sometimes hindered rather than helped the promotion of trade by assuming a superior and forceful approach in their personal dealings with local Latin American officials. Invariably appointed for political reasons in accordance with the dictates of 'spoils politics' and the presidential election cycle, they frequently lacked diplomatic or consular experience. They were also typically representative of American society in rarely possessing either knowledge of Spanish or Portuguese or even much of an acquaintance with Latin American domestic affairs or culture. When John W. Foster was offered the Mexican mission in 1872 he confessed his inexperience in diplomacy and his lack of foreign languages, but he related that his patron, Senator Levi Morton of Indiana, 'only smiled at my hesitation, reasserted his confidence in my ability, and said I was much better fitted than most of those who were appointed to our diplomatic service'.[14]

For Foster the Latin American posting marked the beginning of a distinguished diplomatic career, eventually leading to the office of secretary of state. For others, the lack of diplomatic experience and skill, and sometimes even of good moral character, resulted all too often in social isolation, frustration, inefficient work and, on occasion, costly diplomatic blunders. A common feeling of insecurity was increased by the fact that length of office was uncertain and was largely determined by political favour and the duration of the presidential administration that had made the original appointment. Indeed, inadequate pay, low prestige and poor working conditions reflected the practical aspect of American diplomacy in which political and economic constraints undermined the effective implementation of policy. In addition, the Latin American states were linked in the American popular mind with inherent political and economic disorder and were perceived as particularly unattractive posts. For example, James Watson Webb did not disguise his personal disappointment at being offered a posting to Brazil in 1861. On his arrival at Rio de Janeiro, Webb freely admitted that he had no knowledge of the Portuguese language and had no desire to learn. Webb's insensitivity exemplified a style of behaviour that was not uncommon among American officials serving in Latin America.

American territorial expansionism

The occurrence of the French Revolutionary Wars and especially the resulting military and financial weakness of Spain had greatly assisted American territorial expansion during the first two decades of the nineteenth century. A similar advantageous position for the United States arose as a result of the weakness of Mexico, whose early years of independence were marked by internal political conflict culminating in a series of civil wars. In contrast to the rest of mainland Latin America, however, Mexico's geographical proximity meant that it was, and would remain, the one nation that the people and government of the United States did not consider as distant and remote. In fact, the exact location of the border between the two countries had long been a matter of some uncertainty. The 1803 Louisiana Purchase had considerably extended the south-western borders of the United States and stimulated a territorial dispute with Spain over the boundary between the Louisiana Territory and the frontier province of Texas in northern Mexico that was seemingly resolved by the Adams–Onís Treaty of 1819.

In the negotiations for the 1819 treaty the United States was principally concerned about the transfer of the Spanish Floridas to its possession and made no claim to Texas. During the 1820s, however, that territory experienced steady encroachment by Americans (Anglo-Americans or 'Anglos'), mostly taking the form of peaceful settlement. In 1821, shortly before the establishment of Mexican independence, Moses Austin secured permission from the Spanish colonial authorities for 300 ostensibly Catholic families to migrate from Louisiana to take up grants of cheap land in the arid and sparsely populated province of Texas that had been attracting only small numbers of Spanish settlers (Tejanos) since the 1790s. Moses Austin died before the expedition could be organized. His son, Stephen Austin, acquired the concession and subsequently founded settlements in the province. The Anglo settlers formed successful agricultural communities and soon outnumbered the Tejanos in the region. The Anglo population had grown to around 7,000 by 1830 when further immigration was halted by the Mexican government. The policy of colonizing a remote frontier province with Anglos had produced dangerous consequences. No longer poor and destitute, the Anglos were increasingly difficult to control, not only in terms of their growing numbers and economic independence but because their political loyalty was also uncertain so long as they insisted on retaining their separate Anglo identity, religion and culture and resisted pressure for 'Mexicanization'.

Even though it was now technically illegal, the influx of Anglos into Texas continued after the 1830 prohibition with the result that the Anglo population rose to 30,000 by 1835 compared to a Tejano population of less than 10,000. Joining in the internal political struggle that was taking place against the centralizing policy of the dictator Antonio López de Santa Anna, the Anglos proclaimed the Texas Revolution in November 1835. Their aims were not just federalist reforms for their province but outright secession from the Mexican Union. As Stephen Austin observed, the Anglos wished to affirm their separate national identity because they felt 'in danger of becoming the alien subjects of a people to whom they deliberately believed themselves morally, intellectually, and politically superior'.[15] The Mexicans, however, viewed the Anglos as aggressive and untrustworthy. An army under Santa Anna marched north with the aim of crushing the rebellion. Despite an initial defeat at the Alamo in San Antonio in March 1836, the Anglos defiantly proclaimed the independent republic of Texas. On 21 April they achieved a notable military success at San Jacinto under the command of Sam Houston. Santa Anna was captured while trying to escape from the battle. In return for his release he agreed to the secession of Texas from the Mexican Union. The new nation was officially recognized by the United States on 3 March 1837 and later by Great Britain and France but not by Mexico. Fearful of Mexican counter-attack and conscious of the difficulty of preserving their independent status as 'the lone star republic', the Texans desired annexation by the United States. Annexation attracted considerable support, but it did not immediately take place on account of sectional political differences between the North and the South relating to the admission to the Union of such a large state in which the controversial institution of slavery was allowed. 'We cannot consent', declared the New England Unitarian leader William E. Channing, 'that the South should extend its already disproportionate power by an indefinite extension of territory'.[16] There was also awareness in the United States that the act of annexation must inevitably bring about war with Mexico because the Mexican government continued to claim authority over what it regarded as a rebellious province and one that was still an integral part of the Mexican Union.

During the 1840s the issue of annexing Texas to the United States became fused with the powerful movement of people westwards across the North American continent that was popularly known as Manifest Destiny. Westward expansion predated the 1840s, but the public imagination was captured, if only briefly, by the new term. It was famously coined in July 1845 by the magazine editor, John L. O'Sullivan, who justified America's territorial expansion and transformation into a transcontinental nation on the grounds that it was 'our manifest destiny to overspread the continent allotted by Providence'.[17] The movement also had significant diplomatic consequences because European powers were warned not to interfere. Seeking 'to reiterate and reaffirm the principle avowed by Mr. Monroe', President James K. Polk vigorously asserted in 1845 'that no future European colony or dominion shall with our consent be planted or established on any part of the North American continent'.[18] Polk's specific reference to the 'North American continent' showed that he was actually concerned about rumoured European, rather than Latin American, designs on Texas, Oregon and California, but his statement was notable in drawing public attention and attaching special significance to Monroe's 1823 message.[19] As a result, from the mid-nineteenth century onwards American politicians and public began to refer to the principles expressed in the 1823 message as the 'Monroe Doctrine'.

When Texas was eventually incorporated into the United States by a Joint Resolution passed by the US Congress in March 1845, the Mexican government protested and refused to recognize the Rio Grande River as marking its new border with the United States. The Mexican minister in Washington, Juan Almonte, declared that the annexation was 'an act of aggression, the most unjust which can be found recorded in the annals of history'.[20] Continued friction between Mexico and the United States eventually resulted in the Mexican–American War, which broke out between the two countries in May 1846. While most of the initial fighting took place in northern Mexico, a separate American military force under General Winfield Scott landed at and captured the port of Veracruz in March 1847. After a slow inland advance to Mexico City, the capital was stormed and occupied in September. An American army of around 10,000 troops defeated a Mexican force of 30,000 soldiers defending the city. It was an outstanding American military success and a tribute to the skill of General Scott. The Mexican army, however, relied heavily on Indian conscripts and, in terms of military resources and training, it was ill prepared for war.

The fall of the capital was decisive and resulted in the resignation of Santa Anna and his replacement by a new Mexican government that decided to seek peace terms. The war ended in February 1848 with the signing of the Treaty of Guadalupe Hidalgo by which a vanquished Mexico accepted the Rio Grande River as its border with Texas and also ceded to the United States a vast portion of territory extending from the modern state of New Mexico to California. The United States paid $15 million for what was equivalent to half the territory of the Mexican nation in 1848. Additional land was gained later by the Gadsen Purchase in 1853 in which the American minister to Mexico, James Gadsen, arranged the purchase of the Gila River Valley in Arizona and New Mexico for the price of $10 million.

The advocates of American territorial expansionism were greatly encouraged by the Texas question and the conflict with Mexico. Prior to the conclusion of the 1848 peace treaty, an 'all-Mexico' movement lobbied for total annexation of the whole of Mexico to the United States. One strong argument in favour was to point out to Americans that they had a revolutionary duty to replace Spanish despotism with freedom. This attitude reflected a patronizing American sense of democratic mission and racial superiority that had been markedly strengthened by recent military successes in the Mexican–American War. The editor of the *New York Sun* wrote on 22 October 1847:

> The [Mexican] race is perfectly accustomed to being conquered, and the only new lesson we shall teach is that our victories will give liberty, safety, and prosperity to the vanquished . . . To liberate and ennoble – not to enslave and debase – is our mission.[21]

A belief in the historical inevitability of Manifest Destiny was also invoked because Mexico was regarded as part of the North American continent. 'To attempt to prevent the American people from taking possession of Mexico, if they demand it, would be as futile in effect as to undertake to stop the rushing of the cataract of Niagara', stated the Democratic political leader Lewis Cass in the US Congress in December 1847.[22] But the annexation of all Mexico potentially contained heavy costs and liabilities that ultimately proved to be unacceptable to the US Congress. In the opinion of the former American minister in Mexico Waddy Thompson, taking additional Mexican territory was akin to conquest and:

> will add a large population, alien to us in feeling, education, race, and religion – a people unaccustomed to work and accustomed to insubordination and resistance to law, the expense of governing whom will be ten times as great as the revenues derived from them.[23]

While the all-Mexico movement failed to achieve its territorial objectives, the war and its outcome clearly confirmed the relative military weakness and economic backwardness of Mexico and its inability to prevent the emergence of the United States as the pre-eminent military power in the Central American–Caribbean region.[24] It also served to strengthen the American attitude of military and cultural superiority over the people of Mexico and by extension to Latin Americans in general. In addition, the acquisition of large amounts of Mexican territory was a demonstration that American political leaders did not regard the proscriptions contained in Monroe's 1823 statement as applying to their country. The United States was evidently free to acquire territory, whether by military conquest or purchase, and establish its own 'colonies' in the New World.

The filibusters

In fact, the United States was also interested in obtaining possession of Cuba. That island was only a short sailing voyage – less than 100 miles – from the Florida Keys. Its strategic and commercial importance was underscored by the geographical fact that it commanded the sea routes that led to and from the Mississippi River and the Gulf of Mexico. Thomas Jefferson noted in 1823:

> I candidly confess that I have ever looked on Cuba as the most interesting addition which could ever be made to our system of States. The control of which, with Florida Point, this island would give us over the Gulf of Mexico, and the countries and the Isthmus bordering on it, as well as all of those whose waters flow into it, would fill up the measure of our political well-being.[25]

Indeed, after the purchase of the Louisiana Territory in 1803 and the Spanish Floridas in 1819 it seemed that Cuba would be next in the list of American territorial acquisitions. In a celebrated statement made in 1823, John Quincy Adams referred to the 'laws of gravitation' and thereby added an element of scientific certainty to the inevitability of American expansionism:

> There are laws of political as well as physical gravitation; and if an apple severed by the tempest from its native tree cannot choose

> but fall to the ground, Cuba, forcibly disjointed from its own unnatural connection with Spain, and incapable of self-support, can gravitate only toward the North American Union, which by the same law of nature cannot cast her off from its bosom.[26]

Spain was determined, however, to retain possession of Cuba because it was economically valuable and a visible remnant of its once great American empire.[27] But Spain's evident and continuing decline as a great power made it seem only a matter of time before the island would be lost either to an internal rebellion or handed over to a stronger foreign power such as Great Britain. The prospect of Cuba falling under British control gave most concern to American diplomats. Not only would this be economically damaging but it posed the strategic threat of the island being used as a base for hostile military operations. Various attempts were made to forestall this contingency and gain possession of Cuba for the United States. The favoured method of governments in Washington was to buy the island from Spain. American interest and activity increased as a result of success in the Mexican–American War. In 1848 President Polk offered $100 million, and this figure was raised to $130 million by President Franklin Pierce in 1854. But Spain revealed no disposition to give up control of what its people regarded as their 'ever-faithful isle'. American frustration was illustrated by the Ostend Manifesto that was initially drawn up at a meeting in the Belgian city in 1854 by the American diplomats, Pierre Soulé, James Buchanan and John Mason. They sought to justify incorporation into the United States and threatened Spain with forceful annexation of the island if the offer to purchase was rejected. But the ministers had exceeded their instructions. The Pierce Administration (1853–7) quickly disavowed the Manifesto. Secretary of State William L. Marcy acknowledged that Cuba:

> would be a very desirable possession, if it came to us in the right way, but we cannot afford to get it by robbery or theft . . . I am for getting the Island, if it can be acquired fairly and honestly, not otherwise.[28]

Marcy's comments on 'robbery or theft' referred to military expeditions that were organized and funded by private individuals in the United States who became known as filibusters. Mostly composed of groups of adventurers and soldiers of fortune, filibusters were intent on using force to seize land, mostly in Mexico and Central America. Aims were varied and ranged from a nationalistic desire to fulfil America's Manifest Destiny to assisting the spread of democracy, establishing colonies of settlers (sometimes as a means of perpetuating the institution of slavery) or the purely mercenary motive of taking possession of any easily available precious metals such as gold or silver. Filibusters attracted most support in the southern states on account of geographical proximity to Central America and because they were viewed in the South as a means of bringing new slave states into the Union and thereby adding vitality to and strengthening the controversial institution of slavery. In this respect, Cuba was regarded as potentially a very valuable political asset. Prominent leaders such as the Venezuelan-born Cuban patriot Narciso López and Mississippi Governor John Quitman advocated the annexation of Cuba to the United States by force, and from 1848 to 1854 they launched a succession of unsuccessful military expeditions starting out from New Orleans. In the 1851 expedition López was captured and publicly executed in Cuba.

The activities of the filibusters were often represented as in keeping with America's traditional sense of democratic mission. Their declared aim was to liberate Cuba from Spanish tyranny, establish democratic self-government for the Cuban people and secure annexation to the United States. But successive American governments did not wish to be seen to be endorsing forceful annexation because such action would almost certainly provoke war with Spain and might also arouse possible retaliation from Great Britain. Moreover, under existing American neutrality legislation it was illegal to organize military expeditions to invade countries with which the United States was not at war. The federal authorities, however, did not always vigorously enforce the law, a practice that understandably raised suspicions in Spain and in Latin America of American hypocrisy and ulterior motive.

Despite the publicity accorded to the filibusters, the mass of the American people showed little sustained interest in overseas affairs. Any special significance that might be attached to Cuba's geographical proximity was offset by the fact that it was not a contiguous territorial part of the North American continent. Cuba was perceived, therefore, as an offshore island whose absorption, in contrast to the adjacent territories of Texas or California, could not so easily be justified by appeals to America's continental 'Manifest Destiny' and seemed more like the acquisition of an overseas colony. Furthermore, just like the Texas question, account had to be taken of the highly sensitive political question of race and slavery. The controversy provoked by the desire of the southern states to extend their economic system of plantation agriculture into Cuba during the mid-nineteenth century not only underscored the large number of slaves and blacks in the Cuban population but also made annexation an explosive political issue because it would entail the admission of a new slave state to the Union. Consequently, Adams's 'laws of gravitation' went into abeyance as American public attitudes and government policy towards Cuba preferred a continuation of the status quo and thereby implicitly acknowledged Spain's control and retention of sovereignty over the island.

The Central American Canal

Ever since the Spanish explorer Vasco Núnez de Balboa had glimpsed the Pacific Ocean in 1513 the dream of constructing a sea-level canal across Central America to link the oceans of the Atlantic and the Pacific had gone unrealized. The project was so vast that it made the Erie Canal look small by comparison. It was simply too big and daunting, both in terms of discovering a feasible route through extremely difficult terrain and in attracting sufficient capital for a speculative venture in such a remote part of the world. Government financial guarantees were not forthcoming because governments, both in Europe and the United States, were reluctant to become actively involved in canal projects beyond their own national borders. The policy of the United States was, in principle, to support private efforts from whatever country to construct a canal across Central America but to insist that it should be open on equal terms to the shipping of the world. Consequently, in his instructions to the US delegates appointed to attend the 1826 Panama Congress, Secretary of State Henry Clay had remarked that his government approved the idea of an international canal in principle and believed that any completed waterway across Central America should be open to the shipping of all nations and not be under the exclusive control of any one country. Despite various expressions of interest by canal promoters, however, no serious scheme was forthcoming.

American canal policy was modified by chance rather than design in 1846 when the American minister in Bogotá, Benjamin Bidlack, responded to the initiative of the Colombian foreign minister, Manuel Laria Mallarino, and negotiated a treaty with New Granada (renamed the United States of Colombia in 1863). The treaty was mostly concerned with commercial matters, but in article 35 the United States agreed to guarantee Colombian sovereignty over the isthmus of Panama and the protection of isthmian transit from external or internal interference. The isthmus was the shortest land route between the Atlantic and the Pacific and was located in Panama, the most northerly province of the Colombian Union. The stipulation of an American guarantee would have considerable significance in the future history of the canal but in 1846 it was very much at the instigation of the government in Bogotá, which at the time desperately wanted an American undertaking to protect its possession of the isthmus from possible European aggression. This ulterior motive of the Colombians, however, was understood in the US Senate where, despite the expression of some concern and the holding of lengthy debates over the dangers of contracting an 'entangling alliance', the treaty was eventually ratified in 1848. The United States, however, was not claiming a special or privileged position in isthmian affairs because it was expected that Great Britain and France would conclude similar treaties with Colombia and also join in the guarantee of Colombian sovereignty. Indeed, the new administration of Zachary Taylor

(1849–53) had misgivings over the arrangement. 'The guarantee in the treaty with New Granada', remarked Secretary of State John M. Clayton, 'is a conspicuous exception to our usual cautious and wise policy' and should not be considered as 'a safe precedent'.[29]

The transit issue suddenly and unexpectedly attracted considerable attention after the discovery of gold in California in 1848 and the ensuing gold rush in 1849 which resulted in a greatly increased use of the isthmus as the quickest means of travelling to and from the east and west coasts of the United States. Numerous canal schemes were vigorously announced and promoted, ranging from locations in the isthmus of Panama to Nicaragua and Tehuantepec in Mexico. Conscious of close British diplomatic interest in the question and the fact that the involvement of British financiers was essential to ensure the successful construction of the canal, the United States sought cooperation rather than confrontation. A treaty to this effect was negotiated with Great Britain in April 1850. Known as the Clayton–Bulwer Treaty, after Secretary of State Clayton and the British minister to the United States Henry Lytton Bulwer, it included terms that amounted to an Anglo-American undertaking to respect and to guarantee the neutrality of the projected isthmian canal with a joint disclaimer that neither power would ever erect fortifications or seek to acquire exclusive privileges or control. Despite the treaty providing what amounted to an unprecedented Anglo-American political undertaking to cooperate in canal construction, engineering difficulties still appeared as an insuperable barrier to proceeding with any serious canal works. Moreover, funding for such an enormous project was not forthcoming from either private or public sources. By contrast, American financiers were willing to invest in the more modest but still expensive undertaking of the construction of the Panama Railroad, whose successful completion in 1855 greatly reduced the need for and therefore the public interest in a sea-level canal. The later development of intercontinental railroads across the United States also provided alternative and effective means of passenger and freight transit between the east and west coasts.

During the 1850s the pursuit of some more fanciful canal schemes in Central America became linked with the activities of filibusters, many of whom were now drawn from the growing ranks of disappointed goldminers in California and veterans of the Mexican–American War. The most famous leader of these filibusters was William Walker, a lawyer based in California but originally from Tennessee. After a failed expedition to Baja California in Mexico, Walker looked for economic opportunity further to the south. In 1855 he arrived in Nicaragua with just over 50 men. This small group evolved into an 'army' of over 2,000 that took advantage of local political rivalry between Liberals and Conservatives to take control of the government and enable Walker to declare himself as dictator. In 1856 Walker organized elections to secure his confirmation as the country's president. For a while Walker's exploits attracted considerable public attention in the United States where he became something of a popular hero, especially in the South when it was learned that he had a southern background and had reintroduced slavery into Nicaragua. Walker also decreed that English should become the second official language of the country. The Pierce Administration, however, was placed in a dilemma over Walker's activities. Adopting the same attitude that was shown towards similar expeditions destined for Cuba, the US government declared that the organization of filibusters contravened American neutrality laws. President Pierce gave Walker no direct support, but his action in receiving a representative from the government that Walker established in Nicaragua in 1856 revealed an element of official encouragement, if not approval, for filibustering schemes that involved American territorial and commercial expansion.

Walker called himself 'the grey-eyed man of destiny', a reference to the oral traditions of the local Indians which predicted that they would be liberated from Spanish oppression by 'the grey-eyed man'. Sharing the racist attitudes of many of his countrymen, however, Walker believed in the superiority of 'the pure white American race' and had little sympathy for the Indians, whose future he envisaged as that 'of an inferior race yielding meekly and peacefully to the controlling influence of a superior people'.[30] The same racist theme was taken up and placed in the context of the American sense of democratic mission by the *New York Evening Post* in 1855:

> He may fail but there is reason to believe that in Nicaragua at least the sceptre has departed from the degenerate descendants of the Spanish conquerors, and that the destiny of Central America is now more manifestly than ever placed in Anglo-American hands. An efficient republican system may yet be adopted there under Yankee auspices, and the perplexed 'Central American question' . . . may be settled by the irresistible law of modern colonization.[31]

The idea of American filibusters exercising permanent control over the countries and peoples of the Central American region, however, had little basis in reality. Despite assuming the title of president of Nicaragua, Walker's authority did not extend very far beyond his headquarters, which he had established in the city of Granada. With financial and military support from the government of Costa Rica, the political factions in Nicaragua joined together in a common cause to drive out the foreign intruders. Moreover, a clash with the powerful American financier Cornelius Vanderbilt over the allocation of a steamship contract greatly strengthened Walker's enemies. Walker was forced to flee from Nicaragua in 1857 and return to the United States. Undaunted, he continued his filibustering activities until they eventually came to an end in 1860 when he was captured and executed by a firing squad in Honduras. News of Walker's passing was not greatly regretted in the United States. *Harper's Weekly* judged that 'Walker was undoubtedly a mischievous man, better out of the world than in it' and concluded: 'His works, from first to last, have been injurious rather than beneficial to the world.'[32]

In spite of the treaties negotiated by the United States with New Granada in 1846 and with Great Britain in 1850, a Central American Canal came no nearer to actual realization. Private schemes continued to be proposed, but an official survey by the British Admiralty in 1853–4 dismissed them as a 'useless and expensive waste of time'.[33] Moreover, American interest was distracted by the domestic political tensions over slavery that resulted in the outbreak of the Civil War in 1861. After the war ended in 1865 Secretary of State William H. Seward showed a personal interest in the question and adopted a new approach that abandoned the idea of an international canal expressed in the 1850 Clayton–Bulwer Treaty in favour of an 'American' canal, whose construction, operation and ownership would be largely determined and dominated by the views of the US government. Treaties to secure the rights to build a canal in the isthmian region were negotiated with Colombia in 1869 and, after Seward left office, by the administration of President Ulysses S. Grant in 1870. The timing of the negotiations was inopportune because the completion of the first transcontinental railroad in May 1869 diminished the commercial attraction of all isthmian canal projects. It also led to the formation in the United States of influential vested railroad interests opposed to alternative transit systems. In addition, the Colombian Senate proposed several amendments to the original treaties. 'The real cause of the rejection of the [1869] Treaty is the absence of any ready money payment to Colombia', explained the British minister at Bogotá, Robert Bunch, and he added: 'Had this been promised the other objections would have disappeared.'[34]

In fact, both canal treaties were given a very low order of political priority in Washington with the result that neither treaty was ever brought to a vote for ratification in the US Senate. However, the successful opening of the Suez Canal in 1869 meant that public and business interest in canal schemes was not deterred by the congressional setbacks. Indeed, both Houses of Congress established committees to investigate canal projects, the most important of which was the Interoceanic Canal Commission under the chairmanship of Admiral Daniel Ammen. Congressional appropriations were also voted for extensive geographical and scientific surveys of the whole Central American region from Tehuantepec in Mexico to Panama. At the same time several politicians and newspapers stressed the benefits and necessity of an 'American' canal, and companies were formed in the United States to prepare to carry out the work.

Unfortunately for the canal promoters, once again the initial surveys did not prove to be very encouraging. A canal was believed to be practicable at the narrowest point of the isthmus of Panama, but the expense involved in construction was still estimated as enormous. Consequently, the second Grant Administration (1873–7) began to show less and less active interest in the question. In February 1876 the Interoceanic Canal Commission recommended a canal to be constructed through Nicaragua, a much longer route than the isthmus but less expensive to build because it contained more easily navigable rivers linking up with a large inland lake. In what was essentially a reversion to the policy of an international canal, the report added that the scheme would be facilitated if all nations intending to use the waterway would join together to guarantee its neutrality and protection and, most importantly, share the costs of construction. In what was the Grant Administration's final year of office, Secretary of State Hamilton Fish somewhat reluctantly opened negotiations first with Costa Rica and then with Nicaragua to secure the necessary territorial concessions and legal rights to build a canal. However, discussions proved difficult because both Central American governments were unwilling to give up their sovereign rights in the proposed canal zone. The result was a diplomatic impasse. After he left presidential office, Grant commented that he had given 'much thought' and had worked hard to make progress on the canal issue, but he revealed that 'Mr. Fish did not feel the same interest'.[35] Whatever the explanation, the fact was that a decade of American canal diplomacy ended with the record of two unperfected treaties and no canal.

Diplomatic disengagement

Great Britain was the most powerful foreign influence upon the Latin American nations during their first half century of independence. By contrast, Latin Americans were generally ambivalent towards the United States and still wary of dealings with a people who were largely Anglo-Saxon and Protestant in their background. Nevertheless, so considerable was the territorial expansion of the United States during the mid-nineteenth century that the country could not be easily ignored. In particular, acute alarm was aroused by the conquest and incorporation of huge amounts of Mexican territory resulting from the Mexican–American War of 1846. Also disturbing were the notorious activities of American filibusters such as William Walker in Central America that revived memories of Drake and Morgan. The American chargé d'affaires in Buenos Aires, William Harris, noted in 1847:

> The strongest feelings and prejudices exist here, with all classes of Spaniards, against our people and government in regard to the Mexican war . . . They look upon the war as one of mere conquest, and as an act of the grossest and most cruel oppression . . . so strong has this prejudice become, and so hurtful is it to our interests and standing with these people.[36]

American territorial expansionism appeared to have no set limits. The Chilean minister in Washington, Manuel Caravallo, alarmingly predicted: 'What today they are doing to Mexico by taking over California, they will do to us tomorrow for frivolous reasons if it occurs to them.'[37] Latin American concern was publicly demonstrated when the governments of Chile, Peru and Ecuador organized a conference at Santiago de Chile in 1856 to which the United States was not invited. The delegates condemned American aggression and discussed ways of organizing defence against filibusters, but none of the agreements that they made were later ratified or acted upon.

Despite the apprehension expressed at the 1856 conference in Santiago de Chile, the actual examples of American filibusters and their seizure of territory were limited both in duration and geographical location. They were, in fact, confined to Mexico, Central America and the Caribbean islands. By contrast, the South American countries that were more distant geographically from the United States were relatively immune from direct American military action throughout most of the nineteenth century. Brazil's declaration of neutrality in the American Civil War in 1861 is an example of the latitude of diplomatic manoeuvre that could be exercised by Latin American governments. Like the European powers, Brazil granted belligerent rights to the Confederate States. Consequently, Confederate ships were able to enter Brazilian ports to refit and take on supplies. The administration of President Abraham Lincoln (1861–5) was annoyed, but did not regard the Brazilian government as unfriendly. In fact, the Brazilian emperor, Pedro II, privately expressed his wish that the Union would be victorious. In one instance, however, Brazil's sovereign rights were infringed in October 1864 when an American warship, the *Wachusett*, captured the Confederate cruiser *Florida* at dock in Salvador da Bahia and towed the vessel from the port. The incident was a sobering demonstration to Brazilians of how the United States could project its superior naval power with virtual impunity in Latin American waters. Nevertheless, the Brazilian government resolutely declared that the Brazilian national flag had been insulted and demanded that the United States must make an official apology. Secretary of State Seward was conciliatory and explained that the naval action had been unauthorized.

Seward wanted friendly relations with Brazil. In fact, as the Civil War came to a close in 1865 he was increasingly concerned with what seemed to be growing European designs upon acquiring territory in the Western Hemisphere. A show of naval force in Mexico in 1862 to collect debts owed to French bondholders became an ambitious imperial adventure in 1864 when Emperor Napoleon III of France sent troops to occupy the country and install an Austrian prince, Archduke Maximilian, as emperor. In 1865 Spain formally proclaimed the reincorporation of the Dominican Republic into its colonial empire and dispatched a small military force to occupy the island. A Spanish naval expeditionary force also appeared in the Pacific and temporarily occupied the Chincha Islands off the coast of Peru. American energies had been absorbed internally by the Civil War (1861–5), but after the war ended the US government put diplomatic pressure on France to withdraw its military forces from Mexico. Seward instructed the American minister in Paris to inform the French government that:

> the presence and operations of a French army in Mexico, and its maintenance of an authority there, resting upon force and not on the free will of the people of Mexico, is a cause of serious concern to the United States.[38]

Seward also wanted Spain to withdraw from the Dominican Republic and abandon its Pacific naval expedition. In a note to the Spanish government, he remarked that the Latin American nations 'allege that several of the European states, which once had colonies here, are now seeking to reduce them again to the condition of dependencies'. Adopting a tone reminiscent of Monroe's 1823 message, the secretary of state remarked: 'The proceedings of Spain in Peru give them a color which is deeply to be regretted.'[39]

Unable to defeat the Mexican resistance forces led by Benito Juárez and concerned at the geopolitical implications of Prussia's victory over Austria in the Austro-Prussian War of 1866, Napoleon III required little persuasion to abandon his disastrous overseas adventure. Further humiliation followed for France when Maximilian, who had decided to remain in Mexico, was captured and executed in 1867. While the awareness of American military power was not the determining factor, it was a consideration in inducing both France and Spain to comply with Seward's requests and withdraw their military forces from Latin America. The external threat to the Central American–Caribbean region persisted, however, in the form of rumours of European designs upon Samaná Bay, the strategically located naval base in the Dominican Republic. In 1870, in what would be the last of the nineteenth-century political debates over the annexation of territory in the Central American–Caribbean region, President Grant unsuccessfully attempted to persuade the US Senate to ratify a treaty by which the United States would annex the Dominican Republic by purchase. Senators appreciated the strategic value of Samaná Bay as a naval outpost en route to and from a projected isthmian canal, but they were wary of annexing an island territory that was some distance from the United States. Moreover, the purchase of non-contiguous territory in Alaska in 1867 still remained a controversial issue. Senators were also aware of allegations made against the Grant Administration that the proposal was motivated by land speculation and financial corruption. In addition, there was the belief that the population of the island was predominantly black. In the aftermath of the Civil War and the contentious debate over civil rights, it was argued that, for political and moral reasons, these people should be left undisturbed and allowed to rule themselves. 'Already by a higher statute', stated the chairman of the Senate foreign relations committee and celebrated anti-slavery politician, Charles Sumner, 'is that island set apart to the colored race.'[40]

The debate over the annexation of the Dominican Republic was significant in that it prompted President Grant to send a Special Message to the US Senate on 31 May 1870 in which he added the 'no-transfer' corollary to Monroe's 1823 message. 'I now deem it proper', he informed Congress, 'to assert the equally important principle that hereafter no territory on this continent shall be regarded as subject of transfer to a European power.'[41] While Grant's message was politically motivated in attempting to gain support for his annexation treaty, it also possessed diplomatic ramifications. In European eyes, such statements appeared self-righteous and annoying, but nevertheless they were considered worthy of more respect in the mid-nineteenth century than Canning had given to Monroe's statement only a few decades earlier. In 1857 the British prime minister, Lord Palmerston, had pointed to the reason why when he said: 'These Yankees are most disagreeable fellows to have to deal with about any American question. They are on the spot, strong, deeply interested in the matter, totally unscrupulous and dishonest and determined somehow to carry their point.'[42]

Reality differed, however, from political rhetoric. The United States was clearly a substantial local regional power, but the practical exercise of that power was limited by geographical distance, lack of military capacity, preoccupation with internal development, the tradition of avoiding entanglements in foreign affairs and the possibility of political conflict between the executive power and Congress. As a result, the treaties negotiated with Colombia to construct an isthmian canal encountered congressional resistance and were shelved. The treaty to annex the Dominican Republic also failed to secure ratification. Although its power was in decline, Spain was able to maintain control over Cuba in the face of strong American criticism of Spanish political oppression and expressions of public sympathy for Cuban attempts at liberation especially during the Ten Years' War that took place on the island from 1868 to 1878.

Nor was American influence very evident in South American affairs. Argentina, Brazil and Uruguay invaded Paraguay in the War of the Triple Alliance from 1865 to 1870. Despite his active interest in Central American and Caribbean affairs, Seward sought to prevent the United States from becoming diplomatically entangled in the major conflict in South America. This contrasted with the views of his minister-on-the-spot, James Watson Webb, who was fearful of European diplomatic meddling in the war and proposed American mediation to bring the belligerents together to discuss peace. 'We should impress all the American governments with a conviction that it is alike in their interest and their duty to look to the United States for protection and advice', affirmed Webb.[43] But Seward rejected the idea of taking a pro-active diplomatic role in South American questions. Like John Quincy Adams some forty years earlier, he was also inclined to be circumspect, especially when there was little likelihood of intervention by the European powers. Seward believed that the United States should not interfere unless formally requested to do so by the belligerents. 'It is not within the province of the United States', he informed Webb, 'to pronounce an opinion upon either the original merits of the war, or upon the wisdom or necessity of its longer continuance.'[44]

Despite the vigorous advocacy of territorial expansionism within the North American continent and the development of the Monroe Doctrine, American politicians and diplomats were generally indifferent to Latin American diplomatic issues during the period from 1830 to the 1870s. This was a consequence of domestic political circumstances, the particular personalities and attitudes of various American diplomatic officials, and, most of all, the desire of the United States to maintain a unilateral and independent policy that stressed the avoidance of overseas entanglements. With the exceptions of Mexico, the Central American Canal, Cuba and the occasions when there were reports of European territorial designs, the people of the United States continued in their role of a distant neighbour and were not greatly concerned over Latin American affairs. Their priority was to deal with their own domestic preoccupations arising from sectional divisions leading to the Civil War, the resulting problem of the reconstruction of the Southern states, and the challenges of westward expansion, the agricultural revolution and rapid industrialization and urbanization. Successive presidential administrations wanted friendly relations with the Latin American countries and, most of all, welcomed opportunities to increase commercial contact. But they also had a low opinion of the ability of Latin Americans to establish viable systems of democratic self-government. Examples ranging from the debate over participation in the 1826 Panama Congress to Seward's decision not to interfere in the War of the Triple Alliance demonstrated that American political leaders felt no compelling desire to enter into close political cooperation with the countries and peoples beyond the Central American–Caribbean region.

3

PAN-AMERICANISM (1879–1900)

The Isthmian Canal

After a period of apathy towards foreign affairs in the aftermath of the Civil War, the attention of the American public was noticeably drawn to a series of major political events occurring in parts of Latin America during the last quarter of the nineteenth century. Domestic political and economic considerations and increased coverage in the daily press influenced the official American responses to these events and formed the basis for a change in the foreign policy attitudes of both the American public and politicians. Consequently, the closing decades of the nineteenth century were marked by a more pro-active diplomacy that resulted in confrontation with certain European powers, the revival of the Monroe Doctrine and the assertion of American claims to political pre-eminence in the Western Hemisphere.[1]

Concern over the threatening prospect of a foreign power being in control of the construction and ultimately the operation of a Central American Canal was primarily responsible for the reawakening of American public interest not only in Latin American affairs but also in the Monroe Doctrine. After decades characterized by a succession of abortive schemes, an ambitious French canal project that promised success suddenly emerged in 1879. An international congress was held at Paris in May and decided in favour of constructing a sea-level canal close to the existing Panama Railroad on the isthmus of Panama. Admiral Ammen, who was in attendance as an unofficial observer from the US government, unsuccessfully advocated the Nicaragua route that had already been chosen by the Interoceanic Canal Commission. On his return to the United States, Ammen complained that the selection of Panama had been forced upon the congress. It was evident, however, that the French organizers of the congress had out-manoeuvred the American delegates and had achieved an impressive victory over the Nicaraguan scheme. The Panama Canal Company was quickly formed and the celebrated French entrepreneur and builder of the Suez Canal, Ferdinand de Lesseps, was appointed as its president. The canal was scheduled for completion in 1889, fittingly in time to commemorate the centenary of the French Revolution.

News of the proceedings at Paris soon aroused a critical public response in the United States. Ignoring the fact that the French canal company was a private capitalist venture and that Americans had attended the congress, Senator Ambrose Burnside of Rhode Island introduced on 25 June 1879 the first of several resolutions in Congress stating that any attempt by the European powers to construct an isthmian canal under their protection would be a violation of the Monroe Doctrine. The reference to the venerated Monroe Doctrine illustrated the significance attached to the issue and reflected popular suspicions that the de Lesseps project would provide the means by which France would establish a protectorate over the isthmus. Memories still lingered of Napoleon III's attempt to impose a European monarchy on Mexico during the 1860s. 'It is certain', remarked the *New York Herald* on 3 July 1879, 'that our government will neither recognize nor respect or tolerate any European interference in the matter.'[2] The past policy of American governments had been to welcome proposals from private capitalists to build an international canal provided that conditions of open access to the completed waterway were assured. This was the first time, however, that a proposal had progressed to the stage of actual implementation. As a result, national security concerns had to be addressed. In his diary entry for 20 February 1880, President Rutherford B. Hayes wrote that 'the United States cannot consent that it [the canal] shall be under European control' so that, in his view, a straightforward choice existed between 'either an American canal or no canal'.[3] A few weeks later on 8 March the president sent a Special Message to Congress declaring that the completed canal would be 'virtually a part of the coastline of the United States' and that 'the policy of this country is a canal under American control'.[4]

The Special Message was notable because it contained the assertion by Hayes that his government had the right to exercise authority over territory beyond its borders as if that land was within the United States. To justify this claim Hayes cited not the Monroe Doctrine but article 35 of the 1846 treaty with New Granada in which the United States had undertaken to guarantee the protection of isthmian transit from external interference. The broad implications of the president's message attracted criticism in the British press. 'The Washington protest', remarked an editorial in *The Times*, 'is a claim to indefinite suzerainty from Mexico to Patagonia, though throughout the vast region the Government at Washington exercises no power, and to its populations it acknowledges no duty.'[5] In practice, however, the impact of the message was limited because it did not specifically call for any immediate action or even response from Congress, the American public or even interested foreign governments located in either Central America or the rest of the world. Moreover, Hayes refrained from criticizing the French scheme by name and made no mention of seeking to prevent a private company from proceeding with its normal commercial activity. He was aware, however, that de Lesseps intended to invite Americans to invest in the canal company by public subscription. Although the Hayes Administration was not actually claiming a veto power on isthmian canal-building, it was definitely seeking to discourage potential American investors from giving any financial support to the French scheme.

Nevertheless, there was a very real risk that the presidential message might actually obstruct the building of what promised to be a very valuable means of communication between the east and west coasts of the United States, an object that had long been desired. Indeed, de Lesseps astutely read the mood of American public opinion and cleverly responded to the Special Message with a speech welcoming the president's statement as adding to 'the political security of the canal'.[6] Although the amount of American financial subscriptions proved relatively meagre and disappointing, the alluring prospect of a 'second Suez' and the fact that de Lesseps was in charge of the project attracted sufficient capital from French investors so that survey teams were sent to Panama and actual construction work was begun on schedule by the end of 1881.[7]

In the meantime, the new administration of President James A. Garfield came into office in March 1881 and reaffirmed the 'American' canal policy of its predecessor. On 24 June 1881 Secretary of State James G. Blaine sent a note to the leading European governments stating that the United States would resist any diplomatic interference by European powers on matters of transit affecting the isthmian area and based this stand upon 'the pronounced adherence of the United States to principles long since enunciated by the highest authority of the Government'.[8] In contrast to President Hayes, Blaine was therefore directly asserting that America's special canal rights were sanctioned by the Monroe Doctrine. The allusion to European meddling, however, had little substance in reality. Those governments sensibly preferred to wait and see if any progress was made at Panama by de Lesseps. The major difficulties that the French canal company soon encountered proved the wisdom of this pragmatic approach. Meanwhile, the British government effectively countered Blaine's note by reminding the secretary of state that Great Britain also possessed canal rights under the terms of the 1850 Clayton–Bulwer Treaty and relied 'with confidence upon the observance of all the engagements of that Treaty'.[9] The diplomatic correspondence initiated by Blaine in 1881 continued back and forth between his successors at the state department and the British Foreign Office throughout the 1880s. Despite American objections, so long as the Clayton–Bulwer Treaty remained in existence its terms were binding on both parties and thereby effectively prevented the United States from securing exclusive control of the canal.

Blaine and the War of the Pacific

Blaine assumed office as secretary of state in March 1881. The shooting of President Garfield by a disappointed office-seeker in July 1881 and the president's subsequent death in September elevated Vice-President Chester A. Arthur to the presidency. The change of president represented a serious loss of political influence for Blaine and brought an abrupt end to his period as secretary of state. Nevertheless, in only a few months his Latin American policy had aroused considerable controversy and debate both within and beyond the United States. Indeed, Blaine was similar to Henry Clay in being unusual among leading politicians in giving any special attention to events in Latin America. Reviving the concept of the separation of the hemispheres that had been popular earlier in the nineteenth century, he was convinced that the New World must remain inviolate from the corrupt and sordid influences of the Old World. Blaine considered the Latin American republics to be 'younger sisters' of the United States and 'far removed from the European system'.[10] It was also his belief that the United States must protect and lead its sister nations and that Great Britain posed the biggest threat to these aspirations. Indeed, Blaine's political career exhibited a strong anti-British bias and a good deal of his popularity within his home state of Maine, the Republican party and the nation at large, lay in his reputation for 'twisting the British lion's tail'. This was particularly evident in his attitude and policy toward the War of the Pacific that he described after leaving office as 'an English war on Peru, with Chile as the instrument'.[11]

The War of the Pacific had originated initially as a local dispute between Bolivia and Chile over the level of nitrate export taxes levied by the Bolivian authorities on Chilean merchants. Fighting broke out in February 1879, and Peru joined Bolivia against Chile in March 1879. The story that followed was one of steady and virtually uninterrupted Chilean military success in destroying the Peruvian navy, taking possession of the nitrate-rich Bolivian province of Tarapacá and culminating in the invasion of Peru and the occupation of Lima in January 1881. But Chile lacked the resources to maintain a lengthy military occupation of Peruvian territory. Nevertheless, peace terms proved elusive and a diplomatic impasse ensued over Chilean demands for the cession of the southern Peruvian provinces of Tacna and Arica. Blaine showed a close interest in developments in the war and, in contrast to his most recent predecessors at the state department, believed that American diplomacy, even if uninvited by the belligerents, should become actively involved in an existing conflict in order to facilitate a peace settlement. Blaine was personally sympathetic towards the plight of Peru. A principal reason was his suspicion that British business interests were secretly supporting Chile in order to gain control of the local nitrate industry. Blaine's political enemies, however, were not convinced and suspected that he sought to enrich himself by 'guano diplomacy'.[12] Whatever the secretary's motives, the diplomatic reality was that the Chileans had won a right of military conquest and that this might necessitate the cession of Peruvian territory. Nevertheless, seizing upon the fact that Chile had originally denied that it was involved in a war seeking the acquisition of territory, Blaine argued that Peru should therefore be allowed to pay a financial indemnity to Chile rather than give up Tacna and Arica.

Acting on his own personal initiative in early December 1881, Blaine sought to assist a peace settlement by dispatching a special commission to Santiago de Chile headed by William H. Trescot, an experienced state department official. Should Chile prove to be uncooperative and insist on retaining Peruvian territory, Blaine told Trescot that the United States:

> will hold itself free to appeal to the other republics of this continent to join it in an effort to avert consequences which cannot be confined to Chili and Peru, but which threaten with extremest danger the political institutions, the peaceful progress, and the liberal civilization of all America.[13]

This was a reference to an idea proposed earlier by Blaine of assembling a Pan-American peace conference in Washington at which the differences between Chile and Peru might be settled. The Chilean government was alarmed by Blaine's unilateral intervention and interpreted the Trescot mission as part of a calculated American strategy of aggressively exerting diplomatic pressure in order to help Peru. But the initiative was badly timed. Blaine left the state department on 19 December 1881 so he was out of office when the Trescot mission reached South America in January 1882. Moreover, the decision to send the mission was known to be under the careful scrutiny of the new secretary of state, Frederick Frelinghuysen, who decided to repudiate his predecessor's controversial policy. Frelinghuysen released to the press the instructions that Blaine had given to Trescot and later also withdrew the invitations to the proposed conference. The Chilean government was informed of these developments by telegraph prior to Trescot's arrival. Consequently, the Chileans were able to put aside their apprehensions and ignore the veiled threat of censure from a Pan-American conference. As the British minister in Peru, Spenser St John, gloatingly remarked, the results were 'most humiliating' for American diplomacy.[14] Furthermore, Blaine had incurred a reputation for aggressive and unpredictable diplomacy that was to last throughout his lifetime and served to spread and confirm the anti-American suspicions of Latin American political leaders.

A peace settlement was eventually arranged in 1883 between the Chileans and the Peruvians without the mediation of, or even consultation with the United States or the great European powers. Peru secured the withdrawal of Chilean troops but at the price of ceding Tacna and Arica to Chile. The outcome was merely another assertion of the independence of action that Chile had enjoyed and maintained ever since the beginning of the war. The one restraint to this had been the possibility of US intervention, either diplomatic or military, on the side of Peru and Bolivia, but this contingency had disappeared after Blaine's departure from office. It was most unusual for American diplomats to become actively involved in South American affairs. In the case of the War of the Pacific, American intervention appeared ill considered and insensitive. Consequently, the United States suffered a good deal of diplomatic embarrassment, and a legacy of bitterness was provoked between America and Chile that was to affect their relations for some years. Peru would seek to take advantage of this discord by cultivating friendly relations with the United States, not because of a strong belief in an 'American' system but rather with the ulterior motive of enlisting American influence to regain the lost provinces of Tacna and Arica from Chile.

The Pan-American Conference, 1889–90

The active interest taken by the United States in Latin American affairs as exemplified by the Central American Canal and the War of the Pacific contributed to the development of 'Pan-Americanism', the general term used at the time to describe a policy that sought a hemisphere of prosperous, secure and democratic sister nations. While there were similarities with the ideas of Henry Clay, the concept emerging at the end of the nineteenth century was more practical in seeking to establish an informal political alliance and commercial union of all the American republics. Pan-Americanism was effectively an attempt to put the Monroe Doctrine into action. This was demonstrated by the fact that the United States consciously took the lead and claimed to act the part of a friendly sister. The concept was particularly associated with Blaine and became a prominent feature of his campaigns for his party's presidential nomination, including a narrow defeat for the presidency in 1884, and also of a Republican electoral platform that pushed Latin American affairs to the forefront of domestic political debate. Although he was concerned over European political designs on Latin America, Blaine placed particular stress on the recent marked increase in European economic influence and the urgent necessity for Americans to counter and reverse this development. 'If these tendencies are to be averted, if Spanish–American friendship is to be regained, if the commercial empire that legitimately belongs to us is to be ours', Blaine combatively argued in 1882, 'we must not lie idle and witness its transfer to others.'[15]

To an extent Pan-Americanism reflected the understandable but selfish desire of American political leaders to take direct action to alleviate their own country's economic depression.[16] The American economy grew steadily throughout the late-nineteenth century, but not without periods of recession and, in the case of the years from 1893 to 1897, severe depression. The economic crisis was attributed rather simplistically to chronic overproduction, especially of agricultural produce, and the solution was logically seen as disposing of the surplus in the form of increased exports not only of agricultural but also of manufactured goods. Not for the first or last time in the view of American politicians and business leaders, the geographical proximity of Latin America made that region appear as a natural and very accessible market for American exports. Moreover, the region was also known to be enjoying its own industrial boom and was therefore perceived as particularly receptive to foreign trade and investment. For example, President Arthur envisaged the prospect of securing a special and mutually beneficial commercial relationship when he declared in his Annual Message to Congress in 1884:

> The countries of the American continent and the adjacent islands are for the United States the natural marts of supply and demand. It is from them that we should obtain what we do not produce or do not produce to sufficiency, and it is to them that the surplus productions of our fields, our mills, and our workshops should flow, under conditions that will equalize or favor them in comparison with foreign competition.[17]

In contrast to the contentious debates over the 1826 Panama Congress and the isthmian canal treaties, Pan-Americanism was not a divisive political issue in the US Congress. During the 1880s there was frequent discussion of proposals for an inter-American customs union on the lines of the successful German Zollverein, the negotiation of bilateral reciprocity treaties to stimulate trade, and especially the improvement of railroad and steamship communications. In 1884 an appropriation was voted to dispatch a special commercial commission to tour Latin America and investigate ways of promoting more trade. The decision to send an official commission was unusual and aroused considerable interest on the part of Latin American governments. 'In every country that we visited except, perhaps, Chile,' reported the commission, 'we found the authorities and the people desirous of strengthening the relations between their country and the United States.'[18] The commission recommended that a most promising area for American diplomatic action was that of increasing trade by means of the negotiation of bilateral reciprocal trade agreements. But the implementation of commercial reciprocity normally meant each country revising its tariff schedules downwards. In the United States, however, the tariff had become a highly sensitive political issue. Despite the existence of general approval in principle on the need to cultivate more trade with Latin America, the passage of reciprocity legislation in Congress faced opposition from powerful business lobbies and political interests in both parties that were unwilling to allow any change to the existing policy of tariff protection. On the other hand, there was increasing bipartisan political support for the much less controversial proposal that the United States should host a meeting of all the American nations for the purpose of discussing commercial matters. In early 1888 agreement was reached in the US Congress on an Act authorizing the president to invite Latin American governments to an 'international American Conference' to be held in the nation's capital in 1889.[19]

The proposed agenda of the conference was extremely broad and included specific items such as steamship and railroad communication, customs regulations, weights and measures and copyright agreements, but also much more general and potentially controversial questions such as the project for an inter-American customs union, the adoption of a silver coin as the common unit of currency and an arbitration scheme to resolve inter-American disputes. Congressman James McCreary of Kentucky expressed the aims of the conference in purely commercial terms. 'The countries of Central and South America', he declared, 'need the products of our furnaces, of our factories, and of our farms.'[20] In effect, the meeting was regarded as a positive step towards American displacement of the existing European commercial ascendancy in Latin America. 'We should not only have a larger share of that trade than any country but we should be able to control most of it', remarked Congressman Richard Townshend of Illinois.[21] Indeed, the deliberate exclusion of Canada and the British West Indies from the conference pointed to the anti-British nature of US policy. The ambitious proposals to form a customs union and to establish arbitration machinery also signified a determination to exclude European political and commercial influence from the Western Hemisphere and were in keeping with the Monroe Doctrine and the idea of a New World separate from the Old World.

For a nation that had only very reluctantly sent representatives to the 1826 Panama Congress and which had regularly declared a desire to avoid foreign entanglements, the decision of the United States to call an inter-American conference was most unusual and an event of major diplomatic significance in the Western Hemisphere. It also attracted considerable notice in Europe where the London Chamber of Commerce concluded that the importance of the development could 'hardly be overestimated'.[22] While the Latin American nations were aware of the commercial aspects of the conference, they were also suspicious of American motives and wondered why exactly the United States was reversing its policy of neglect and seeking instead to alter the historical pattern of inter-American relations. Nor was this apprehension allayed by the election of the Republican candidate, Benjamin Harrison, as president in 1888 and his subsequent decision to appoint the controversial Blaine as secretary of state. This meant that the task of organizing and hosting the conference would fall to Harrison and Blaine.

With the sole exception of the Dominican Republic,[23] all the Latin American countries accepted the invitations, and their delegates assembled in Washington for the opening of the conference in October 1889. The reasons for Latin American acquiescence were varied. First, there was the sheer difficulty of turning down an invitation made by the United States because such a refusal could be interpreted as lack of diplomatic courtesy. Furthermore, the original invitation had stressed that the conference was 'consultative and recommendatory only' so that no obligations were incurred by acceptance.[24] Attendance at the conference also had undoubtedly attractive aspects. There was widespread support for the development of steamship communication with the United States and keen interest among silver producers in the proposal to establish a silver coin as common currency throughout the hemisphere. Eager to find alternative markets for its declining sugar industry, Brazil was rumoured to be willing to negotiate a commercial treaty with the United States. Moreover, item eight of the agenda allowed virtually any subject to be raised at the conference and so presented valuable political opportunities. Venezuela used this item to publicize its long-standing boundary dispute with Great Britain. The timing of the invitation was also opportune in that there was no major military or diplomatic conflict pending in Latin America to prevent countries from attending.

The new Harrison Administration (1889–93) saw the conference as an opportunity for mounting an impressive public relations spectacle. William E. Curtis, a journalist who had been the secretary of the trade commission that had visited Latin America in 1884–5, was placed in charge of the administrative preparations for the 1889 conference. 'The constitutional centennial of this, the mother of republics,' wrote Curtis in June 1889, 'could not be celebrated in a more appropriate manner than by bringing her children together.' Curtis publicly praised the 'phenomenal foresight' of Bolívar in convening the 1826 Congress of Panama and, although it distorted the historical record, traced a direct link between that meeting and Blaine's revival of the idea in 1881 and the congressional appropriation voted in 1888.[25] In an attempt to impress not only American public opinion but also the Latin American delegates, he was instructed by Blaine to organize a pre-conference deluxe railroad tour of the United States for the visitors. But the itinerary of the excursion had a specific commercial purpose in mind that reduced its initial attractiveness. The *Boston Journal* noted that the delegates would see 'the mines and iron mills, the factories, gas wells, cotton plantations and all the other wonders of American agricultural methods'.[26] The English-language *Rio News* similarly remarked:

> We do not understand that these delegates have gone to Washington to buy a stock of goods, nor did we believe that the United States proposed to play the part of a professional drummer. We were

> of opinion that this congress was designed to discuss a number of important international questions, some political, some financial, and some commercial.[27]

Argentina emerged as the focus of opposition to the United States at the conference and thereby set a precedent for a competitive and, at times an adversarial relationship that would last well into the twentieth century.[28] A relatively big country with a flourishing economy largely based on exports to Great Britain, Argentina attracted substantial numbers of immigrants from Europe and was proud of its close and expanding ties with the Old World. It also considered itself to be the leading nation in South America and expected to play an important role at the meeting in Washington. The two Argentine delegates, Manuel Quintana and Roque Sáenz Peña, were conspicuous in adopting an independent and highly professional approach to the business of the conference. Indeed, they were extremely critical of the time allotted to the railroad excursion and believed that it had distracted delegates from their main purpose, which was to discuss only those items listed on the agenda. The American organizers were taken to task for their procedural errors. The opening session of the conference was conducted entirely in the English language until Quintana requested that a translation be made and asked why bilingual secretaries had not been appointed for this purpose. Sáenz Peña even questioned the reasons of the United States for organizing the conference. He alleged that the American delegates were motivated by a selfish concern to redress their country's adverse trade balance with the Latin American nations. While acknowledging the existence of a problem of economic overproduction and the consequent American need for foreign markets, he also pointed out that the recent tariff history of the United States was characterized not by free trade but by protectionism and high duties. In his view, the pursuit of an inter-American customs union was misguided because it ignored the economic reality that most Latin American trade was currently conducted with Europe. 'Between us, the American nations,' Sáenz Peña declared, 'interchange is the exception, and non-communion the rule.'[29]

While the speeches and actions of Sáenz Peña and Quintana indicated the existence of a significant divergence of national interests between Latin America and the United States, their intention was not to disrupt the conference. The two Argentine delegates had come to Washington and remained at the conference because their country had something to gain. Increased trade with the United States, improved credit and banking facilities, better steamship communications and a common silver coin were included among the prospective benefits. On the other hand, the American delegates were not able to take full advantage of this opportunity for constructive discussions on account of domestic political pressures, especially emanating from the US Congress, whose legislative proposals often ran counter to everything the conference was trying to achieve. For example, while the conference was in session and debating ways of improving inter-American trade, the new Republican-controlled Congress began to prepare, under the leadership of Congressman William McKinley of Ohio, a tariff bill that aimed to increase rather than decrease existing duties on goods imported into the United States. Sáenz Peña sarcastically remarked that when he returned home, he might find that American duties on Argentine products were even higher than before he had left Argentina to attend the conference.

The conference came to an end on 19 April 1890. The meeting was adjudged to have promoted Pan-American fellowship, so much so that, in reporting the event, the American press preferred to adopt the term 'Pan-American Conference' instead of the official title of 'International American Conference'. Despite the flattering reporting of the press, the substantive results were slight. Indeed, divergence had been more often in evidence than convergence. The customs union never materialized. While seven delegations, including Peru, agreed in principle to Blaine's scheme for providing compulsory arbitration to settle disputes, Chile remembered the diplomacy of the War of the Pacific and remained firmly opposed. Although the Latin Americans had generally deferred to the wishes of the host nation, the actions of the Argentine delegates in criticizing and even resisting American attempts to stage-manage and manipulate the proceedings, revealed a determination to affirm the equality of states. In fact, the sole tangible achievement of the conference was the establishment of a small commercial information bureau located in Washington that struggled in its early years to attract funding but would ultimately grow into the Pan-American Union. In general, muddled and, at times insensitive management of the conference combined with domestic political pressures arising principally from the US Congress had provided an effective barrier to the achievement of Pan-American aims. Nevertheless, the very fact that the conference had actually taken place not only provided a precedent for future meetings[30] but was also a significant demonstration of the prestige and powerful influence of the United States within the Western Hemisphere. That influence now took another form in the shape of the revival and implementation of the policy of commercial reciprocity.

Commercial reciprocity

Republican leaders in Congress were made aware that their high tariff proposals were damaging the Pan-American policy of the Harrison Administration. 'There is not a section or a line in the entire [McKinley Tariff] bill that will open the market for another bushel of wheat or another barrel of pork', declared Blaine.[31] In order to limit the political damage to their party and to stimulate external trade, Republican leaders agreed to requests from Harrison and Blaine to include the reciprocity amendment in the McKinley tariff bill that was signed into law by Harrison on 1 October 1890. The amendment empowered the president to negotiate and conclude reciprocal commercial agreements with foreign nations by executive action and without therefore requiring the uncertain and time-consuming process of Senate ratification. Blaine was especially keen to use the reciprocity amendment to carry out his long-held plans to expand trade with Latin America and, in the process, to oust European competitors by creating a hemispheric commercial system ultimately dominated by the United States. A treaty with Brazil was negotiated in early 1891 and came into effect on 1 April 1891. In return for admission to an American list of goods free of import duty, including sugar and coffee, Brazil reciprocated by removing duties on its imports of American machinery and foodstuffs and granting a 25 per cent reduction of duty on a large number of manufactured goods. Similar arrangements followed with Spain (for Cuba), the Dominican Republic, Guatemala, Honduras, El Salvador, Costa Rica, Nicaragua and Great Britain (for the British West Indies).[32]

'If the merchants and manufacturers of the United States utilize the advantages secured for them,' predicted Curtis, 'the ultimate effect will be to confine American trade almost entirely to American waters.'[33] But the network of reciprocity treaties never extended very far beyond the Caribbean and Central American countries whose trade was already mostly with the United States. Moreover, no treaties were concluded either with Mexico or with any of the nations of Spanish South America which stood to gain relatively little from admission to the American free list. The treaties were also in force for only a short period of time on account of the defeat of Harrison by Grover Cleveland in the 1892 presidential election. This resulted in the return to power of a Democratic administration (1893–7) that set the reversal of the Republican policy of tariff protection, including commercial reciprocity, as one of its priorities. Consequently, all the reciprocity treaties were unilaterally terminated by the passage of the Wilson Tariff Bill in August 1894.

The cavalier manner in which the treaties were abruptly terminated not by diplomatic agreement but by the action of the US Congress demonstrated that the policy of commercial reciprocity, both in formulation and execution, had been primarily dictated by internal political pressures. Indeed, the policy all too often had assumed an inconsistent and aggressive character that openly clashed with the proclaimed policy of cultivating Pan-American goodwill. In the opinion of the British Foreign Office, the developments of these years were a 'most extraordinary series of legislative and political manoeuvres'.[34] In effect, the aims of American commercial diplomacy as articulated by Blaine were too ambitious and premature. Pan-American conferences and reciprocity agreements were a beginning, but they were no substitute for the essential elements of conducting business that the United States still conspicuously lacked in its commercial relationship with Latin America. The limited provision of steamship shipping services, banking and credit facilities, continued to serve as severe obstacles towards the expansion of American trade and business in Latin America. Consequently, the American economic challenge to well-established European business interests in Latin America was not very effective in the short term. As the British minister to Washington, Lionel West, had noted in 1885: 'The inauguration of an American hemispherical policy does not seem to meet with much favour . . . The channels of trade cannot be so easily diverted by insisting on national exclusiveness as was anticipated.'[35]

Indeed, European economic influence was further reinforced by the evident desire of Latin Americans to maintain close links with Europe. The late-nineteenth century saw the emergence of a flourishing world economy in which Europe exported large quantities of manufactured goods, investment capital and immigrants to areas such as Latin America and in return imported essential raw materials and primary goods. Latin Americans admired the undoubted achievements of 'the colossus of the north', but they admired the Old World, too, and were very much aware that their economic fortunes were tied as much as ever to Europe rather than to the United States. The mutual economic benefits of increased inter-American contact were not disputed, but ironically Pan-Americanism contributed to making Latin Americans even more aware of their bonds with Europe. Far from desiring a New World isolated from the Old, Sáenz Peña had eloquently reminded Americans at the Washington Conference that 'Europe extends to us her hand, sends us her strong arms, and complements our economic existence, after apportioning to us her civilization'. As a counter to the popular slogan appearing in the American press of 'America for the Americans', Sáenz Peña urged: 'Let America be for humanity.'[36] The British minister at Washington, Julian Pauncefote, even believed that the cultural ties with Europe had never been stronger. 'South American travel and social and intellectual intercourse', he remarked, 'are with Europe and not with North America.'[37]

Diplomatic crises in Chile, Brazil and Venezuela

During the last quarter of the nineteenth century Latin American affairs intruded into the very essence of American domestic politics, helped by the growth of popular journalism whose daily tabloid editions often added heavy doses of drama and sensation to the reporting of events. The result was a greater public awareness of the region that did much to dispel previous indifference and lack of information. During the 1890s, in particular, a series of political crises occurred in certain countries of Latin America that made front-page news in the United States and even provoked calls for a vigorous American diplomatic and military response. Notably, governments were overthrown in Brazil in 1889, Argentina in 1890 and Chile in 1891.

The change of regime in Chile culminating in the suicide of President José Manuel Balmaceda was particularly significant because relations between that country and the United States had been difficult ever since Blaine's controversial diplomatic intervention in the War of the Pacific. Relations were further embittered by the 'Baltimore Incident'. In October 1891 a group of American sailors from the cruiser *Baltimore* on shore leave in Valparaíso were involved in an affray with a Chilean mob in which one American sailor was killed and five seriously wounded. The commander of the *Baltimore*, Captain Winfield F. Schley, reported to Washington that his men had been unarmed and had given no provocation for the attack. Public excitement reached such a height that the body of the murdered American sailor, Charles Riggin, was returned to the United States and for a while lay in state at Independence Hall, Philadelphia. President Harrison interpreted the incident as a 'savage, brutal' and 'unprovoked' assault.[38] Even though Secretary of State Blaine favoured moderation, the president chose to react in an assertive and aggressive manner to Chile's reluctance to give a full apology by sending warships and threatening to break off diplomatic relations. Weakened by its recent civil war and without allies, the Chilean government did not want war with the United States and agreed to pay financial compensation to the injured American sailors. The British press expressed surprise that 'intelligent and fair-minded Americans' should 'raise a tavern brawl to the dignity of an international question'.[39] Harrison, however, had no doubts. His insistence on receiving an apology and reparation was motivated by his aggrieved sense that American honour and the rights of American citizens had been infringed. It did not go unnoticed in Latin America, however, that Harrison's resort to the threat of force and evident determination to humiliate Chile contradicted the Pan-American rhetoric and affirmations of sisterly goodwill that had marked the beginning of his administration.

The defeat of Harrison by the Democratic candidate, Grover Cleveland, in the 1892 presidential election appeared to signal a change to a more cautious and restrained American foreign policy. This was exemplified by the principled decision of the new Cleveland Administration (1893–7) to reject the treaty held over from the Harrison Administration proposing that the United States annex Hawaii. 'I am unalterably opposed', declared Cleveland's secretary of state, Walter Q. Gresham, in 1894, 'to stealing territory, or of annexing a people against their consent, and the people of Hawaii do not favor annexation.'[40] The Cleveland Administration adopted a similarly legalistic and reactive attitude to the Brazilian Naval Revolt of 1893–4. By overthrowing the empire in 1889, Brazil had become a republic. Though regret was expressed in the United States for the deposition of the much-admired Emperor Pedro II, the victory for republicanism was welcomed, especially as it finally signified the end of the last monarchical system of government in Latin America. 'Nothing so grand or so excellent has ever been achieved in the history of any nation', enthused Senator John T. Morgan of Alabama.[41]

American politicians were dismayed, however, by evidence that the switch from empire to republic did not automatically bring political stability. 'What at present confronts us in Brazil', remarked the *New York Sun* a month after the coup, 'is a military dictatorship.'[42] The threat by the Brazilian navy to bombard Rio de Janeiro in November 1891 brought about the resignation of the first president of the republic, Deodoro da Fonseca. In September 1893 the Brazilian navy mutinied again and mounted a naval blockade of the harbour of Rio de Janeiro. The government of Floriano Peixoto alleged that the revolt represented a European plot to restore the monarchy and requested overseas support, including American military assistance, to defeat the naval rebels. The conspiracy theory extended to reports that the British navy was secretly giving aid to the insurgents. But Gresham was sceptical. He questioned the 'patriotism' of the Brazilian people and told the American ambassador in London: 'I do not believe Great Britain, or any other European Power, will attempt to re-establish the Monarchy in Brazil.'[43] The policy adopted by the Cleveland Administration towards the revolt was pragmatic and legalistic. Two warships were sent to Rio for the purpose of protecting American commercial operations in the bay. By January 1894 this number was increased to five. The small American squadron commanded by Admiral Andrew Benham was involved in an act of limited military intervention when it exchanged shots with insurgent ships in escorting an American merchant vessel to the docks. The incident was brief but locally significant. By preventing the insurgents from stopping and searching American ships, and by implication all foreign merchant shipping, 'Benham's action' effectively broke the attempted blockade and rendered the position of the insurgent fleet in the harbour untenable.

The Brazilian Naval Revolt finally collapsed in March 1894. A constant factor throughout the conflict was the combination of firmness and skilful diplomacy shown by Floriano Peixoto that defeated the strategy of the insurgents and made it only a matter of time before they capitulated. But Floriano was also grateful for Benham's action and demonstrated this by making 4 July 1894 a national holiday. Secretary of State Gresham, however, was careful to stress that the aim of American naval action had not been to take sides in what he judged was an internal dispute but to assert the right of American merchants to carry out commercial operations without hindrance from insurgent ships. In fact, the collapse of the blockade was of more immediate benefit to European rather than American trade. At the end of the revolt, the American minister at Rio recalled that there were only five merchant ships in the harbour flying the American flag while he counted more than 100 British vessels.[44] Whatever the exact motive, the naval action in Brazil, coming so soon after the Baltimore Incident, effectively demonstrated the growing military power of the United States and how it could be projected, if required, to assert American rights in Latin America. In commending Benham's conduct, Cleveland's secretary of the navy, Hilary A. Herbert, declared that his action would 'have a far-reaching and wholesome influence in quite a number of countries where revolutions are so frequent as to almost constantly imperil the rights of American citizens'.[45]

Another troublesome diplomatic issue to confront the Cleveland Administration and to attract the attention of the American daily press was the long-standing dispute between Venezuela and Great Britain over the exact location of the boundary in the remote and virtually inaccessible jungle region separating Venezuela and the British colony of Guyana. The question had persisted since the 1840s and attracted added significance during the 1880s after discoveries of gold were reported from the disputed area. From 1876 onwards, successive Venezuelan governments frequently looked to the United States for diplomatic support against Great Britain. They received, however, little more than polite expressions of sympathy. The likelihood of some form of American diplomatic intervention in the dispute began to look much more probable in 1895 after the Venezuelan government enlisted the lobbying services of a former American diplomat, William L. Scruggs, who had previously served as American minister to Colombia and Venezuela. Scruggs's masterstroke was to raise the Monroe Doctrine. He prepared a historical pamphlet that was provocatively entitled 'British Aggression in Venezuela, or the Monroe Doctrine on Trial', and was widely circulated in Washington. Scruggs argued that Great Britain was violating the Monroe Doctrine by deviously seeking to acquire territory at Venezuela's expense. In addition, he claimed that the British aimed to establish control over the Orinoco River in order to dominate the trade of northern South America.[46]

The reference to the Monroe Doctrine exercised a decisive influence. On 20 July 1895 Cleveland's secretary of state, Richard Olney, dispatched a diplomatic note to the British Foreign Office. Its central theme was a requirement that other nations recognize the principles of the Monroe Doctrine. Without any forewarning Olney demanded that Great Britain agree to submit the boundary dispute to arbitration. 'Today the United States is practically sovereign on this continent, and its fiat is law upon the subjects to which it confines its interposition', he declared.[47] The sweeping implication was that the United States, by reason of its geographical position, possessed an inherent right to intervene in diplomatic questions relating to the Western Hemisphere even if it was not a party to the dispute. Great Britain's reply, however, challenged the applicability of the Monroe Doctrine to the boundary issue and, in so doing, actually sought to protect the sovereign rights of the Latin American nations. The British foreign minister, Lord Salisbury, argued:

> The Government of the United States is not entitled to affirm as a universal proposition, with reference to a number of independent States, for whose conduct it assumes no responsibility, that its interests are necessarily concerned in whatever may befall those States simply because they are situated in the Western Hemisphere.[48]

President Cleveland was annoyed at Salisbury's apparently unyielding response. He was also aware of criticism in the press and from Republicans in Congress of his Administration's 'weak and un-American' foreign policy.[49] As Hayes had done in March 1880 over the canal issue, Cleveland decided to transform a minor Latin American question into one of pressing domestic importance by sending a Special Message to Congress on 17 December 1895. In what was a resounding reaffirmation of the principles of the Monroe Doctrine that he described as 'of vital concern to our people and their government',[50] the message requested congressional funds to set up an American commission to investigate and decide the boundary dispute. The tone was similar to that adopted by Harrison only a few years earlier in the Baltimore Incident. Right was assumed to be assuredly on the side of the United States, and there was no place for compromise. The message was interpreted in the British and American press as a virtual ultimatum to accept arbitration, which if rejected, must pose the possibility of war between the United States and Britain. 'Nothing is heard', reported British Ambassador Julian Pauncefote, 'but the voice of the Jingo bellowing out defiance to England.'[51]

The war scare was short-lived much to the relief of both governments. Confronted simultaneously with a difficult crisis in South Africa resulting from the ill-fated Jameson Raid, the British government did not want to become embroiled in a distant 'American' question and chose to send a conciliatory response to Cleveland. It agreed to his proposal for arbitration and thereby acknowledged the right of the United States to intervene in the boundary dispute. For the United States, the episode represented an important historic victory. The Monroe Doctrine was vindicated and American political pre-eminence in the Western Hemisphere was finally recognized by Great Britain and by implication, the other European powers, too, because they would surely follow Britain's example. Ironically, this successful outcome aroused apprehension in Latin America. The United States claimed to be acting selflessly on behalf of its Latin American sisters in defeating European imperialism, but the apparent altruism was strongly tinged with national self-interest. It was also exercised in a characteristically unilateral and arrogant manner. Olney and Cleveland did not consult the Venezuelan government over their policy, and the arbitration procedure was virtually imposed upon a reluctant Venezuela. That country's sense of grievance was heightened when the arbitration commission announced its award in 1899 and granted Great Britain most of the disputed territory.

The Spanish–American War

The ability of the United States to deploy naval forces in Chilean and Brazilian waters was a consequence of the steady build-up of the American navy during the last two decades of the nineteenth century. The development owed much to a growing economy that led the world in iron and steel production, political pressures from shipyards and armaments manufacturers, and especially the teaching and writings of Admiral Alfred Thayer Mahan that emphasized the strategic and commercial necessity of constructing a strong American navy in response to the formation of military alliances in Europe. The 'new' American navy that came into being, with its powerfully armoured first-class battleships, not only gave international prestige to the United States but also served as a valuable instrument of diplomacy, especially in Latin America. Indeed, an influential argument in favour of a strong American navy and the acquisition of overseas naval bases for coaling and repairs was the need to counter possible European imperialistic designs on the Western Hemisphere. During the last half of the nineteenth century vast areas of territory in Africa, Asia and the Pacific were falling under European colonial control and there were rumours of similar European designs on Latin America. American public opinion was influenced by popular writers and lecturers such as John Fiske who revived and expanded the ideas and the spirit of Manifest Destiny and democratic mission when he argued that the United States should not neglect its duty and that:

> the work which the English race began when it colonized North America is destined to go on until every land on the earth's surface that it not already the seat of an old civilization shall become English in its language, in its religion, in its political habits and traditions, and to a predominant extent in the blood of its people.[52]

There was actually little substance to rumours of European governments plotting to acquire territory in Latin America. As the Venezuela boundary dispute demonstrated, clashes with the United States could be painful diplomatic experiences, but the overall implications of American claims to political pre-eminence in the Western Hemisphere were neither disturbing nor threatening to European nations, who attached, after all, only marginal strategic significance to the area. The reckoning was, however, to come brutally for Spain in 1898 over Cuba. The US government had long shown a desire to acquire the island, but active political interest in annexation had diminished after the 1854 Ostend Manifesto. Instead, the emphasis was on promoting and developing closer economic ties. By the last quarter of the nineteenth century, the United States had replaced Spain as Cuba's largest trading partner and was purchasing from 80 to 90 per cent of Cuba's total exports. Like its neighbours in the Caribbean and Central America, Cuba now formed part of an 'informal' American economic empire that was being steadily established in the region by the policy of commercial reciprocity. Indeed, the prosperity of the Cuban economy became dangerously dependent on continued access to the American market. This was underscored in 1894 by the passage of the Wilson Tariff that unilaterally removed the duty-free status previously conferred on imports of Cuban sugar. The resulting collapse of the sugar industry in Cuba contributed significantly to an increase in political and economic unrest, which led to the outbreak of a major rebellion in February 1895 initially led by the Cuban poet and patriot José Martí and the mulatto general Antonio Maceo, whose aim was to achieve freedom for Cuba ('Cuba libre'). Martí, however, was one of first casualties in the fighting when he was killed in an ambush on 19 May 1895.

President Cleveland preferred to take a detached view of the civil war unfolding in Cuba. Although he did not doubt that Spanish rule was oppressive, he showed no desire to meddle in Cuban affairs nor any particular sympathy for the insurgents and their aspirations for Cuban independence. Like Cuba, the United States was also experiencing an economic depression. Already alarmed by the threat to property and order posed by social and economic agitation at home, Cleveland was suspicious of similar troubles elsewhere and appeared comfortable with the official explanation of the Spanish government that the disorder on the island was the work of bandits and outlaws. On a later occasion he privately referred to the insurgents as 'the most inhuman and barbarous cutthroats in the world'.[53] There were also disturbing reports that the real aim of the revolt was to overthrow the white Cuban-Spanish elite and set up a black republic. In June 1895 Cleveland issued a proclamation of neutrality to prevent the launching of filibusters from the United States. The pursuit of neutrality, however, was made extremely difficult by the close geographical proximity of Cuba and the determination of Cuban exiles and their American sympathizers to send aid to the revolt.

Cleveland and his successor, William McKinley, also had to take into account the excitable mood of American public opinion. Americans were naturally sympathetic towards what they perceived as one more stage in the historic struggle of the Cuban people for freedom from Spanish tyranny. Although the conflict was marked by brutality and savagery on both sides – insurgents and government – traditional American prejudices against Spain and Spaniards were revived and reinforced by sensational reports in the press of the Spanish army and especially their commander, General 'Butcher'

Weyler y Nicolau, resorting to widespread torture and summary execution not only of captured insurgents but also of civilians who were suspected of aiding the rebellion. 'These revolting details of unspeakable cruelty', noted the *Chicago Tribune*, 'show how close is the Spaniard of today at heart to the Spaniard of two and one-half-centuries ago.'[54]

The American press, notably led by the rival New York newspapers of William Randolph Hearst (*New York Journal*) and Joseph Pulitzer (*New York World*), often exaggerated the Spanish atrocities, but, even so, the sufferings of the Cubans were horrible enough to arouse deep sympathies. Moreover, they were the sufferings of a neighbour, and they were incurred in a fight for independence from a manifestly unjust European imperial ruler. American public opinion increasingly believed that their government had a moral duty to compel Spain to stop the suffering and destruction. It was also greatly incensed by the blowing up in suspicious circumstances of the US battleship *Maine* in Havana harbour in February 1898 with the loss of 266 American lives. The assistant secretary of the navy, Theodore Roosevelt, privately informed a friend that the sinking was the result of 'an act of dirty treachery on the part of the Spaniards'.[55] 'The Whole Country Thrills With War Fever', stated a typical banner headline in the New York press.[56] The intensity of public interest was revealed a few weeks later when Hearst proudly disclosed that the daily circulation of morning and evening editions of the *Journal* had reached one million and that this represented an increase of more than 250,000 from the previous year's figure.

In spite of enormous political and public pressure for immediate military retaliation against Spain for its presumed complicity in the destruction of the *Maine*, President McKinley preferred to use America's influence to achieve a resolution of the civil war by peaceful diplomatic means. The president's aim was to secure a cease-fire as a prelude to negotiations for a political settlement leading to independence and an orderly Spanish military withdrawal from the island. But neither the Cuban insurgents nor the Spanish government were prepared to compromise. Encouraged by the recall of General Weyler to Spain in October 1897, the insurgents sensed victory and would not stop fighting unless independence was guaranteed. But a similar determination to keep fighting prevailed in Madrid. The abandonment of the 'ever-faithful isle' was unacceptable to the Spanish monarchy, government and, most of all, the senior army officers for whom it would signify military defeat and professional dishonour. Conscious of the likelihood of American military intervention, the Spanish queen appealed for the support of the great European powers, but they were unwilling to challenge the United States in what was regarded as an 'American' question.

McKinley chose to ignore the Cuban insurgents and concentrated his diplomatic efforts on the Spanish government in Madrid. He finally lost patience with Spanish promises to end the fighting and in April 1898 recommended in a 'War Message' that the US Congress recognize Cuban independence. 'In the name of humanity, in the name of civilization, in behalf of endangered American interests which give us the right and the duty to speak and to act,' McKinley told Congress, 'the war in Cuba must stop.'[57] A Joint Congressional Resolution was passed affirming America's commitment to spreading democracy and stating: 'the people of the island of Cuba are, and of right ought to be, free and independent.'[58] The US Congress empowered McKinley to use armed force to secure Spanish political and military withdrawal from the island. But it also placed what would turn out to be a major constraint on his future actions. Despite the strong support for the president's War Message, the fact that he refused to recognize the insurgents as the provisional Cuban government had created a suspicion in Congress that he privately favoured not independence but the annexation of Cuba to the United States. To satisfy any doubts on this question, the Senate approved an Amendment proposed by Senator Henry Teller of Colorado stating that the United States 'disclaims any disposition or intention to exercise sovereignty, jurisdiction, or control over said Island except for the pacification thereof, and asserts its determination when that is accomplished to leave the government and control of the Island to its people'.[59] Spain responded to the Joint Resolution by declaring war on the United States. Both Cleveland and McKinley had sincerely worked for peace, but their policy of exerting diplomatic pressure on the Spanish government to stop what was perceived as an increasingly destructive and futile conflict eventually collapsed in the face of Spain's refusal to abandon its most valuable and revered colonial possession.[60]

By early July and within ten weeks of the declaration of war, the fighting was over and the victory won. For Americans, it was truly a 'splendid little war'. The Spanish–American War was arguably the most 'popular' of American wars because it brought not only the glory of Commodore George Dewey's magnificent naval victory at Manila Bay in the Philippines and the bravery of the Rough Riders at the San Juan Heights, outside Santiago de Cuba, but it was also over before weariness or discontent could set in. The reason for rapid success in Cuba lay not so much in the undoubted bravery of the US military forces, but in the fact that the large Spanish army on the island had become severely crippled with sickness and low morale. Even before the outbreak of war with the United States, Spanish forces had proved increasingly reluctant to venture outside their protected forts and garrisons, so control over much of the countryside was handed by default to the insurgents. 'This war cannot last more than a year', predicted the insurgent leader, General Máximo Gómez y Báez, at the beginning of 1898.[61] When the United States entered the war, the American navy soon gained control of the seas around the island, while the Spaniards compounded their own inefficiency by immobilizing their warships in Santiago de Cuba. The American Expeditionary Force, with the aid of the local insurgent army, was therefore allowed to land in eastern Cuba with little Spanish resistance. After the destruction of the Spanish fleet and the fall of Santiago de Cuba, Spanish forces surrendered in July and peace was signed in August 1898. In the Treaty of Paris that formally ended the war, Spain accepted the loss of Cuba and Puerto Rico, its last colonies in the New World.

According to the wording of the Joint Congressional Resolution and the Teller Amendment of April 1898, the United States had entered into war against Spain with the proclaimed intention of bringing peace and freedom to the Cuban people. Having achieved victory over Spain, it was widely assumed that McKinley would quickly declare the formation of an independent Cuban republic and withdraw American troops from the island. José Martí had always feared, however, that a close association with Americans would compromise the fight for 'Cuba libre' and ultimately result in the island's annexation to the United States. 'To change masters', he once noted, 'is not to be free.'[62] Martí's fears were borne out as an internal civil conflict was transformed into a war of American military conquest in which the United States used its superior power to dictate the terms of the peace settlement. On 1 January 1899 McKinley formally replaced Spanish rule in Cuba with a military government headed by General John R. Brooke. Although the Teller Amendment stipulated that such an administrative arrangement must be temporary, its exact duration was not specified. Consequently, the future political status of Cuba remained uncertain.

The delay in handing over government and sovereign rights was explained and complicated by the low opinion which Americans possessed concerning the capacity of the Cuban people to govern themselves. American soldiers and journalists who had been on the island during the war had already communicated highly unfavourable accounts of their personal encounters with the local population. Their superior and contemptuous attitude was also fuelled by the discovery that the large majority of Cubans were illiterate and apparently black or of mixed race. The journalist George Kennan expressed a common American reaction of surprise when he observed that 'fully four-fifths' of the insurgent army in eastern Cuba were mulattos or blacks. 'If their rifles and cartridge-belts had been taken away from them,' he added, 'they would have looked like a horde of dirty Cuban beggars and ragamuffins on the tramp.'[63]

Conditioned by Anglo-Saxon racist prejudice towards blacks and Social Darwinist ideas of racial progress based on the idea of 'the survival of the fittest', Americans readily believed that independence for Cuba was premature and, if granted too soon, would result in the island becoming poor and politically unstable like the notorious black republic of Haiti. The American military commander, William R. Shafter, was quoted as saying: 'Self-government! Why, these people are no more fit for self-government than gun-powder is for hell.'[64] But the Teller Amendment ruled out annexation. The solution to the quandary was to establish American civil and military administration, while providing Cubans with uplifting instruction in the art of government until such time as they were deemed ready for independence. 'Under our supervision, and with firm and honest care for the future', remarked the US Commissioner, Major George M. Barbour, 'the people of Cuba may become a useful race and a credit to the world, but to attempt to set them afloat as a nation, during this generation would be a great mistake.'[65] There was virtually no organized Cuban resistance to American occupation because the insurgent forces were no longer able to forage and live off the land. They had become increasingly destitute and willingly gave up their weapons in exchange for rations and jobs. In fact, reports from American officials in Cuba reassuringly suggested that there would be local acceptance of a period of tutelage. Indeed, many leading Cuban politicians and businessmen were known to favour the continuation of both an American governmental role and a military presence as a safeguard against the recurrence of economic and social disorder. In effect, they wanted the United States to replace Spain as the guarantor of order and stability on the island. 'The American authorities', observed an insurgent general, 'are surrounding themselves with the people of most worth.'[66]

For more than three years, from 1 January 1899 to 20 May 1902, the people of Cuba were ruled by the US army. A military governor was appointed by the president of the United States and was directly accountable not to the Cuban people but to the US secretary of war. The question of allowing Cuba's independence while at the same time ensuring and managing future political stability on the island was eventually resolved by granting the United States a constitutional right to intervene by armed force. This was contained in article 3 of the Platt Amendment which stated: 'The government of Cuba consents that the United States may exercise the right to intervene for the preservation of Cuban independence, the maintenance of a government adequate for the protection of life, property, and individual liberty.'[67] The amendment was named after Senator Orville H. Platt of Connecticut and was passed by the US Congress in March 1901 and later approved by a vote of 16 to 11 in the Cuban constitutional convention in June 1901. Almost one year later, at a ceremony in Havana on 20 May 1902, the occupation was formally declared over and the powers of government were transferred to Tomás Estrada Palma, the elected president of the new Republic of Cuba. Estrada Palma had lived in New York for a number of years and held strong pro-American sympathies. He represented, therefore, not the lower orders but the 'better class' of Cuban, much preferred by the American military authorities.[68]

The Platt Amendment was essentially a substitute for formal annexation and provided the means by which the United States granted independence to Cuba but effectively withheld full sovereignty from the new republic. In reality, the new state of Cuba was an informal American protectorate and would serve as a prototype for a system that would be established throughout much of the Central American–Caribbean region in the early twentieth century. 'There is, of course, little or no independence left Cuba under the Platt Amendment', frankly admitted the US military governor, General Leonard Wood.[69] The possession of a constitutional right to intervene provided the ultimate safeguard should the island collapse into disorder and threaten to become another Haiti. Moreover, the United States would be able to protect life and property on the island and thereby obviate any need for intervention from any foreign power. Despite criticism that it betrayed the spirit of the Teller Amendment, the Platt Amendment was attractive to American political leaders because it promised future political stability and a privileged access to economic markets. It also brought an end to the lengthy and increasingly expensive military occupation of the island. On the other hand, Cubans had virtually no alternative but to accept the Amendment and the limitations that it placed on their sovereign rights. If they refused, the American military occupation would be maintained for an indefinite period. Cubans generally felt humiliated by the imposition of the Platt Amendment and came to regard it as a supreme symbol of American oppression. In 1902, however, it gave them a measure of self-government and an opportunity to affirm their own national identity for the first time.

4
DOLLAR DIPLOMACY (1900–28)

Consequences of the Spanish–American War

A distinguished professor of history at Harvard wrote at the beginning of the twentieth century that the United States had 'assumed a new position among nations' and should now be considered 'as one of the chief forces in international affairs.'[1] Although American interest in the wider world of Europe and, notably, the Far East was increasing, most diplomatic activity was still concentrated within the Western Hemisphere, especially the Central American–Caribbean region. The 'splendid little' Spanish–American War not only underscored and enhanced the strategic significance of this region for the United States but it also reawakened the sense of American mission to spread freedom and democracy. American trade and investment benefited significantly from this pro-active attitude that would soon be popularly referred to as 'dollar diplomacy'. The term derived from a speech in 1911 by Assistant Secretary of State Francis Huntington Wilson, who remarked that 'the substitution of dollars for bullets' was an aim of American foreign policy.[2] Indeed, the booming American economy was eager to take advantage of the growing commercial opportunities so close to home. Between 1900 and 1910 American trade and investment with Latin America more than doubled and grew at a faster rate than with other areas of the world. The growing importance of the region was reflected in the fact that the state department established a separate Latin American Bureau in November 1909. Taft's secretary of state, Philander C. Knox, remarked:

> With the creation of the Latin-American Bureau, the producers of the United States will have at their command facilities which will enable them to understand just the sort of market offered to them and what is to be done in order to secure customers in that quarter.[3]

Going to war against Spain required the projection of American military power, both army and navy, beyond the borders of the United States. The subsequent military victory not only facilitated but was also used to lend justification to the development of the Caribbean as an 'American lake' or 'American Mediterranean', a sphere of influence that successive presidential administrations sought to insulate from foreign interference while seeking to dominate politically, militarily and economically. Although the government and people of the United States rejected the creation of formal colonies as an undesirable and undemocratic practice associated with the Old World, Spain's former colonial possessions of Cuba and Puerto Rico were firmly placed under American protection and tutelage. In the case of Cuba, the country was legally independent but, in reality, it was a protectorate of the United States. The latter's influential role was illustrated by Cuba adopting the political system of the United States, agreeing not to make treaties of military alliance with foreign powers, handing over the naval base of Guantánamo Bay to the American navy and accepting the Platt Amendment that allowed the United States a constitutional right of intervention in Cuban political affairs. Under the protection of the Platt Amendment and with the cooperation of the Cuban elite, American trade and capital investment flowed into Cuba. US investment in Cuba rose to $200 million in 1911 and increased further to more than $1 billion in 1925. With Cuba as the prototype, a system of informal rule based on protectorates was extended throughout much of the Central American–Caribbean region. This interventionist policy reflected not only America's greatly increased naval and economic power but also the influence of progressive ideas that advocated the imposition of political stability and financial rectitude in those republics considered guilty of irresponsible behaviour. The idealistic and well-meaning aspects of progressivism, however, were belied by the implicit assumption of American superiority and the frequent use of force rather than persuasion to implement the policy.[4]

The Latin American countries were generally dismayed by the new activism shown in American foreign policy. Fully aware of the geopolitical might of the United States, these governments, and especially those closest in geographical proximity, were wary of provoking the 'colossus of the north'. In the case of the Spanish–American War, this had shown itself in the adoption of policies of neutrality towards the conflict in Cuba. Nevertheless, the outward show of official neutrality concealed strong undertones of anti-American sentiment among the educated elite who made up the ruling class in Latin America. Although the Latin American elite was generally critical of Spanish political repression in Cuba, once American military intervention occurred there was considerable private sympathy with Spain rather than the United States. Part of the reason was the longstanding tradition of regarding the United States as an expansionist and aggressive power with particular designs on acquiring territory in the Central American–Caribbean region. Some Latin Americans instinctively distrusted, therefore, the idealistic motives proclaimed by President McKinley in justifying war against Spain in April 1898 and his later evangelical enthusiasm when advocating the annexation of the Philippines. But not all Latin American opinion was hostile. The notable exception was Brazil, whose Portuguese background and diplomatic ambitions to become a greater hemispheric power than its archrival Argentina resulted in the adoption of a conspicuously friendly and helpful Brazilian attitude towards the United States. Two warships were sold to the American navy and ships of the US fleet were allowed to take on fuel and to refit in Brazilian ports during the Spanish–American War.

Nevertheless, the unexpectedly swift military defeat of Spain followed by the denial of home rule to Cuba and Puerto Rico, and the establishment instead of American military governments in those islands, served to confirm and harden anti-American sentiment in Latin America. American troops were withdrawn from Cuba in 1902 but Cuban independence was severely circumscribed by the imposition of the Platt Amendment that ensured the perpetuation of a supervisory US political influence. At the same time, however, Spain was humiliated by a crushing military defeat that its people called 'the disaster of 98'. The final removal of Spanish imperial power from the New World was therefore a definite reality and, as a new century began, only made the Latin American nations feel even more isolated and vulnerable to the growing political, economic, military and cultural influence of the Anglo-Saxon United States. The Latin American predicament was eloquently expressed by the Uruguayan writer, José Enrique Rodó, whose celebrated work *Ariel* was published in 1900. Echoing the warnings made by the Cuban poet and national hero José Martí, Rodó likened the United States to 'Caliban', a character taken from Shakespeare's play *The Tempest* and representing a monster that was respected for its great energy and strength but feared for its insensitivity and seemingly insatiable appetite for material expansion. 'In spite of its titanic accomplishments and the great force of will that those accomplishments represent, and in spite of its incomparable triumphs in all spheres of material success,' stated Rodó, 'it is nevertheless true that as an entity this civilization creates a singular impression of insufficiency and emptiness.'[5] In similar vein the Nicaraguan poet Rubén Darío lamented: 'The United States is grand and powerful. Whenever it trembles, a profound shudder runs down the enormous backbone of the Andes. If it shouts, the sound is like the roar of a lion.'[6] For salvation, Darío looked to Argentina for leadership:

> On the balance scales of the American continent, it is the Argentine Republic that gives us the counterweight to Yankee power. This is the country that will rescue the spirit of our race and put an end to present and future imperialist ambition.[7]

Dollar diplomacy

Despite Great Britain's acceptance of arbitration in the Venezuela boundary dispute in 1896 and Spain's military defeat in 1898, American political and military pre-eminence in the Western Hemisphere was once again, if only briefly, put to the test by Europe in the Venezuela Incident of 1902–3. Venezuela was similar to a number of countries in the Central American–Caribbean region that had built up large foreign debts mainly owed to European banks and bondholders. The outbreak of internal civil war at the close of the nineteenth century, however, meant that Venezuela lacked both the financial means and the political will to service its foreign debt. In November 1902 Great Britain, Germany and Italy demanded financial compensation for their nationals and, when this was refused by the Venezuelan government of Cipriano Castro, a small squadron of gunboats was sent to impose a punitive naval blockade of the main Venezuelan ports. The blockade was eventually lifted in February 1903 after all parties to the dispute agreed to seek binding arbitration at The Hague Court of Permanent Arbitration. At first, Germany had declined to go to arbitration, but it later consented to do so after (so President Theodore Roosevelt later claimed) being threatened by American naval intervention in the dispute. In fact, the European powers needed little persuasion because it was evident that none of the countries involved, including Venezuela, stood to gain very much either economically or politically from a continuation of the blockade. Indeed, arguably the United States was the principal beneficiary of the crisis. 'We have succeeded in . . . getting England and Germany explicitly to recognize the Monroe Doctrine', Roosevelt informed Grover Cleveland.[8]

The ruling of The Hague Court on 22 February 1904 found in favour of the European powers and stated that they should be given preferential treatment over other nations in the settlement of the existing financial claims made against Venezuela. The ruling raised the prospect of an increasing resort to 'gunboat diplomacy' by European powers because it appeared to give legal justification to the use of military intervention to collect unpaid debts in cases where arbitration was refused. Latin American nations were disturbed by the clear threat the ruling posed to their sovereignty and independence. They sought recognition of the Drago Doctrine, named after Argentine Foreign Minister Luis María Drago, which had argued at the time of the Venezuelan blockade that foreign nations did not automatically possess the legal right to use force to recover public debt. Moreover, the employment of force was not regarded as a simple technical issue because it contained many dangerous ramifications directly affecting the principle of non-intervention and respect for the sovereignty of nations. 'The collection of loans by military means', explained Drago, 'implies territorial occupation to make them effective, and territorial occupation signifies the suppression or subordination of the governments of the countries on which it is imposed.'[9]

Prior to the blockade, President Theodore Roosevelt had been informed privately by the German government of the intention of the European powers to issue an ultimatum to Venezuela. At the time Roosevelt had expressed no objection to this proposed course of action because no acquisition of territory was envisaged. Nevertheless, he was alarmed by the example of European gunboat diplomacy employed against Venezuela and was concerned at the prospect of its repetition, especially in the unstable republics of the strategically important Central American–Caribbean region. He refused, however, to endorse the Drago Doctrine and was unwilling to adopt an inter-American approach to resolving the issue. It was Roosevelt's belief that the United States was already bound by the Monroe Doctrine to ensure order in the Western Hemisphere and that his government must retain complete freedom of action in foreign affairs and be prepared to act unilaterally if necessary. In his Annual Message to Congress on 6 December 1904, Roosevelt patronizingly declared that Latin American nations that conducted their affairs with 'reasonable efficiency and decency', maintained political stability and paid their debts need not fear interference from the United States. The United States, however, had a duty to intervene in cases where governments acted irresponsibly and committed 'chronic wrong-doing'.[10] Roosevelt's argument was that international incidents such as the one that had occurred in Venezuela were dangerous to hemispheric security because they had provoked European intervention and thereby presented a challenge to the Monroe Doctrine. In his opinion, such incidents could be best avoided not by collective inter-American action but by pre-emptive unilateral US intervention. Indeed, the United States must be prepared to intervene in Latin American affairs if it wished to be sure of keeping other nations out. Roosevelt was referring to the particular threat posed by the powers of the Old World, but Great Britain and the European powers were not displeased by his comments. In fact, they welcomed what became known as the 'Roosevelt Corollary' to the Monroe Doctrine or the policy of the 'Big Stick' because it meant that the United States would act as a self-appointed policeman to ensure that Caribbean and Central American countries acted responsibly and, most importantly, met their financial obligations to foreign investors.

The right of intervention claimed by Roosevelt had already been written into the Cuban Constitution in the form of the Platt Amendment and would provide the justification for sending marines to restore political order in Cuba in 1906. The passage of a similar constitutional or congressional sanction, however, was not necessary to justify intervention in the Dominican Republic in 1905. Faced with imminent national bankruptcy and rumours of European military intervention, the Dominican government of Carlos Morales Languasco suggested that Roosevelt establish American supervision of the collection of the country's customs duties. American officials and financial experts accordingly carried out this task and set up a depository fund to ensure repayment of the mainly European-held debt. Under American tutelage the Dominican Republic became politically stable and attractive to investors and business interests. Furthermore, European intervention was prevented and 'wrong-doing' was punished. Responding to criticism that his aim was to acquire overseas territory, Roosevelt denied any such intention and explained that the United States 'was simply performing in a peaceful manner not only with the cordial acquiescence, but in accordance with the earnest request of the government concerned, part of that international duty which is necessarily involved in the assertion of the Monroe Doctrine.'[11]

Perceived revolutionary disturbances in the Central American–Caribbean region resulted in subsequent presidents making even more complete use of the Roosevelt Corollary than Roosevelt had done. William H. Taft ordered marines to Nicaragua in 1912 to suppress political revolt and ensure an orderly presidential election. 'Not to do so and to sit by', warned Huntington Wilson, would 'be a blow to our prestige in all the neighboring republics.'[12] In 1915 serious rioting and disorder in Haiti, including the brutal killing of the president by a mob in broad daylight, prompted Woodrow Wilson to send in marines to impose martial law, disarm and disband military forces, and establish a financial receivership. A proper legal basis was also secured to justify American actions. A treaty was signed which legalized American military occupation and allowed continued American control over Haitian finances. These powers were retained until 1934 and included the creation, training and direction of a Haitian non-political police force (Gendarmerie). Under the command of Lieutenant Colonel Smedley D. Butler of the US Marine Corps, the Gendarmerie maintained order in the countryside and, in suppressing a local rebellion, was held responsible for the deaths of several thousand Haitians during the 1920s. A non-political police force or 'National Guard' (Guardia Nacional) was similarly created in the Dominican Republic where Wilson suspended the government for 'chronic wrong-doing' in 1916 and turned over the administration of the republic's affairs to American naval officers; an American Rear-Admiral, William B. Caperton, served as acting-president. Government was returned to the Dominicans in 1924 though the 'financial protectorate' was not formally ended until 1941.

The Panama Canal

A major strategic issue for the United States at the beginning of the twentieth century was the construction of the Panama Canal. Despite continued congressional interest and lobbying by canal promoters, presidential administrations from Hayes onwards had generally preferred to neglect the canal question primarily on account of the mounting evidence of the engineering and financial difficulties faced by the French canal company in attempting to build a sea-level canal at Panama. The ending of construction work in 1889 was followed by the bankruptcy of the French company and revelations of financial corruption that resulted in the prosecution and conviction of several company executives including de Lesseps. Although the French canal company was reorganized and talked of resuming construction work, the Panama project appeared to be defunct. American interest in canal projects, however, notably revived during the Spanish–American War. That conflict illustrated the potential military value of a canal as a means of making possible the implementation of a two-ocean naval strategy in which the American navy could operate simultaneously in both the Atlantic and the Pacific. The need for easier and faster transit between the two oceans was also underscored by the annexation to the United States of Hawaii, the Philippines and Guam in the Pacific Ocean. In addition, the war resulted in the United States acquiring naval bases in Cuba at Guantánamo Bay and in Puerto Rico, both of which were strategically located on the eastern approaches to the Caribbean and the projected isthmian waterway. Instead of looking to private enterprise as in the past, the McKinley Administration decided that, if a canal was to be successfully constructed, the US government must become directly involved in the project. To achieve this, however, required considerable diplomatic and political effort. The first step was to remove the barrier of the 1850 Clayton–Bulwer Treaty in order to allow the canal to be constructed and controlled exclusively by the United States. During the 1880s British diplomats had vigorously resisted American attempts to revise the 1850 Treaty. Not wishing to obstruct the building of the canal and impressed by the display of American military power in 1898, the British government adopted a more accommodating response and approved the negotiation of a new treaty in 1901. Known as the Hay–Pauncefote Treaty, the new arrangement abrogated the 1850 Clayton–Bulwer Treaty and meant that the United States could now build and fortify a canal and exercise exclusive control so long as full provision was made for international shipping to use the completed waterway.

At the same time as negotiations were taking place to abrogate the 1850 Clayton–Bulwer Treaty, an Isthmian Canal Commission of professional engineers, which had been formed by Congress in 1899, was examining possible canal routes. Reporting in November 1901 the commission initially preferred the Nicaraguan route over that of Panama, but then switched to the latter when it was learned from the skilful agent of the French company, Philippe Bunau-Varilla, that the Panamanian concession could be purchased on very reasonable financial terms. In fact, the French asking price was slashed from $102 million to $40 million. In June 1902 after some contentious debates, the US Senate approved the Spooner Act (named after Senator John C. Spooner of Wisconsin), which authorized the Roosevelt Administration to buy out the French Panama Canal Company and to negotiate a treaty with Colombia that would transfer the existing French canal rights to the United States. Negotiations between Roosevelt's secretary of state, John Hay, and the Colombian minister in Washington, Tomás Herrán, resulted in the Hay–Herrán Treaty in January 1903. The treaty was ratified by the US Senate in March but defeated by the Colombian Senate, which asked for more generous financial terms and greater rights of sovereignty over the proposed Canal Zone in which the waterway would be located. Roosevelt was angry and refused to reopen negotiations with the Colombian government. He privately belittled the Colombian politicians and let it be known that he would be pleased to deal with Panama as an independent state. 'I do not think that the Bogota lot of jack rabbits should be allowed permanently to bar one of the future highways of civilization', he stressed.[13]

The collapse of the Hay–Herrán Treaty would mean no canal and was a considerable blow to the future economic prospects of the Panamanian political and business elite. On 3 November 1903 demonstrations calling for independence from Colombia erupted in the province. Acting in accordance with article 35 of the 1846 treaty with New Granada requiring the United States to maintain order on the isthmus, the American gunboat *Nashville* prevented Colombian troops from putting down the revolt at Panama. In the protective presence of the American navy, the rebels declared an independent Panama. On 6 November Theodore Roosevelt officially recognized the new republic. A canal treaty was quickly concluded between Hay and Bunau-Varilla, who represented the new republic in Washington, and the treaty was ratified by both governments in February 1904. It granted the United States rights 'as if it were the sovereign of the territory' to administer, fortify and defend an area of land ten miles wide across the isthmus that would become known as the Panama Canal Zone.[14] In contrast to similar arrangements concerning Louisiana in 1803 and Alaska in 1867, the United States paid Panama for canal rights but did not purchase actual territory. In fact, the question of defining sovereign rights would prove to be a very contentious issue between the United States and Panama throughout the twentieth century. Nevertheless, from its inception in 1904 the Canal Zone was administered essentially as a 'colony' of the United States, and American authority was strictly imposed on the inhabitants. Senator John T. Morgan of Alabama recommended that 'the Government of the United States had absolute charge of every foot of it in every respect' in order to deal with 'as uncontrollable and as mischievous a rabble as ever collected at any place in the world'.[15] The task of construction was assigned to the US Corps of Engineers under whose direction the canal was successfully completed and opened on 15 August 1914. The work also involved massive improvements to the region in terms of the provision of housing, social and welfare facilities, and public health, especially sanitation and the successful treatment of tropical diseases.

In a speech delivered in 1911 Roosevelt boasted that he had 'taken' the Canal Zone in 1903.[16] While most Americans supported his action and believed that it brought peace, prosperity and security to the Central American–Caribbean region, deep resentment against the United States was stirred not only among Colombians but also in the rest of Latin America at what was regarded as another example of blatant American aggression. 'The Government of the United States, invoking and putting into practice the right of might', declared the Colombian political leader, Rafael Reyes, 'has taken from us by bloodless conquest – but by conquest nevertheless – the most important part of the national territory.'[17] While Panamanians welcomed their separation from Colombia and the construction of the canal with all its financial benefits, there was also concern that the Hay–Bunau-Varilla Treaty infringed their country's sovereign rights and had turned Panama into an American protectorate. Indeed, the events occurring at Panama served to reinforce the basic Latin American suspicion of the United States and to vindicate the warnings made by such writers as Martí, Rodó and Darío. First, the imposition of military government in Cuba then 'the taking of Panama' were examples of how so-called Pan-Americanism had given way to 'the American peril' expressed in the establishment of protectorates in the guise of 'dollar diplomacy' and characterized by the sending in of marines and financial supervisors.[18]

The pursuit of dollar diplomacy reflected the expanding geopolitical power of the United States and conversely the relative weakness and vulnerability of the Latin American countries. The policy consciously sought to overcome European rivals and to establish an undisputed American sphere of influence especially in the Central American–Caribbean region. It was also imperialistic in that it was designed to provide a framework of political order and stability that would assist and encourage the development of American business and financial interests. For example, the inflow of American capital was so visible in Haiti that the country was popularly referred to as the 'territory of the National City Bank of New York'.[19] A considerable increase in American capital investment and a somewhat modest increase in American trade with Latin America directly resulted from dollar diplomacy, but US policy was influenced by more than simply the desire to open and to control new fields for American business enterprise. Other objectives were: first, the protection of American lives and property in areas of political and civil disturbance; second, the reduction of governmental chaos, especially financial difficulties that threatened to provoke European military intervention; and third, the need to protect the construction and security of the Panama Canal. Secretary of State Philander C. Knox noted in 1912:

> The logic of political geography and of strategy, and now our tremendous national interest created by the Panama Canal, make

> the safety, the peace, and the prosperity of Central America and the zone of the Caribbean of paramount interest to the Government of the United States.[20]

The policy of establishing protectorates by direct military intervention was, notably, limited to the Central American–Caribbean area. By contrast, there were no similar military incursions into South America where most nations were considerably larger, more politically and economically stable and potentially capable of mounting effective military resistance to external encroachment. In fact, the Roosevelt and Taft administrations displayed a desire to develop closer relations with Argentina, Brazil and Chile, the leading countries of South America known as the 'ABC'. Relations were especially friendly with Brazil, whose distinguished diplomats, the Baron do Rio Branco and Joaquim Nabuco de Araújo, advocated a strategy of 'approximating' Brazil's diplomatic goals with those of the United States. The highlight of this policy was the upgrading of diplomatic relations with Brazil to ambassadorial rank in 1905, only the second Latin American country (after Mexico) to be given this distinction, and Secretary of State Elihu Root's attendance at the Third Pan-American Conference held at Rio de Janeiro in 1906. Nabuco regarded Root as a personal friend and described him as 'a unique type in his interest in Latin America'.[21] But considerations of national interest prevailed over friendship. To Brazil's disappointment, the United States drew back from showing any special diplomatic favour in order to avoid upsetting Argentina and becoming entangled in South American rivalries. 'The Argentines have a strong impression that the US shows a preferential friendship for Brazil', wrote Second Assistant Secretary of State Alvey A. Adee in October 1908. 'Is there', he asked Root, 'any way of convincing them that we love them just as much as the Brazilians?' The secretary of state instructed that an even-handed attitude be displayed towards the two South American rivals.[22]

Woodrow Wilson

During the second decade of the twentieth century the policies of President Woodrow Wilson exerted a major influence on the course of inter-American relations. By nature and background, Wilson had little personal interest in foreign policy. His priority on assuming the presidency in 1913 was the legislative enactment of the domestic programme of progressive reform known as the 'New Freedom'. Nevertheless, early in his first administration (1913–17), he publicly declared his intention of reversing the aggressive foreign policies associated with his Republican predecessors. The United States would seek a new relationship with its Latin American 'sister republics' that was firmly based upon reason and trust. This was made apparent in Wilson's celebrated speech delivered to the meeting of the Southern

Commercial Congress at Mobile, Alabama, on 27 October 1913. Proclaiming that 'the future is going to be very different for this hemisphere from the past', Wilson sought to reassure the Latin American nations by stating that 'we must prove ourselves their friends, and champions upon terms of equality and honor'. The United States, he affirmed 'will never again seek one additional foot of territory by conquest'.[23]

Wilson's idealistic rhetoric interacted, however, with his more pragmatic considerations of national self-interest as exemplified by his decisions to intervene with armed force in Haiti and the Dominican Republic. In his first year in office, however, the most pressing problem in foreign affairs that he identified was the instability and violence occurring in Mexico as a result of the overthrow of the dictator Porfirio Díaz in May 1911 and the ensuing period of revolutionary change known as the Mexican Revolution. Only a few weeks before Wilson became president, a diplomatic crisis arose when General Victoriano Huerta staged a military coup in February 1913 that resulted in the murder of the democratically elected president, Francisco Madero. Wilson condemned the assassination of the legally elected president and refused to recognize the new military government, which he declared was 'stained by blood'.[24] Wilson's moralistic attitude, however, reflected a simplistic interpretation of Mexican and also Latin American domestic politics. It was particularly evident in a self-righteous determination to educate the people of Latin America in the ways of democracy that was summed up in one of his celebrated and notorious statements: 'I am going to teach the South American republics to elect good men.'[25] Wilson found that his good intentions were not so easy to put into practice. Frustrated in his efforts to force Huerta's voluntary resignation and restore democratic government by the application of diplomatic persuasion, the president's personal antipathy towards the Mexican general eventually resulted in a unilateral decision to order a naval bombardment and occupation by marines of the port of Veracruz in April 1914. Although Wilson publicly announced that the act of intervention was in response to Huerta's failure to apologize for an incident involving the arrest of American sailors at the nearby oil terminal at Tampico, its timing was also dictated by the need to prevent the arrival at Veracruz of a German ship carrying weapons for the Mexican general. But Wilson's meddling in Mexican domestic politics proved to be a miscalculation. Mexico was a large country and not a small Caribbean island. Indeed, the American chargé d'affaires in Mexico City, Nelson J. O'Shaughnessy, believed that Huerta actually welcomed and stood to benefit from American intervention. On being told about the imminent arrival of the American warships, Huerta was reported to have said: 'It is the best thing that could happen to us.'[26] From being an unpopular general, Huerta suddenly acquired in the eyes of the Mexican people the image of a national hero resisting American military invasion. Reports from Mexico suggested that Huerta's opponents were prepared to make common cause with him to fight the foreign invader. The potential escalation of the conflict at Veracruz into a full-scale war between Mexico and the United States became a distinct possibility and was avoided by the timely diplomatic intervention of the three leading Latin American nations – Argentina, Brazil and Chile (the ABC).

The ABC governments sought to exert a moderating influence by proposing their joint mediation of the dispute on the grounds that a war would be harmful to all the nations of the hemisphere. As Roosevelt had demonstrated over the Drago Doctrine, the United States was traditionally reluctant to accept Latin American diplomatic initiatives. However, the offer was speedily accepted by Wilson in 1914. While this reflected his awareness of the influence of the leading South American nations, he was also motivated by personal dismay at the moral consequences of American armed intervention, which had resulted in the deaths of 19 US sailors and more than 200 Mexicans. He was also surprised at the unfavourable response the incident had evoked both at home and overseas. From Wilson's point of view, the multilateral action of the ABC countries conveniently served the immediate and useful purpose of restraining any further extension of hostilities and allowing the peaceful withdrawal of American troops by an agreed deadline of November 1914. Despite its success, however, the mediation did not lead to any further substantive inter-American cooperation nor did it deflect Wilson from his central objective of driving Huerta from the Mexican presidency.

By taking control of Veracruz, Wilson blocked funds and arms shipments going to Huerta and thereby contributed to the general's resignation in July 1914. This outcome failed, however, to bring an end to the violent struggle among the various revolutionary factions in Mexico. With the qualified permission of the Mexican government another limited American military intervention took place in 1916 when 6,000 American troops, under the command of General John J. Pershing, pursued the Mexican leader, Pancho Villa, into northern Mexico. The action was in retaliation for Villa's incursion across the border into New Mexico during which a number of American civilians had been killed. After almost a year of pursuit Pershing gave up his attempt to capture Villa. Wilson was ostensibly seeking to maintain order along the US–Mexican border and to promote democracy in Mexico, but his aggressive actions and violation of Mexico's sovereignty only further antagonized Mexican nationalism and anti-American opinion. This was exemplified in 1917 by the interception by British intelligence officers and the publication in the American press of the Zimmermann Telegram. The secret telegram revealed that the German foreign minister, Alfred Zimmermann, had instructed the German ambassador in Mexico to promise the Mexican government the restitution of territory lost as a result of the Mexican–American War should Mexico join Germany in a war against the United States. While the Mexican president, Venustiano Carranza, had apparently stated that Mexico would not initiate a war against its northern neighbour, he had continued to hold meetings with the German ambassador.

A more serious threat to relations between the United States and Mexico was the 1917 Mexican Constitution, especially article 27, which placed the ownership of the country's oil, water and natural resources in the Mexican nation and put severe restrictions on foreign investment and concessions. The article was deliberately intended to assert Mexican sovereign rights over its own national resources and to define and reduce the economic influence of foreigners. American citizens and companies, especially those involved in the flourishing oil industry, the major foreign investment in the country, expressed concern that Mexico was adopting the dangerous ideas of Bolshevism that condemned free-enterprise capitalism and the ownership of private property. They feared that the enforcement of the constitutional provision would damage future profits and might lead to the expropriation of their existing assets. Although Mexico claimed possession of the oil, it was independently unable to operate the oil fields or to export and sell the oil. For the time being, therefore, article 27 was not enforced so long as Mexican oil revenues were dependent on the cooperation of the foreign oil companies. This suited Woodrow Wilson, for whom events in Mexico in 1917 were overshadowed by the fighting in Europe and the decision of the United States to join the world war. Wilson favoured a policy of accommodation and dismissed the suggestion of sending American troops to take control of the oil fields, an idea that he likened to Germany's pre-emptive and ruthless invasion of Belgium in 1914. In the circumstances, American diplomats sought to avoid a clash over the provisions of article 27. 'During the war my job was to keep Mexico quiet, and it was done', remarked the American ambassador to Mexico, Henry P. Fletcher.[27]

The First World War

Despite his lack of personal interest in the details of foreign policy, Woodrow Wilson found that his presidency was increasingly dominated by diplomatic and strategic issues arising from the outbreak of war in Europe in August 1914. At first, all the countries of the Western Hemisphere sought to avoid any direct military involvement in what appeared initially as a purely European conflict. Wilson, for example, declared that the United States would adopt a policy of strict neutrality. But the conflict could not be limited to Europe. By directly affecting so many nations, the ensuing world war elevated the importance of Pan-American solidarity and provided a test of the sincerity of Wilson's intention that he had proclaimed at the beginning of his presidency to cultivate more cooperative relations with Latin America. 'The sentiment', noted Wilson's secretary of state, William Jennings Bryan, in December 1914, 'is unanimous among the South American countries that something ought to be done to protect the neutral nations if the war is to continue.'[28] Indeed, the Latin American countries looked to the United States for guidance and leadership. But suggestions that the president call a conference of neutral nations to be held in Washington were dismissed by state department officials as 'undesirable and inexpedient'.[29] In characteristic fashion, the declaration of neutrality by the US government in August 1914 had been a unilateral act. Moreover, Wilson also preferred to deal directly with the leaders of the European belligerent powers and proved unwilling to provide the positive leadership that would facilitate the formulation of a common hemispheric policy. The period of neutrality from 1914 to 1917 was therefore marked largely by diplomatic indecision and confusion.

The Wilson Administration, however, showed a very keen interest in promoting closer economic links that even included the holding of inter-American conferences. Indeed, the serious economic dislocation caused by the war provided a signal and historic opportunity for the extension of US commercial influence throughout Latin America at the expense of its European competitors. In a matter of a few months American business was able to make advances that would ordinarily have taken several years to achieve. Wilson's secretary of the treasury, William McAdoo, was enthusiastic about the historic opportunity: 'The South Americans were like the customers of a store that has burned down, they were looking around for a place to spend their money.'[30] Already alarmed by the onset of domestic economic recession and the likelihood that the war would cause a severe contraction of American trade with Europe, the Wilson Administration was eager to support the search for alternative markets in Latin America. An unusual sense of common purpose infused the activities of American business executives, politicians and government officials. Advantage was taken of the provision in the 1913 Federal Reserve Act allowing American banks to open overseas branches, most of which would be located initially in Latin America. Decisions were implemented with remarkable speed. It had taken more than a year to complete arrangements for the 1889 Washington Conference. In marked contrast, less than two months after the passage of its congressional appropriation, the Pan-American Financial Conference speedily assembled at Washington in May 1915. A product of the initiative and energy of McAdoo, the meeting was welcomed by Latin American governments and was attended by business executives as well as diplomats and finance ministers. Compliments were even forthcoming from the Argentine delegate. 'The suggestion of the holding of this Financial Conference, made by the Government of the United States has come at a propitious moment, and its success already in this very hour is assured by the presence here of the representatives of so many American nations', he remarked.[31]

Wartime conditions boosted American trade and investment particularly with the countries of South America where Europeans had traditionally been predominant. In April 1915 the British minister at Rio de Janeiro reported that 'the United States are making great efforts'.[32] He jealously noted the frequent arrival of commercial missions, the opening of an American branch bank in the capital, and the proposal to establish a direct steamship line between Rio de Janeiro and New York. The seriousness of the challenge to Great Britain's economic influence in Brazil was most vividly illustrated by the coal trade. Prior to 1914 Brazil had been dependent upon British imports. The impact of war brought about a complete reversal of market share so that by 1916 American sales of coal to Brazil were four times those from Great Britain. For the region as a whole, American exports tripled during the decade and by 1920 amounted to more than 40 per cent of all goods imported into South America. Substantial economic gains were made during the war at the expense of European competition, but further American advances were constrained by the relative lack of shipping and credit facilities. Moreover, while economic opportunities undoubtedly existed in South America, the market was new and relatively unknown for American business. In addition, the frequent reports of local political and economic instability reinforced the financial conservatism and caution of American merchants and investors. By contrast Europe was much safer and more attractive. In fact, the outbreak of war brought a boom in American trade with Great Britain and France. Compared to the vast and highly profitable European market, Latin America was of considerably less value and a much greater financial risk.

Although the war definitely stimulated closer commercial contact between Latin America and the United States, the diplomatic consequences were harder to evaluate. While the opinion of the Latin American elite generally favoured Great Britain and France and was hostile to Germany, the Latin American governments showed no desire to become directly embroiled in the European conflict and naturally expected the United States to lead the defence of neutral rights during time of war. President Wilson publicly championed these rights but, in practice, took little account of Latin American views in his own discussions with Great Britain, France, Italy and Russia (the Allies) and Germany and Austria (the Central Powers). As the role of the world's peacemaker came increasingly to absorb the president's attention, the various suggestions for inter-American diplomatic action made from time to time by Latin American statesmen were either politely rejected or studiously ignored. With the exception of the abortive proposal for a Pan-American treaty with the ABC nations to provide for the compulsory arbitration of inter-American disputes,[33] Wilson appeared indifferent to Latin American opinion and left those nations to evolve their own separate policies of neutrality towards the war.

The Latin American governments were therefore spectators rather than participants in Wilson's policy of initiating a peace process to end the war. The Brazilian foreign minister, Domício da Gama, summed up the president's mediation efforts as 'sympathetically humane, though still perhaps impracticable'.[34] His description reflected the detached attitude that most Latin American diplomats had adopted towards a process from which they were effectively excluded. However, events in Europe took a dramatic turn in January 1917 when the German government declared its intention of enforcing unrestricted submarine warfare in the war zone which it had established around the British Isles. This ultimatum signified the withdrawal of Germany's earlier pledge to allow the safe passage of unarmed merchant ships from neutral countries. The nations of Latin America reacted with apprehension and naturally feared for the continuance of their overseas trade. There was also the distinct prospect of the United States being drawn into the war, a development whose economic consequences were likely to be catastrophic. The whole of Latin America anxiously awaited Woodrow Wilson's response to the submarine threat. Led by the Argentine ambassador, Romulo Naón, the Latin American diplomatic representatives at Washington lobbied for the maintenance of hemispheric unity.

On 3 February Wilson decided to break off diplomatic relations with Germany. The subsequent sinking of American merchant ships by German submarines resulted in the president appearing before Congress on 2 April and urging America to fight to 'make the world safe for democracy'. On 6 April Congress declared war on Germany. Although the decision to go to war had not involved consultation with the Latin American governments, Wilson hoped that they would support his action by joining the war against Germany. But Wilson's idealistic justification for America's entry into war evoked a limited response from the rest of the hemisphere. Only eight nations joined the Allied side, seven of which were Central American–Caribbean states already strongly under American influence – Costa Rica, Cuba, Guatemala, Haiti, Honduras, Nicaragua and Panama. Mexico conspicuously chose to remain neutral. 'We cannot afford to participate in the war on one side or the other, if we can possibly avoid it', stated the Mexican ambassador in Washington.[35]

Brazil was the only South American country to declare war on Germany. Brazil's course of action contrasted markedly with that of Argentina, who typically took an independent line and insisted on maintaining normal diplomatic relations with all the nations at war. On 22 April the Argentine government had raised the idea of hosting a Latin American peace conference from which new belligerent powers such as the United States would be pointedly excluded. Brazil's decision to go to war effectively sabotaged the conference and consequently rekindled the traditional suspicion and rivalry between the two countries. Nevertheless, American officials believed that Brazil's action in joining the war would be imitated by Argentina and Chile. The belief was ill founded and revealed a characteristic American misunderstanding of South American politics. Indeed, the fact that countries such as Argentina, Chile, Mexico and Colombia remained neutral throughout the war showed that there were not only strong misgivings in Latin America over Wilson's policy but also that the memory of their recent conflicts with Washington on a variety of issues still rankled and placed definite limits on America's diplomatic influence.

The Latin American countries that joined the war were not expected to make an actual military contribution to the war effort. Only Brazil and Cuba considered taking on an active military role. A small Brazilian naval squadron of destroyers and cruisers was prepared and eventually sent out for wartime service in August 1918. The signing of the armistice intervened before the ships reached Gibraltar so that the squadron did not actually experience active service in the war. Plans to dispatch a contingent of Cuban troops to France were similarly cancelled by the unanticipated early end to the fighting in Europe. The Wilson Administration valued the Latin American countries that declared war on Germany for the symbolic support that their decision showed for the sanctity of international treaties and neutral rights. They were also appreciated for their economic cooperation, especially the provision of important raw materials and minerals for the war effort. Entering the war, however, conferred no special trade benefits. For example, Brazil suffered the imposition of a trade embargo on its exports of coffee because it was considered a luxury and therefore a non-essential item. Indeed, Brazil complained bitterly that during the war American trade increased with Argentina as much as with Brazil.

When the world war came to a close in November 1918, Woodrow Wilson astounded opinion at home and overseas by announcing his intention to leave the United States in order to lead the American delegation personally at the forthcoming Versailles Peace Conference. A month later the man who had promised the world 'peace without victory' was greeted by enormous public interest and enthusiasm on his arrival in Europe. Throughout Latin America, too, Wilson was popularly acclaimed a hero and a great statesman. But Latin American diplomatic opinion was inclined to be more critical. Wilson's high moral principles and his image as a peacemaker were already tarnished by his record of military interventions in Mexico, Central America, and the Caribbean. Prior to entering the war he had consistently rejected Latin American proposals to hold a peace conference of neutral nations and clearly preferred to avoid meetings that he could not personally control and manipulate. Consequently, his attendance at the Versailles Peace Conference was not regarded as having any tangible material benefit for Latin America. Despite his grand rhetoric about the equality of nations, Wilson clearly believed that the great powers, one of which was the United States, should monopolize the main business of the conference. American influence was occasionally used to help the Latin American countries. For example, Wilson intervened to secure an increase in the size of the Brazilian delegation from two to three members. Although the eleven Latin American nations that had declared war on or severed relations with the Central Powers participated by right in the conference, they found themselves relegated to a very subordinate role in the proceedings.

The 1920s

In 1921 Wilson's presidency came to an end at a time when the era of progressivism was drawing to a close in the United States. A decade of Republican political ascendancy followed during which the presidential administrations of Warren G. Harding (1921–3) and Calvin Coolidge (1923–9) stressed not 'Democratic' moral righteousness but the simpler 'Republican' virtues of economy and efficiency. For the majority of Americans this brought a time of unprecedented affluence. In foreign affairs an inward-looking mentality prevailed, symbolized by the decision not to join the League of Nations and the start of what would be a protracted and soul-searching investigation into why the United States had entered the war. But the apparent aloofness from international relations, which became known as 'isolationism', was superficial. The long-standing suspicion of overseas entanglements certainly existed, but it was balanced by awareness that the United States was now indisputably a great power with worldwide political, economic and strategic interests and must act accordingly.

Within weeks of assuming office, President Warren G. Harding announced America's determination to work for world peace by concentrating on naval disarmament. A conference to limit the size of the navies of the great powers was subsequently held at Washington in November 1921. The meeting revealed, however, that the primary concern of American officials was to achieve a reduction of naval force levels in the Pacific Ocean. The South Atlantic was accorded only a passing mention. Consequently, all the nations of Latin America found themselves ignored and pointedly excluded from the conference. It was apparent that the Harding Administration intended to continue the traditional American diplomatic strategy of acting unilaterally and taking little account of Latin America. The course of events was also painfully reminiscent of the indifference shown to the Latin American countries by the great powers at the Versailles conference.

The Latin American nations approved, however, the proposal made at Versailles to create a new world organization to be known as the League of Nations with its headquarters located in Geneva, Switzerland. They all duly became members of the Assembly of the League and Brazil, as the largest Latin American nation and a co-belligerent in the war, was honoured with a temporary seat on the Council. Moreover, the Latin American nations welcomed the creation of the League because membership conferred international recognition and prestige. 'Now we have become a nation that reaches beyond its continent to take part and be heard in the deliberations that concern the world', proudly boasted a Brazilian diplomat.[36] The League also appeared to provide a means of reducing American political and military interference in hemispheric affairs. But the belief that the new organization might provide a valuable countervailing power to the 'colossus of the north' was not realized because the United States did not join and was not therefore bound by the rules or the resolutions passed in Geneva. Indeed, it soon became evident that the Council of the League was dominated by the European powers. With the exception of colonial possessions in Africa, the Middle East and Asia, they showed little interest in affairs beyond their own continent.

Moreover, the European powers had no desire to cause conflict with the United States. Indeed, the recognition of American political pre-eminence in the Western Hemisphere was made evident by the inclusion of article 21 in the original League Covenant: 'Nothing in this Covenant shall be deemed to affect the validity of international engagements such as treaties of arbitration or regional understandings like the Monroe Doctrine, for securing the maintenance of peace.'[37] The failure of Argentina's attempt to secure the removal of the specific reference to the Monroe Doctrine at the first session of the League showed that the great powers intended to avoid discussion of controversial Latin American questions. In 1921 Peru and Bolivia withdrew their membership of the League over the refusal to allow a debate on their dispute with Chile over the possession of Tacna-Arica. Another disillusioning experience was the controversy over Brazil's claim to permanent membership of the Council that indicated the lack of importance which the great European powers attached to the Latin American countries. Complaining of unequal treatment, Brazil dramatically left the League in 1926. 'The action of Brazil', a British diplomat claimed, 'was largely due to American edging at the psychological moment.'[38] While the actual role of the United States was hardly so decisive in explaining Brazil's action, American officials were content with the evolution of the League into a forum that was dominated by the European powers and focused mainly on their particular affairs.

The formation and activities of the League of Nations did little to alter the fact that the world war had clearly boosted the economic and political influence of the United States in the Western Hemisphere. No longer so fearful of European challenge to the Monroe Doctrine, officials in Washington complacently regarded the whole region as securely within the American sphere of influence. As their absence from the Washington naval conferences demonstrated, the nations of Latin America were generally accorded little military or diplomatic significance by the United States. Notably, Latin American resentment surfaced when those nations confronted the United States in the Pan-American conference system that resumed at Santiago de Chile in 1923. This meeting had originally been scheduled for 1914, but had been cancelled as a result of the outbreak of war in Europe. The Harding Administration showed little enthusiasm for the conference. The agenda was held to contain too many potentially controversial political items, including a Uruguayan project to set up a separate Pan-American League of Nations. President Harding, however, believed that the conference had good public relations value and tried to persuade Secretary of State Charles Evans Hughes to attend. However, it was quite evident that the secretary of state's personal sympathies and priorities lay elsewhere. In 1922 he had attended Brazil's centennial celebrations. The British ambassador at Rio de Janeiro, Sir John Tilley, reported that 'Mr Hughes, who has a stiff manner, speaks no language but his own, did not appear to go out of his way to make himself particularly agreeable'.[39] Replying to Harding's suggestion that he should attend the Santiago Conference, Hughes stated that he 'had no love whatever for speechmaking trips' and declined to undertake another journey to South America so soon after having visited Brazil.[40] The negative response considerably diminished the importance of the conference and revealed the lack of importance that the United States attached to meetings with its southern neighbours.

Nevertheless, during the 1920s Republican administrations pursued a less forceful policy towards Latin America than their Democratic predecessors had done.[41] The presence of US marines in some Latin American countries was no longer seen as necessary for political stability or helpful for American economic interests. The conciliatory but businesslike tone was expressed by Hughes at the Brazilian centennial celebrations in 1922: 'We covet no territory, we seek no conquest; the liberty we cherish for ourselves we desire for others; and we assert no rights for ourselves that we do not accord to others.'[42] In substantive terms, the Harding and Coolidge administrations did attempt to improve relations with Latin America by supporting US Senate approval of the 1921 treaty giving compensation of $25 million to Colombia for the loss of Panama in 1903, announcing and arranging the formal withdrawal of garrisons of American marines from Cuba in 1922, the Dominican Republic in 1924 and Nicaragua in 1925, and securing an agreement with Mexico in 1923 to secure recognition of American property rights in that country.

The conciliatory policy, however, was not intended to signal an abandonment of American national interests. Consequently, Haiti remained an American protectorate throughout the decade. The withdrawal of marines in the Dominican Republic was not accompanied by the end of American financial supervision. More controversial was the quick return of American marines to Nicaragua in 1926 to support the conservative government of Adolfo Díaz against a liberal revolt. The decision to send a substantial force of marine reinforcements to Nicaragua in the following year caused considerable criticism especially when local guerrilla resistance was organized by the Nicaraguan political leader Augusto César Sandino. Indeed, far from achieving political order the intervention provoked further instability and an upsurge in anti-Americanism so that the local conflict soon took on the epic proportions of a battle between 'Ariel' and 'Caliban'. Sandino denounced the US marines as 'barbarians' and 'invaders'. 'We must fight without respite until we are free from Yankee imperialism, because it and its government are the enemies of our race and our language', he declared.[43] In Nicaragua, Sandino took on the image of a patriot and hero, but in the opinion of the American minister in Nicaragua, Charles Eberhardt, Sandino was 'an erratic Nicaraguan' who had 'preached Communism, Mexican brotherly love and cooperation, and death to the Americans, until the rabble of the whole north country joined him in his plan to massacre Americans there and set up his own government'.[44] The head of the American military mission in Nicaragua, General Frank Ross McCoy, remarked, however, that Sandino's fame had spread so widely that he had become 'the symbol of opposition to the United States policy throughout Latin America and at home, a useful figure to those who desire to attack us'.[45] For a while, one of Sandino's most prominent regional allies was the Salvadoran socialist and peasant leader Augustín Farabundo Martí. So long as Sandino remained at large, the United States was compelled to maintain a sizable military presence in Nicaragua. In 1929 the number of US marines reached 5,000. The military burden was gradually reduced by following the same policy as in the Dominican Republic and Haiti of recruiting and training local forces to form a National Guard (Gardia Nacional). At the same time a schedule was established for the withdrawal of American marines from Nicaragua, and this was eventually completed in January 1932. Sandino subsequently negotiated peace terms with the Nicaraguan government, but was murdered in 1934 on the instructions of the commander of the National Guard, Anastasio Somoza García.

New difficulties between the United States and Mexico also erupted in 1925 when the government of President Plutarco Elías Calles declared that, based on Article 27 of the 1917 Mexican Constitution, rights to property acquired by foreigners prior to 1917 were to be limited to a time period of fifty years, after which ownership would revert to the state. American oil companies complained that Calles was influenced by anti-capitalist Bolshevist dogma. They also pointed out that the proposed action was retrospective and that their rights predated the 1917 Constitution. If implemented, its impact beyond the United States and Mexico would be severely detrimental to business and financial investment. 'Any weakness in our attitude here', argued the American ambassador in Mexico, James R. Sheffield, 'is certain to be reflected almost immediately in other foreign countries.'[46] Diplomatic relations became strained as the Coolidge Administration sought to protect the interests of the American oil companies. But officials in Washington did not automatically side with the American companies. The state department official, J. Reuben Clark, later reminded them that the 'adoption by other countries of theories of nationalization is not our business; our only concern is with specific cases of injury and violations of legitimate rights'.[47] Indeed, Coolidge ruled out proposals for military intervention and sent his personal friend, Dwight Morrow, to Mexico to negotiate a peaceful solution. A compromise was reached in December 1927, stating that foreign interests that had already begun work on their sub-soil properties should retain their existing property rights. The fact that an agreement could be reached was a success for Coolidge and a positive sign for the current state of inter-American relations. As the Mexican Revolution demonstrated, however, the desire of a government to control its own national resources and to implement radical policies of economic development raised issues of potential conflict with the large American economic interests that had spread throughout the hemisphere. It was also similar and often likened to Bolshevism in presenting an economic ideology that competed with the free-enterprise capitalist system favoured by the United States and especially the Republican administrations of the 1920s.

Latin American governments were so openly critical of American diplomacy and especially of dollar diplomacy that American representatives had to endure a series of unpleasant debates on this subject at the Pan-American conferences which were held at Santiago de Chile in 1923 and Havana in 1928. Several months before the Havana conference assembled, Coolidge's secretary of state, Frank Kellogg, wrote apprehensively to the state department diplomat, Henry Fletcher:

> The next meeting of the Pan American Conference is going to be more important and probably more difficult than any we have had in many years . . . There is no use disguising the fact that there are liable to be elements going to the next Conference purely for the purpose of making trouble for the United States. You know how difficult it was to suppress some of this even at Santiago, where there was a much better feeling towards us than there is now.[48]

In order to impress and conciliate the Latin American delegates, it was decided to schedule a brief visit by President Coolidge to the opening ceremonies at Havana. In marked contrast to the previous meeting at Santiago de Chile, the country's most distinguished statesman, Charles Evans Hughes, agreed to head the American delegation on this occasion.

Unfortunately, the attempts of Coolidge and Hughes to be conciliatory at the Havana Conference coincided with Latin American anger at the administration's military intervention in Nicaragua and what was believed to be unreasonable diplomatic pressure on Mexico over disputed oil rights. As usual, the most contentious and, on this occasion, acrimonious debate concerned the question of armed intervention. The Argentine delegation was characteristically prominent in supporting a resolution which contained the clause that 'no state may intervene in the internal affairs of another'. American policy was clearly on trial. While Hughes accepted that international law should be upheld, he also defied the assembled critics of US policy with the statement that, in cases where government breaks down and is unable to function:

> it is a principle of international law that in such a case a government is fully justified in taking action – I would call it interposition of a temporary character – for the purpose of protecting the lives and property of its nationals.[49]

The majority of Latin American nations voted for the resolution that was critical of intervention. The United States voted against and was supported by only four nations – Panama, Cuba, Nicaragua and Peru. The vote was interpreted as a major defeat for the United States. Indeed, the American policy of dollar diplomacy was under such severe attack at Havana that it was generally held at the time that the Pan-American conference system, which had started with the Washington Conference in 1889, had come to an end.

Economic ties

The First World War greatly strengthened American economic influence in the Western Hemisphere. One of the most notable developments was the increase in American capital investment. Prior to 1914 the United States had been a net importer of capital from Europe. At the end of the war in 1919 Wall Street had replaced the City of London as the world's leading money market and financial centre. This position was further exemplified in Latin America during the 1920s when total American investment more than tripled from $1.6 billion in 1914 to $5.3 billion in 1929. Indeed, American investment in the region grew at a faster rate than that of Great Britain and for the first time constituted a larger proportion of the new capital issues. By the end of the decade the United States had finally replaced Great Britain as the nation with the largest total investment in Latin America. A significant development was the geographical spread of American investment to include South America instead of concentrating as before mainly on the Central American–Caribbean region. For example, American capital investment rose in Argentina from $40 million in 1913 to $611 million in 1929, and doubled in Chile from $200 million in 1920 to $400 million in 1928.

Support for the expansion of American trade with Latin America was a theme of the Republican era. Referring to the Western Hemisphere in his inaugural address in 1921, Harding stated that 'in the new order of finance and trade we mean to promote enlarged activities and seek expanded confidence'.[50] During the war the federal government had taken on a more open and defined role in promoting the expansion of American trade and investment in Latin America. This was continued by the Harding and Coolidge administrations. A particular feature was the contribution of the Department of Commerce under the dynamic leadership of Secretary of Commerce Herbert Hoover. Officials sought commercial opportunities all over the world, but Latin America was regarded as particularly important because it was a vital source of raw materials and was eager to attract American investment capital.

During the 1920s important inroads were made into South America, a region in which the United States had traditionally lagged behind its European rivals.[51] For example, in Brazil the United States had made a considerable economic advance during the war due largely to the remarkable rise in value of American exports, whose share of the Brazilian market increased from 15 to 48 per cent. However, the wartime gains were soon challenged by the revival of strong European competition, especially from Great Britain. But American exports began to rise again in the second half of the 1920s. It was evident that a new pattern of trade, in which the United States was pre-eminent, was establishing itself. Whereas Great Britain's commercial dominance in Latin America had been largely based on the export of coal and textiles, Brazil and other countries in the region now looked to the United States to supply the new products of the twentieth century such as automobiles, films, radio and telephone communications, petroleum products and electrical goods. The demand for these items was constantly growing and was restrained only by the financial inability of the local population to buy.

In its ever-widening search for markets and raw materials, American business invested directly in Latin America to finance the acquisition and establishment of local subsidiary companies. Indeed, British and foreign competitors found themselves overwhelmed by the financial resources available to the giant American corporations. The latter included Armour, Ford, General Electric, General Motors, International Telephone and Telegraph, Radio Corporation of America, Standard Oil, Swift, United States Steel and Westinghouse. Corporate investment brought cash for new factories and jobs. It also spread American business skills and cultural values. The building of 'outposts of Yankee enterprise'[52] was most vividly symbolized by Henry Ford and his Ford Motor Company in Brazil. At its São Paulo plant in 1919, the company assembled just over 2,000 automobiles in the year. In 1925 production had increased to the same figure per month with an annual capacity of 45,000. Model Ts, Fordson trucks and tractors became a regular sight on the roads of Brazil. By 1928 the Ford Motor Company had authorized 700 agencies and more than 2,000 garages all over Brazil to market, distribute and repair its products. Henry Ford's ambitions knew no bounds. Acquiring a concession of territory almost the size of the state of Connecticut, he ordered work to commence in 1928 on his ultimately ill-fated scheme to create a prosperous rubber plantation in the new city of 'Fordlandia' located in the Amazon jungle.

Latin Americans were impressed and often overawed by the achievements of American business. They also welcomed increased trade with the United States and the inflow of American capital investment which they valued as an important means of promoting their own domestic economic development. But they could also be irritated by the burgeoning symbols in their countries of the growing American economic presence in utilities such as telephone and electricity, tramways, the radio and film industries. Following a pattern already set by the Mexican Revolution, nationalist sentiment was especially alarmed by American capitalists buying up substantial amounts of national territory and economic resources. For example, the schemes of the American entrepreneur Percival Farquhar to exploit the vast iron-ore deposits located in Minas Gerais, Brazil, excited particular suspicion and prompted the Brazilian Congress in 1926 to pass a constitutional amendment nationalizing all mineral deposits located on federal land. The damage that dollar diplomacy was causing to inter-American relations and to the image of the United States was pointed out in 1924 by the university professor and writer, Samuel Guy Inman:

> In these small countries of the South, controlled by our soldiers, our bankers, and our oil kings, we are developing our Irelands, our Egypts, and our Indias . . . We are piling up hatreds, suspicions, records for exploitation and destruction of sovereignty in Latin America, such as have never failed in all history to react in war, suffering, and defeat of high moral and spiritual ideals.[53]

American diplomatic officials dismissed Inman's charges as inaccurate and unfounded. They could not deny, however, the increase of anti-American feeling in Latin America. Indeed, the disagreeable tone of the debates in 1928 at the Sixth Pan-American Conference at Havana were a stark reminder. By the close of the 1920s it was evident that the aims and conduct of American diplomacy towards Latin America required re-evaluation.

5

THE GOOD NEIGHBOR (1928–45)

Herbert Hoover

Noted for his outstanding personal qualities of industriousness and efficiency as secretary of commerce from 1921 to 1928, Herbert Hoover was elected president by a landslide victory in 1928 on the promise of delivering four more years of 'Republican prosperity' for the American people. While the new president shared the popular mood in not according any special priority to foreign affairs, he was unusually active in attempting to cultivate friendly relations with Latin America. Prior to his inauguration as president he embarked upon a hemispheric tour lasting ten weeks and visiting ten countries. A sincere desire to promote hemispheric goodwill was evident, but there were also other more influential reasons for the trip. Indeed, Hoover's immediate aim was to escape, if only temporarily, from the political jungle of American spoils politics in which the president-elect was besieged by job seekers. 'I agree with you', he informed Elihu Root, 'that I should keep entirely out of Washington and also that I should keep in the background as much as possible.'[1] The president-elect was also a great world traveller, and before he assumed the time-consuming burdens of the presidency, he wished to visit the one continent of the globe with which he was personally unfamiliar. But the American work ethic could never be entirely forgotten. Once the journey was under way, Hoover's speeches and press conferences frequently emphasized his desire to promote hemispheric peace and harmony. From this emerged what would later be called the policy of the 'good neighbor'.[2] Shortly after leaving California he told pressmen on board the *USS Maryland*:

> This is not a commercial trip but one intended to promote friendly relations, and if friendly relations are established, trade relations will follow automatically . . . We must interpret these countries to our own people. We must show them they are entirely out of the state of savagery, although many of them are still in the early stages of development and we need to help them to greater stability

> . . . We must feel our way along. I know we cannot accomplish this in one trip. If we do but part of that, we will have laid a foundation on which we must build for perhaps a century.[3]

Despite all the ceremonial trappings laid out for him, Hoover was careful to stress that he came to Latin America as a private citizen and not as a head of state with executive powers to negotiate and enter into agreements. Nevertheless, throughout the tour he was constantly in the public eye, requiring him to be circumspect in his public behaviour and remarks. Furthermore, the visit of an American president-elect was an unprecedented event and helped to moderate the barriers of indifference and misunderstanding that existed on both sides. For example, as secretary of commerce, Hoover had been openly hostile to Brazil's 'valorization' policy of seeking to prop up the world price of coffee by controlling the supply of that commodity. After an official meeting with Hoover the Brazilian ambassador in Washington had privately described him as 'truculent and arrogant'.[4] However, personal contact with Brazilians at a social level in Brazil achieved wonders for Hoover's image so that he was no longer seen as a foe but a friend. Favourable publicity was given to his smallest actions. The people of Rio de Janeiro warmed to a man who dismissed the bodyguards assigned to his motorcade on the grounds that he needed no protection from Brazilians.

During his presidential administration from 1929 to 1933 Hoover genuinely aimed to implement a conciliatory policy towards the Latin American nations. The long simmering controversy over armed intervention was eased by the publication in 1930 of the 'Clark Memorandum' an official document on the Monroe Doctrine prepared at the close of the Coolidge Administration by Under Secretary of State J. Reuben Clark. The memorandum illustrated the change of thinking in American policy towards Latin America. Not only was the policy of intervention considered damaging to America's image and counter-productive to American national interests but it was also now stated that armed interventions undertaken in the Central American–Caribbean region under the Roosevelt Corollary 'are not within the Doctrine as announced by Monroe'.[5] Hoover put this thinking into action by publicly announcing a schedule for the phased withdrawal of all American marines to be completed in Nicaragua by January 1933 and in Haiti by December 1934. But further diplomatic initiatives to improve hemispheric relations were sidelined by the pressure of domestic events. Within a year of taking office Hoover's dream of eliminating poverty in the United States was shattered by the 1929 Wall Street Crash, to be replaced by the sombre realization that an era of 'hard times' was at hand. Not only the United States but also the whole world was thrown into first economic and then political turmoil. In Latin America the Bolivian government fell in March 1930. In late August the dictatorship of Augusto Leguía was overthrown in Peru. On 6 September a military coup in Argentina compelled the resignation of President Hipólito Irigoyen. Brazil's apparent long-standing immunity from revolutionary disorder was suddenly broken on 3 October when a civil conflict erupted which eventually resulted in the rise to power of Getúlio Dornelles Vargas. In the Central American–Caribbean region a military coup occurred in Guatemala on 16 December and a new government came into power in Panama on 2 January 1931.

American officials were surprised and unprepared for the sudden fall of so many regimes in Latin America. This was notably the case in Brazil where the government that was clearly preferred by the Hoover Administration collapsed in 1930 and was replaced by a self-proclaimed 'revolutionary' regime with pronounced nationalist tendencies. 'Brazil Coup Stuns Washington Circles' read the headline of the *New York Times*.[6] Officials in Washington, however, were preoccupied with the grave economic difficulties facing their own country. Nor were they inclined to revert to the past policies of military intervention in the Central American–Caribbean region. Secretary of State Henry Stimson was known to be particularly critical of Japanese military aggression in China and was concerned that the United States should not be seen to be imitating Japan's example in Latin America. Moreover, the civil disorder and change of regimes in Latin America, though regrettable, did not actually pose an immediate threat to the national security of the United States. Nor was there a real prospect of any opportunistic European diplomatic or military interference. This contingency was greatly reduced by the fact that those powers were also preoccupied with finding ways of alleviating their own severe economic difficulties arising from the Great Depression.

Despite Hoover's good intentions, his administration did not witness a tangible improvement in inter-American relations or understanding. In fact, the amount of actual contact was arguably diminished because economic relations between Latin America and the United States were adversely affected by the depression. From 1929 to 1933 American exports to the region fell in value by more than 75 per cent, while imports declined by 68 per cent. In addition, the United States appeared decidedly unsympathetic to the economic plight of Latin American exporters because domestic political reasons dictated the maintenance of a strongly protectionist attitude that was symbolized by the passage in the US Congress of the Smoot-Hawley Tariff in 1930. While the onset of the Great Depression contributed to diplomatic uncertainty and undermined inter-American relations, it also marked a definite historical watershed for the United States. This occurred in 1932 when Herbert Hoover's electoral defeat brought an end to over a decade of Republican control of the White House and paved the way for the 'New Deal' of Franklin D. Roosevelt.

Franklin D. Roosevelt and the 'Good Neighbor Policy'

Latin Americans were apprehensive over the choice of a 'Roosevelt' as the Democratic candidate in the 1932 presidential election because that surname was firmly associated with the aggressive policy of the Big Stick. Unlike his cousin Theodore, however, Franklin D. Roosevelt publicly announced a desire to act sympathetically towards the Latin American nations.[7] As president, he basically continued Hoover's conciliatory policy although it now acquired a new and fresh name as a result of a section taken from Roosevelt's inaugural address of 4 March 1933: 'In the field of world policy, I would dedicate this nation to the policy of the good neighbor – the neighbor who resolutely respects himself and, because he does so, respects the rights of others.'[8] Though never precisely defined, like many of his political slogans, the concept of acting as a 'good neighbor' was attractive in terms of external public relations because it implied equality and mutual respect among nations. It would be applied by Roosevelt not, as he initially seemed to suggest, to include the whole world but specifically to the countries of the Western Hemisphere. Consequently, it was Roosevelt and not Hoover who has been popularly regarded as the originator of what became known as the 'Good Neighbor Policy'.[9]

In his first few months in the presidency, Roosevelt's actions belied his proclaimed good neighbourly intentions. One of his initial foreign policy crises was the island of Cuba which was in civil and economic disorder resulting mainly from the collapse in the world price of sugar and the severe decline of sugar exports to the United States. President Gerardo Machado, who had been in power since 1924, had adopted ruthless emergency powers and was eventually overthrown in a military coup in August 1933. In the ensuing uncertainty considerable political pressure was put on Roosevelt for American military intervention under the Platt Amendment to restore constitutional government. While Roosevelt duly sent a small number of warships to patrol Cuban waters and present a show of military force, he would not order the landing of marines. 'Despite the legal right we possessed', Roosevelt's secretary of state, Cordell Hull, later explained, 'such an act would further embitter our relations with all Latin America.'[10] On the other hand, Roosevelt would not grant diplomatic recognition to the Cuban provisional government of Ramón Grau San Martín, a university professor and radical social reformer who advocated the nationalization of sugar estates, higher wages and improvements in working conditions. When a military coup led by Colonel Fulgencio Batista y Zalvídar forced a change of regime in January 1934, Grau blamed the non-recognition policy of the US government as the crucial element that was responsible for his overthrow. Although Roosevelt had refused to recognize a government headed by Grau even though it had lasted for four months, he established full diplomatic relations with the new government of President Carlos Mendieta after it had been in office for only five days.

While it did not constitute direct armed intervention, Roosevelt's undisguised meddling in Cuban affairs was reminiscent of the earlier era of dollar diplomacy. It was also inconsistent with the high expectations he had aroused with the 'Good Neighbor' concept. This was partly explained by the fact that the president was new to office and that he was preoccupied with domestic affairs, especially the formulation and implementation of the 'New Deal' to combat severe economic depression at home. In addition, he was influenced by the views of Ambassador Sumner Welles, who visited Cuba as the president's personal envoy. Welles was very suspicious of Grau's radical ideological leanings and pointed out the dangers of the establishment of what he termed 'Communist' influence in an area of vital national security and economic importance for the United States. Indeed, shortly after Grau had come to power in September, Welles had warned Roosevelt of the risk of social revolution and contemptuously dismissed the provisional government as 'an undisciplined group of individuals of divergent tendencies representing the most irresponsible elements in the city of Havana with practically no support whatsoever outside the capital'.[11]

Meanwhile, the Seventh Pan-American Conference took place at Montevideo in December 1933. The fact that Secretary of State Hull headed the American delegation indicated the significance attached to the meeting by the Roosevelt Administration. Hull was apprehensive of Latin American criticism on account of the legacy of ill feeling arising from the previous conference at Havana in 1928 and the current controversy over Cuba where Roosevelt's policy of non-recognition of Grau and the sending of warships were interpreted as evidence of an interventionist attitude and a denial of the 'Good Neighbor' concept. 'The outlook for a successful conference was so completely sterile', considered Hull, 'that I asked the President to issue a statement that would serve to squelch too much optimism as to its possibilities.'[12]

At Montevideo Hull hoped to avoid open-ended discussion of Cuban affairs and to concentrate instead on practical items such as the negotiation of reciprocal trade agreements to promote trade. To an extent he was successful, but he could not prevent the holding of a debate on the intervention issue. This took the form of discussion of a proposal to adopt a 'Convention on the Rights and Duties of States' whose article 8 affirmed: 'No state has the right to intervene in the internal affairs of another.' Hull answered in the affirmative but with a qualification reserving such rights of intervention as the United States possessed according 'to the law of nations as generally recognized and understood'.[13] Hull's general acceptance of the resolution was of symbolic importance, but his attached reservation at a time when the United States was refusing to recognize the government of Grau in Cuba did little to conciliate Latin American antagonism towards the United States. Indeed, the Latin American delegates proceeded to vote in favour of the convention, several adding pointedly 'without reservations'.

As critics of his Latin American policy frequently commented, Roosevelt's inaugural speech in March 1933 referring to the 'Good Neighbor' concept merely affirmed American good intentions and was extremely vague on precise detail. To be successful it was evident that the idea required a more tangible form and this was provided in January 1934 when Roosevelt made the important announcement with regard to Latin American affairs: 'The definite policy of the United States from now on is one opposed to armed intervention.'[14] In fact, as the recent Cuban crisis had demonstrated, the actual deployment of armed force was unnecessary and counter-productive. Moreover, its public abandonment by Roosevelt provided a boost for the 'Good Neighbor Policy' and was further exemplified in a new treaty signed with Cuba in May 1934 abrogating the notorious Platt Amendment. The United States therefore gave up its controversial right to intervene in Cuban affairs, though it still retained its possession of the strategically important Guantánamo naval base. Further conciliatory measures followed. Hoover's announced schedule for the withdrawal of marines from Haiti was brought forward to August instead of December 1934. Treaty rights to intervene in that country were allowed to lapse in 1936 though financial supervision was retained until 1941. A new treaty was signed with Panama in 1936 that abrogated the existing American legal right of intervention and increased annual payments to that country arising from the operation of the canal from $250,000 to $430,000. This arrangement, however, did not disturb American control over the strategically important Panama Canal Zone. Moreover, it was not ratified by the US Senate until 1939 and only after inclusion of the unilateral right of the United States to defend the canal in emergencies.

The new treaties concluded by the Roosevelt Administration were significant in publicly reversing the policy of armed intervention associated with the Roosevelt Corollary and dollar diplomacy, but the desire remained for order and stability in the Caribbean and Central American states. When civil unrest pointed to a change of political regime, the United States – while not intervening with armed force – showed a willingness to accept, if not actively support the rise to power of leaders with military backgrounds such as Fulgencio Batista in Cuba, Anastasio Somoza García in Nicaragua, and Rafael Leonidas Trujillo in the Dominican Republic. In 1933 Sumner Welles had personally told Batista that he was the 'only individual in Cuba today who represented authority'.[15] In 1939 Somoza visited Washington where he was met at Union Station by President Roosevelt and stayed overnight at the White House. Trujillo came to Washington in 1940 and was invited to tea at the White House with the president and his wife. In return, these leaders would prove to be most cooperative in assisting the United States to defeat the Axis powers in the Second World War and later to support policies of anti-Communism during the Cold War. The public praise that they often received from American officials for establishing outwardly stable governments conflicted, however, with reports and evidence of their increasingly corrupt and brutal style of ruling. Instead of advancing democracy in the Central American–Caribbean region, as it claimed to be doing, US diplomacy was more often instrumental in facilitating the rise and consolidation of authoritarian regimes.

Commercial diplomacy

The building up of inter-American friendship and goodwill was a prominent feature of Roosevelt's 'Good Neighbor Policy'. Behind the uplifting rhetoric, however, was an evolving strategy of promoting economic integration within the hemisphere that was designed to increase trade and help the American economy recover from the Great Depression. Particularly influential were the ideas of Cordell Hull in support of liberalizing trade. 'All our political acts in the direction of Latin America', he noted, 'would have lost their true effect if we had not been able to back them up with economic acts.'[16] In terms of practical policy Hull was greatly assisted by the passage in Congress in June 1934 of the Reciprocal Trade Agreements Act that was similar to the 1890 McKinley Tariff in allowing closer economic contact to be secured with foreign nations by authorizing the executive power to negotiate bilateral reciprocal trade agreements. These arrangements put into effect mutual tariff reductions of up to 50 per cent on imports and thereby circumvented the protectionist policies of the past. As in the 1890s, the reciprocity policy of the 1930s was very suitable for, and was mostly aimed at the Latin American nations, where it was believed that the United States was particularly losing market share to European competition. Moreover, reciprocal arrangements with the Latin American countries aroused little political controversy because their economies offered raw materials and staple products that were not major competitors of American goods. Those countries were also in the depths of economic depression and were keen to conclude agreements with the United States that implied equality of commercial treatment and promised financial benefits in the form of increased export earnings and reduced prices of imported American manufactured and industrial goods.

Beginning with Cuba in August 1934, bilateral reciprocity arrangements were concluded with eleven Latin American countries by 1939.[17] Trade was also expanded by the creation in February 1934 of the Export–Import Bank to provide foreign countries with dollar credits for the purchase of imports from the United States. In addition, the bank gave loans for industrial development and thereby served as a useful tool of American diplomacy. Although its share of the Latin American export trade actually declined slightly from 33 per cent in 1930 to just over 31 per cent in 1938, the United States remained the largest single market for Latin American goods. In fact, the reciprocity policy was highly successful because the countries signing the trade agreements became more economically dependent than ever on the American market for their export growth. For example, Cuban exports to the United States almost doubled in value from $57 million in 1933 to $108 million in 1938. Most of the increase, however, was in sugar so that the 1934 treaty actually encouraged more Cuban sugar production while discouraging economic diversification. But American exports to Cuba also benefited and more than tripled during the same period from 1933 to 1938. British officials sadly recognized that the position of American exporters had become 'quite impregnable'.[18] 'In summation,' Hull proudly claimed, 'if the case of Cuba was to be the focus of Latin American scrutiny of our acts and intentions, a happier one could scarcely have been chosen.'[19]

Although Great Britain remained the most well-established economic competitor of the United States in Latin America, the mid-1930s saw a rising threat from other European countries, most notably Germany. The arrival of a German commercial delegation in South America in 1934 marked the beginning of a trade offensive from that nation which resulted in a doubling of German exports to Latin America in the following two years. Among the countries of the region, Brazil presented a foremost example of the extent of the German economic challenge to the United States. Throughout the 1930s the United States remained Brazil's single largest export market and source of new capital investment, so Brazil was receptive to American commercial initiatives and was the first nation in South America to sign a reciprocal trade agreement with the United States in February 1935. The agreement was important for Brazil because it ensured that American imports of Brazilian coffee remained free of duty. But the most notable growth in Brazil's overseas trade during the 1930s was with Germany and not with the United States. In marked contrast to customary trading practices, the National Socialist (Nazi) government that came to power under Adolf Hitler in 1933 required that trade be conducted in what amounted to a barter system using a special German currency known as *aski* or compensation marks. The arrangement was the opposite of free trade but it was attractive to Brazil, and other Latin American nations, because it obviated the need to allocate scarce foreign exchange and gold reserves to finance foreign trade. Moreover, Germany was especially keen to buy Brazilian agricultural goods in exchange for industrial products including arms and munitions that were eagerly wanted by the Brazilian military. In fact, the barter system was so successful that Brazil doubled its exports to Germany from 1933 to 1938. Germany not only purchased large quantities of coffee and rubber but also became the biggest market for Brazilian cotton and cacao. During the same period Germany's share of Brazil's import trade more than doubled from 12 to almost 25 per cent.

The visible growth of German interest in Brazil was not just limited to commerce. Brazil was also one of a number of Latin American countries whose friendship the Nazi government wished to cultivate because its population contained a substantial number of immigrants of German extraction, amounting to almost one million. In addition, Germany sought to revive its pre-First World War influence over the Brazilian military by supplying weapons and training and issuing invitations to senior officers to attend German army manoeuvres. American diplomats anxiously observed these developments, which they regarded as a serious challenge to their country's political and economic influence in Brazil. Their concern was further heightened by the creation in 1937 of a new political regime, the *Estado Nôvo* ('New State'), and its close association with the ideas and practices of European fascism. Despite its acknowledged fascist sympathies, however, the *Estado Nôvo* pursued a nationalist policy of *brasilidade* and vigorously repressed pro-Nazi activities in Brazil. Moreover, Brazilian diplomacy carefully avoided becoming identified with the international ambitions of Nazi Germany and continued to value close diplomatic relations with the United States. The Brazilian ambassador in Washington, Oswaldo Aranha, informed a Brazilian journalist in 1937 that his government would be 'very pleased, if all countries treated Brazil on the same friendly terms that the United States has . . . for many years, and now more than ever'.[20]

Accommodation with Mexico

In its attempt to promote the 'Good Neighbor Policy' and to counter the growing influence of fascism during the late 1930s, the Roosevelt Administration sought to moderate any existing tensions with Latin American nations. The adoption of a conciliatory policy was particularly exemplified by Roosevelt's attitude towards Mexico. A major diplomatic crisis emerged in March 1938 when President Lázaro Cárdenas announced the expropriation of the Anglo-Dutch and American-owned oil companies. In effect, this was a continuation of the dispute that had started with the 1917 Mexican Constitution and had been temporarily settled in 1928 at the time of the Coolidge Administration. The oil companies did not contest Mexico's sovereign right to expropriate, but they challenged the decision of the Mexican government to appoint a commission consisting solely of Mexican members to determine the amount of compensation on the basis of existing and not prospective assets. At first, the Roosevelt Administration backed the protests of the American oil companies whose prospective assets were initially estimated at more than half a billion dollars. Not only was a very large financial loss involved but expropriation without adequate compensation could not be accepted in principle. 'We cannot admit', Cordell Hull informed the Mexican ambassador in Washington, 'that a foreign government may take the property of American nationals in disregard of the rule of compensation under international law.'[21] The fear, as always, was that, if the Mexicans were successful, this would not only threaten the confiscation of all American property and investments in Mexico but would also encourage other Latin American nations to take similar action and restrict the access of American companies not only to oil but to other vital raw materials. Particular concerns were the attitudes of Venezuela and Bolivia whose governments were currently involved in negotiations with American companies over concessions to drill for oil.

Mindful of Latin American sensitivity over the issue of American intervention in their internal affairs, Roosevelt ruled out the use of military force and did not follow the action of Great Britain, whose oil companies were also affected, in breaking off diplomatic relations with the Mexican government. But economic retaliation was adopted in the form of an oil boycott and the suspension of the monthly purchases of Mexican silver made by the US Treasury. The sanctions were enforced half-heartedly and were unsuccessful primarily because Roosevelt was personally not sympathetic to the oil companies partly on account of what he believed was their inflated claim for prospective future assets. He was also influenced by the views of the American ambassador in Mexico, Josephus Daniels, who expressed concern about retaining Latin American goodwill and wished to avoid damage to his country's image as a good neighbour. Early in the crisis Daniels advised that 'every possible step should be taken to prevent the threatened break in the relations between the two countries'.[22] In addition, there was anxiety that the dispute was encouraging the advance of fascist influence in Mexico and by implication throughout the whole of Latin America. When the United States refused to purchase Mexican oil, Germany and Italy had come forward to offer shipping facilities and an alternative market. The American financier, Bernard Baruch, was worried that unfriendly European governments would take control of Latin American raw materials so that 'America may readily find herself not alone denuded of the investment represented but also shut off from the supply of those materials, except at prices that can be dictated by others'.[23]

But the principle of expropriation without an agreed procedure of compensation could not be easily accepted so that the dispute dragged on until September 1941. The value of having friendly relations with Mexico, however, was enhanced by the outbreak of the world war. Under the impact of a succession of Nazi military victories in Europe that underscored the need for hemispheric unity and cooperation, including the provision of American access to strategic materials and military bases, a compromise was effected in which the Roosevelt Administration essentially accepted the act of expropriation on Mexico's terms. The US government resumed purchases of Mexican silver while Mexico agreed to pay compensation for seizure of American-owned land as part of a major programme of land reform and redistribution. A joint US–Mexican commission was appointed and determined the amount of compensation owing to the oil companies. They eventually received $24 million instead of the $600 million that they had previously insisted upon.[24] Roosevelt defended the settlement on the grounds that it was important and necessary to secure an understanding with Mexico that would bring an end to past confrontations and set the pattern for future relations. He also insisted that the principle of 'compensation' had been upheld. Although the *New York Times* considered that 'a dangerous precedent' had been set, it explained: 'The best that can be said for it is that it terminates a troublesome controversy with a neighboring country at a time when it is of vital importance to maintain and strengthen relations with Latin America.'[25]

The European war

Although the Roosevelt Administration stressed the importance of consultation and cooperation with the Latin American nations to counter the threat of fascism, American officials were typically determined to assert a leading and predominant role. The concern over growing Axis influence in Latin America and the security challenge that this presented prompted Roosevelt to take the diplomatic initiative and request a Special Pan-American Conference for the Maintenance of Peace to be held in Buenos Aires in December 1936. 'The moment has now arrived', remarked Roosevelt, 'when the American republics, through their designated representatives seated at a common council table' should promote 'the cause of permanent peace on this Western continent'.[26] The president personally attended the conference and was greeted by enthusiastic crowds lining the streets on his arrival in the Argentine capital. 'The primary purpose of this Conference is to banish war from the Western Hemisphere,' declared Cordell Hull, and he added: 'The 21 American republics cannot remain unconcerned by the grave and threatening conditions in many parts of the world.'[27] Good neighbourliness flourished at the conference as delegates welcomed the American proposal that they should be prepared to hold meetings of consultation in the event of a threat to peace either from inside or outside the hemisphere. To Hull's dismay, however, the Argentine delegation 'emasculated' the resolution by adding the qualification 'if they so desire'.[28] There was applause when the American secretary of state signed the protocol affirming that 'the high contracting parties declare inadmissible the intervention of any one of them, directly, or indirectly, and for whatever reason, in the internal or external affairs of any of the other parties'.[29] Under Secretary of State Sumner Welles gratifyingly noted the existence of a more 'objective and unprejudiced' atmosphere than in previous inter-American meetings. He attributed this to 'the practical application of the good neighbor policy', which 'had worked a material change in the sentiments of the other American republics toward the United States.'[30]

Inter-American friendliness and cooperation were evident at further Pan-American conferences, which were held at Lima in December 1938 during the height of diplomatic turmoil in Europe over the Munich Crisis and at Panama City in September 1939 shortly after the outbreak of war in Europe. Although public opinion in both the United States and Latin America generally favoured Great Britain and France and regarded Germany as the instigator of the crises that had led to war in Europe, there was no great diplomatic or public pressure to enter the conflict. Indeed, governments and military leaders were only too well aware of their relative military weakness and ill preparedness for war. They responded therefore to the outbreak of fighting in Europe with declarations of neutrality. The foreign ministers at the Panama meeting in 1939 sought to facilitate the observance of the policy of neutrality by declaring a 'safety' zone averaging 300 miles in width around the coastline of the Western Hemisphere (excluding Canada and European colonies in the Caribbean) into which the warships of the belligerents should not enter.

Roosevelt was very much attracted to the idea of hemispheric isolationism that he hoped would protect and insulate the Americas from the war in Europe. Hull predicted, however, that the vast size of the zone made the declaration practically unenforceable and that it would not be recognized by the nations at war. 'Much would depend on the spirit with which the American Republics sought to maintain it and on the good will of the belligerents', he remarked.[31] This view was echoed in Latin America where a Uruguayan newspaper described the concept as 'absurd'.[32] The pessimism was proved correct in December 1939 when the German battleship *Graf Spee* was engaged in a battle with British cruisers 200 miles off the coast of Uruguay and therefore clearly within the safety zone. A Pan-American note of protest was delivered, but was rejected by both the British and German governments. They simply stated that military actions would take place in international waters as and when necessary.

The rapid success of the German *blitzkrieg* in the spring of 1940 resulting in the fall of France, Belgium and Holland suddenly altered the military balance in Europe and brought the prospect of direct involvement in the conflict much closer to the Western Hemisphere. Growing sympathy for the plight of Great Britain and especially Roosevelt's desire to help that country against Germany, with all material means short of going to war, meant that the concept of the neutrality zone effectively became redundant. In addition, those countries bordering the Atlantic found that their national security was also directly affected, if not threatened, by the expanding conflict at sea especially in the form of the threat of the German submarine to merchant shipping. A particular concern of the Roosevelt Administration was that Germany might convert the French and Dutch colonies in the Caribbean into bases for military aggression in the Americas. In response to this threat, hemispheric unity took even more tangible shape in July 1940 when the Havana Conference of foreign ministers approved an American proposal, which was reminiscent of the 1811 No-Transfer Resolution, that the transfer of European colonies in the Caribbean to a non-hemispheric power would not be recognized.

The success of the Havana Conference demonstrated that the pursuit of the 'Good Neighbor Policy' and especially Roosevelt's successful presentation of that policy had contributed to a distinct improvement in inter-American relations. As a result most Latin American countries joined the United States in organizing resistance against the fascist threat posed by Germany and Italy both before and during the Second World War. The Havana meeting, however, was arguably a highpoint of American diplomatic interest in Latin America because it occurred at a time when American officials were placing great value on the countries of the region as a source of raw materials, vital military bases and diplomatic support against the Axis powers of Germany, Italy and Japan. However, once the United States entered the war in December 1941, American diplomatic interest shifted sharply to Europe and Asia while Latin America moved to the periphery. Once the 'Europe first' strategy was adopted, the holding of Pan-American meetings of consultation and policymaking, which had become a feature of the pre-war period, were regarded as unnecessary and a diversion of diplomatic resources. In fact, after the conference of foreign ministers at Rio de Janeiro in January 1942 the state department discouraged any further Pan-American meetings for the duration of the war.

Diplomatic conflict with Argentina

The United States entered the war in December 1941 as a result of the Japanese surprise attack on the US Pacific fleet based at Pearl Harbor. A Pan-American conference of foreign ministers to discuss measures of common hemispheric defence was immediately scheduled and held at Rio de Janeiro in January 1942. A mood of crisis prevailed. For American diplomats, Japanese aggression had definitively brought a sudden end to the period of neutrality and placed the future security of the hemisphere in the balance. 'This was a life-and-death struggle, the result of which could only mean freedom and advancement for Latin America or domination and probably occupation by the Axis', considered Cordell Hull.[33] Just prior to the meeting at Rio, nine Central American and Caribbean countries had joined the United States in declaring war against Japan and then a few days later taking the same action against Germany and Italy. Once again, however, Argentina was conspicuous in adopting an opposite approach. Bridling against what he considered was attempted American control, the Argentine ambassador in Washington, Felipe Espil, expressed his government's misgivings over the convening of the Rio conference as a forum for discussing future policy when a number of countries had already taken the decision to go to war.

'There is', he informed the state department, 'a certain contradiction in inviting us to participate in the study and adoption of measures of common defense at the same time that nine countries proceed without prior exchange of views' to declare war.'[34]

At the Rio Conference itself the Argentine delegation further angered the United States by its refusal to assent to a unanimous resolution mandating the immediate breaking of relations with the Axis powers. While the action of the Argentine government reflected a proud desire not to be seen as subservient to the United States, its attitude was also influenced by pressure from its own politicians and army officers with pro-fascist sympathies and also from the sizable German ethnic community in Argentina. In addition, Argentine public opinion was very different to that in the United States in expressing doubt over the likelihood of an Allied victory over the Axis and apprehension that abandoning the policy of strict neutrality might provoke German military retaliation. 'The political situation in Argentina', remarked the Republican political leader, Nelson Rockefeller, 'is dangerous to our interests because it involves a weak government which has been relying on the support of pro-Axis elements to keep itself in power.'[35] At the Rio Conference, however, Argentina only gained the support of Chile, whose government was similarly concerned about its own national security because the long Chilean coastline was vulnerable to attack from the Japanese navy. In response to an American undertaking that the US fleet would protect Chile, the Chilean foreign minister, Gabriel Rossetti, privately retorted: 'What fleet? The one sunk in Pearl Harbor?'[36] Both Argentina and Chile, however, became effectively isolated. In contrast to their attitudes during the First World War, and in what was gratifyingly regarded by American officials as a vindication of the success of the 'Good Neighbor Policy', all the other South American nations affirmed their support for the United States by breaking off relations with the Axis powers. Shortly afterwards, in response to repeated attacks by German submarines on their merchant and passenger shipping with loss of civilian lives, Mexico declared war in May and was followed by Brazil in August.[37] Chile was more reluctant, but eventually severed relations in January 1943 and joined the war on the Allied side in February 1945.

Despite the steady escalation of American political and economic pressure, Argentina insisted on its right to maintain normal relations with Germany. The claim to be seeking only to assert its national independence against the United States, however, was undermined by the refusal to place restrictions on the activities of Axis diplomats in Argentina and to assist the Allies in providing naval protection for convoys in the South Atlantic. As a result, the Argentine government made itself vulnerable to charges that it was not neutral but was actually pursuing a pro-Nazi foreign policy. Cordell Hull was increasingly irritated by Argentina's attitude and actions that he described as those of a 'bad neighbor'.[38] This perception was reinforced in June 1943 when the military overthrew the civilian government of Ramón Castillo and installed General Pedro Ramírez as president. The new government included Colonel Juan Domingo Perón who quickly became one of the most influential members of the cabinet. A British diplomat noted in February 1944 that Perón 'is stronger behind the scenes than ever, and if the present régime continues, will become more or less the uncrowned king of Argentina'.[39] American intelligence officials considered the Ramírez government as a pro-Nazi dictatorship and believed that it had coordinated plans with German agents for 'an Axis counter-offensive which would effectively smash the Pan-American bloc and lead to serious diversionary disturbances'.[40] Consequently, the occurrence of a military coup in neighbouring Bolivia in December 1943 was attributed to Argentine instigation. The Roosevelt Administration responded with a publicity campaign condemning Argentine interference in Bolivian affairs. Partly to conciliate the United States and Latin American opinion, Ramírez agreed to break off diplomatic relations with the Axis powers in January 1944.

The abandonment of neutrality, however, was so controversial within the senior military that a few weeks later Ramírez was forced to resign in favour of General Edelmiro Farrell. The United States interpreted the change as a victory for the pro-Nazi element within the military and refused to grant diplomatic recognition to the new government. 'It would be ridiculous', affirmed Hull, 'to recognize and open formal diplomatic relations with a regime known to be working at cross purposes with our war effort.'[41] In what was the antithesis of the attitude of the 'Good Neighbor', the Roosevelt Administration maintained a policy of non-recognition combined with increased economic sanctions on trade and investment in order to bring about a change of government in Argentina. The majority of Latin American countries supported the policy of diplomatic non-recognition, but there was criticism that Roosevelt's strategy of simultaneously escalating economic pressure was too aggressively interventionist. The Farrell government sought to exploit this divergence of opinion and at the same time diplomatically out-manoeuvre the United States by proposing an inter-American conference of foreign ministers to discuss the question of ending Argentina's diplomatic isolation. Acting Secretary of State Edward R. Stettinius denounced the proposal as a 'brazen and insincere move'.[42] While his government was not opposed to the idea of a meeting, Stettinius affirmed that it would not accept the inclusion of a country that had for so long maintained friendly relations with the Axis powers.

The difficulty for the Argentine military was that they suffered from the ignominy of having made a major miscalculation in believing for so long that Germany would actually win the war. In March 1945, at a time when the Axis powers faced imminent military defeat, Argentina finally declared war on Germany and Japan. American diplomatic recognition duly followed in April. After the end of the war, the United States sought unsuccessfully to prevent the election of Perón to the presidency in March 1946. Two weeks before the election the former American ambassador in Buenos Aires, Spruille Braden, released a state department document known as the 'Blue Book' detailing Perón's alleged wartime collusion with the Nazis. But the action only provoked nationalist and anti-American sentiment and proved to be highly counter-productive. Perón accused the United States of blatant interference in Argentine domestic affairs and eagerly grasped the opportunity to state that the election had effectively become a choice between either himself or the American ambassador.

Inter-American cooperation during the Second World War

With the exceptions of Argentina and Chile, the Roosevelt Administration was pleased with the cooperation that it received in Latin America for its policy of forming a united hemisphere in the war against the Axis powers. Sumner Welles had remarked at the 1942 Rio Conference:

> When peace is restored it is to the interest of the whole world that the American Republics present a united front and be able to speak and act with the moral authority to which, by reason of their number and their power, they are entitled.[43]

Although Latin American diplomatic support for the fight against the fascist dictatorships was certainly valued, the United States took the lead in organizing the practical measures for hemispheric defence during the Second World War. After the attack on Pearl Harbor, the US navy took full responsibility for the defence of the sea-lanes in the Caribbean and approaches to the Panama Canal. In 1942 an Inter-American Defense Board was established in Washington to direct military preparations and strategy. Latin American military attachés served on the Board. Though limited to a mainly advisory function, the Board provided a symbol of inter-American unity and military cooperation. In fact, all military aspects involved in prosecuting the war effort were placed very firmly under American control. Just like the First World War, little was required in the way of a Latin American contribution to actual military operations in the Second World War. Latin American militaries would concentrate instead on their local defensive roles. In fact, only Mexico and Brazil actually sent combat troops overseas. Mexico sent an air force squadron to the Philippines while Brazil sent an infantry division to fight under American command in Italy.[44] Several thousand Latin Americans, mostly from Mexico, joined the US armed forces as volunteers.

The wartime policy of close cooperation bordering on subordination to the United States contained distinct material benefits. This was particularly exemplified by Brazil. American perception of Brazil's strategic significance was considerably altered by the outbreak of war in Europe. The geopolitical reality was that Brazil was the largest and, on account of its long coastline bordering the Atlantic, the most vulnerable of the Latin American countries to external aggression. In fact, the Roosevelt Administration became concerned that Brazil's fascist sympathies might lead to a possible alignment with the Axis powers or, after the dramatic collapse of France in 1940, that Germany might use the French colonies in West Africa to launch an invasion of the 'bulge' of north-eastern Brazil with the intention of advancing in force to the United States via Central America and Mexico. Moreover, the onset of war and the resulting disruption of trade with Europe heightened Brazil's value as an important source of agricultural products, raw materials and minerals, especially rubber, iron ore and quartz crystals. President Getúlio Vargas was, therefore, able to conclude an advantageous arrangement in which Brazil agreed to supply raw materials and provide naval and air bases in the north-east of the country in return for American arms and financial assistance including a substantial loan for the projected national steelworks at Volta Redonda. American Lend-Lease aid was also formally extended to Brazil in October 1941. After the United States joined the war in December 1941, Brazil severed diplomatic relations with Germany on 28 January 1942 and formally entered the war on 22 August 1942.[45] By breaking off diplomatic relations with the Axis powers, Brazil was rewarded by the Roosevelt Administration with a doubling of the amount of the Lend-Lease aid that had been initially allocated in October 1941. American assistance was further increased after Brazil's formal declaration of war and grew to such an extent that Brazil received more than $350 million or 70 per cent of the total Lend-Lease aid given by the United States to the whole of Latin America during the Second World War.

The massive war effort was financed and administered from Washington. In a similar fashion to the First World War, the Latin American countries were again highly valued as suppliers of strategic raw materials, especially oil, tin, manganese and copper. For some products such as rubber the significance of Latin American production was greatly enhanced by the closure of access to supplies in South-east Asia as a result of Japanese military occupation. The United States also compensated for the drastic decline of the region's pre-war trade with Europe by purchasing large quantities of Latin American agricultural produce, including sugar, coffee, tobacco and fruit. The American role was paramount. 'Because of our material resources', Sumner Welles remarked, 'the main brunt of the hemisphere effort to maintain the inter-American economic and commercial structure' fell upon the United States.[46] While the resulting economic benefits were considerable for the Latin American economies, traditional links with Europe were greatly reduced and they became noticeably more dependent upon the United

States not only as their biggest single market for exports but also as a source of continuing capital investment. As early as 1940 the Chilean newspaper *La Hora* had predicted that 'excessive cooperation with the United States' would result in a reliance upon 'the benevolence of the financiers of . . . Wall Street'.[47] The prediction was confirmed, as the United States concluded numerous bilateral agreements, in the form of treaties, Lend-Lease arrangements and the dispatch of military and economic commissions that were specifically intended to boost the production and extraction of strategic raw materials. Though some support was given for public works programmes such as the construction of roads and docks and the generation of electricity, these were also mainly designed with the specific purpose of aiding the war effort. Relatively little financial assistance was forthcoming from the United States to help the development of local manufacturing industry or economic diversification away from the traditional staple industries. The Peruvian writer, Luís Alberto Sanchez, summed up the harsh economic reality caused by the war: 'In Latin America, the war has further impoverished the poor and enriched the wealthy . . . The large exporting concerns of Latin America, generally financed with United States and British capital, are making fat profits. Meanwhile, the people, enthusiastically democratic, are doing without essentials.'[48]

Internal security

Another feature of American policy that directly impinged upon Latin America was the determination of the Roosevelt Administration to suppress local Axis activity whether covert or overt. American officials feared that Nazi agents had infiltrated German ethnic communities to organize secret 'fifth columns' that awaited instructions from Germany to create civil unrest and seize political power. The most vulnerable areas were Guatemala, Argentina, Chile and southern Brazil where large German and Italian settlements were concentrated. 'I think there is no doubt', Roosevelt wrote in May 1940 to the American ambassador in Chile, 'that in the event of a continued German victory in Europe, German agents in many Latin American countries will immediately undertake activities with the view to overthrowing existing governments.'[49] The Roosevelt Administration approved a major expansion of cultural activity to counter Nazi propaganda. This task was assigned to the Office of Inter-American Affairs that was created in August 1940 and later renamed the Office of Coordinator of Inter-American Affairs (OCIAA). Nelson Rockefeller, who held the office of coordinator from 1941 until December 1944, saw his primary objective as waging 'psychological warfare in the Hemisphere'.[50] The emphasis was on extolling the virtues of democracy and the American way of life through radio broadcasting, and the distribution of press releases, motion pictures, books and newspapers. Care was taken, however, to stress a sense of mutual interest and common endeavour in keeping with the concept of the 'Good Neighbor'. Programmes were set up to promote hemispheric unity by sponsoring art exhibitions, concerts and educational and cultural exchanges that facilitated the movement of scholars and scientists. OCIAA also brought tangible economic and social benefits. Though usually located in areas containing important strategic raw materials, funds were allocated for public health projects that led to marked improvements in sanitation, water supply and local health-care facilities. For example, in the Amazon region of Brazil several hospitals were built and a major anti-malaria campaign was undertaken. Rockefeller's achievement as both an administrator and a fund-raiser for his agency was impressive. Starting in 1941 with an annual budget of $3.5 million, by 1945 OCIAA had a staff of more than 1,000 in Washington and its activities were costing $45 million.

Prior to the outbreak of war American diplomacy had privately sought to assist American business to compete with its Axis rivals in Latin America. For example, support had been given to Pan American Airways to develop routes to compete with and displace the German and Italian airlines operating in Colombia and Peru. Economic warfare took a more overt form in July 1941 when the state department issued a 'Proclaimed List of Certain Blocked Nationals' popularly known as the 'Black List'. The Black List contained the names of suspected pro-Axis companies and individuals with whom American companies and citizens were instructed not do business with. 'It is a policy designed by us to secure the commercial and financial annihilation of persons resident in and doing business in accordance with the laws of the American republics and against whom we feel that those republics will take no action', explained the state department official, Philip Bonsal.[51] Agents from the Federal Bureau of Investigation (FBI) were dispatched to Latin America to assist governments in identifying local Axis agents and sympathizers and restricting their activities. In what would provide a foretaste of future American clandestine operations, by the end of the war there were 360 FBI agents in Latin America, often conducting independent investigations rather than collaborating with local government officials. The enforcement of the Black List, especially the handing over of hundreds of German nationals for wartime internment in the United States, frequently caused considerable resentment in Latin America. The practice was criticized as unwarranted interference in domestic affairs and contrary to the policy of the 'Good Neighbor'. On the other hand, the restrictions placed upon Axis activities could produce clear benefits for local business interests. Referring to the expulsion of Japanese nationals in Peru, the American diplomat, John Emmerson, remarked:

> To the Peruvians, the war was a faraway fire. Not directly involved, although pro-Allies in sentiment, they set about to enjoy the advantages, and these included war on the Axis economic stake. The

> measures taken against Axis nationals . . . were welcomed for their destruction of unwanted competition.[52]

The Roosevelt Administration was also determined to reduce the influence of Germany and Italy over the Latin American military. A conscious effort was made to persuade Latin American governments to replace any existing military missions from the Axis powers with advisers from the United States. In 1938 American military missions were assigned to only five Latin American countries. In December 1941 American advisers were officially attached to the military of every Latin American country. During the war the United States was also allowed to establish large air and naval bases, especially in Brazil, Mexico and Ecuador, for use in the contingency of an Axis invasion. In return, the Latin American governments received substantial economic benefits. Under the wartime Lend-Lease programme Latin American countries received a total of more than $450 million in military assistance, although this sum was only 1 per cent of the total Lend-Lease aid that was distributed to all recipients. At the same time American military missions concentrated on developing programmes to help modernize military and police forces in terms of their training and equipment. Latin American governments, especially those headed by authoritarian leaders in Central America, saw such American aid as a valuable means of strengthening their own internal security forces. Another visible result was the closer association and identification between Latin American military officers and their counterparts in the United States. A large number of Latin American junior officers received training at US military academies where they often acquired considerable respect and admiration for the United States especially its military and technological skills. In the case of the Italian campaign, the collaboration between American and Brazilian officers forged a significant professional and personal relationship that would last well beyond the period of the actual war.

6

COLD WAR POLITICS (1945–74)

The inter-American system

During the Second World War the United States appeared as the champion of democracy fighting the evil of fascism. Its positive image and prestige both in Latin America and the wider world were boosted by the idealism expressed in President Roosevelt's public espousal of the 'Four Freedoms' of speech, worship, and freedom from want and fear, as well as the universal democratic principles similarly enunciated in the 1941 Atlantic Charter. This favourable image greatly facilitated hemispheric cooperation and compliance as the United States once again during wartime forged unusually close political, economic, military and cultural relations with Latin America. The region was highly significant for the United States as a source of supply of vital war materials and an aid in maintaining military security. In return for their support, the Latin American governments made considerable economic gains. They also confidently expected that the close wartime relationship and the 'Good Neighbor Policy' would continue into the postwar period. Indeed, American assistance was considered a crucial element in preventing a recurrence of the economically depressed years of the 1930s. Most of all, such aid would promote domestic economic development, which was a priority of the new liberal governments that, at the end of the war, had overthrown long-standing dictatorships and risen to political power in several of the Latin American countries. Economic development was widely regarded as the best means to combat the problems of exploding population growth and the rising expectations of the masses for a higher standard of living and social justice. Some American diplomats shared the vision of a flourishing inter-American partnership based on capitalist principles of free trade and open markets. 'The resources of the Americas are unlimited', considered Sumner Welles, and he added: 'They can be developed to the benefit of each nation, with a resulting increase in living standards, if all the Americas share in the enterprise.'[1]

Welles's ideas foreshadowed the Alliance For Progress and were ahead of his time. A very different outcome resulted because the war marked the transformation of the United States from a nation historically on the margin of an international system centred on Europe to the new status of the world's superpower. American economic and especially military power had grown rapidly and massively during the wartime years. But the other great powers had suffered relatively badly. While the United States had escaped the damaging destruction of total war, by contrast Nazi Germany and Japan were devastated and occupied. Moreover, America's principal wartime allies, Great Britain, France and the Soviet Union, had suffered huge economic losses. The new superpower status meant that the United States abandoned its traditional isolationism and policy of avoiding entangling alliances and accepted world-wide commitments notably in western Europe and the Far East. For the first time in the history of the American republic, these commitments even took the form of concluding formal military alliances and were greatly expanded as a result of the outbreak of conflict with the Soviet Union that led to a state of 'Cold War'. Consequently, in the decade after 1945 American foreign policy was truly international in its scope and range. Indeed, the pre-eminence of the United States in the Western Hemisphere was actually more secure than even before the war in that any external threat from the great European powers, either military or economic, was effectively eliminated for at least a decade. In the process, American political and public interest rapidly diminished as Latin America was relegated to the periphery of America's strategic concern. A policy of complacency mixed with indifference was adopted towards the region whose diplomatic support was generally taken for granted and not always given very much significance.

The new stress on internationalism in American foreign policy threatened to upset the existing system of regional organization based upon the regular meetings of the Pan-American (after 1948 replaced by 'Inter-American') conference system which had taken place since 1889. The conference system had proved to be a valuable means by which the Latin American countries could raise common hemispheric issues and debate them with the United States. At times of emergency, meetings of foreign ministers had also been scheduled at short notice. For example, in January 1942, shortly after the Japanese attack on Pearl Harbor, a meeting of foreign ministers was held at Rio de Janeiro. During the war, however, the wider global concerns of the United States were reflected in a marked reluctance to schedule further inter-American conferences.[2] By contrast, a series of often well-publicized meetings were held between American, British and Soviet leaders, showing that American policy and priorities had shifted from regionalism to internationalism. A major conference to discuss the creation of a future world organization to replace the League of Nations was convened at Dumbarton Oaks in Washington in 1944. Only representatives from the United States, Great Britain, the Soviet Union and China attended the conference. Latin American countries were informed of developments but not invited to the meeting. As a result they reacted with understandable suspicion when they learned of the proposal to create a Security Council consisting of the great powers. The new body would not only be separate from the General Assembly but its permanent members would also possess a right to veto all resolutions. This was perceived as a calculated means by which the great powers would use their privileged position to dominate the new organization in contrast to the inter-American system in which all the states were equal members with the same voting rights.

It was only as the war neared its close that the United States finally gave way to Latin America pressure for an inter-American conference of foreign ministers and agreed that a Special Pan-American Conference on the Problems of War and Peace would be held at Chapultepec Palace in Mexico City from 21 February to 8 March 1945. In effect, this meeting provided a timely opportunity for a discussion of post-war matters, especially the new world organization unveiled at Dumbarton Oaks and how this would affect the future working of regional associations such as the existing inter-American system. While expressing a wish for 'amplifying and making more specific the powers of the General Assembly' and also for 'giving an adequate representation to Latin America on the Security Council',[3] the Latin American delegates pleased their American colleagues by agreeing to continue their participation in the preparations for and also to attend the Conference on International Organization scheduled for San Francisco in June at which the actual Charter of the United Nations (UN) would be drawn up.

The delegates also discussed the issue of hemispheric defence and in the Act of Chapultepec agreed that, when the world war came to a formal end, a meeting would be convened to set up a permanent treaty system of military alliance based upon the principle of collective security. Agreement was also reached over the awkward question of future relations with Argentina whose pro-fascist government had not been invited to the conference. On condition that the Argentine government would officially declare war on Germany, the United States undertook to endorse Argentina's admission to the UN. Considerable divergence emerged, however, in the debates over the direction of future economic policy. American diplomats talked in vague terms of accepting broad general principles designed to promote international free trade and private enterprise from which they claimed that not only the United States but also every country in the world stood to benefit. Latin American officials, however, wanted specific programmes of aid for domestic economic development and industrialization and support for fixed international commodity prices.

The future direction of American policy was made more uncertain by Roosevelt's sudden death on 12 April 1945 and his replacement by Harry Truman who was relatively inexperienced in foreign affairs and little known in Latin America. In July 1945, after the end of the war in Europe, the leaders of the 'Big Three' powers of the United States, the Soviet Union and Great Britain met at Potsdam in Germany. The Potsdam Conference was preoccupied with settling the political boundaries of Europe and displayed an attitude of indifference towards peripheral regions of the world such as Latin America. This was especially disturbing to the nations of the region because the Second World War had virtually subordinated the Latin American economy to that of the United States. In terms of trade and investment American influence throughout the whole of the hemisphere had risen to an unprecedented degree. As the Latin American delegates at the Chapultepec Conference had pointed out, for regional economic growth and development to be sustained there was a need for the continuation of American capital investment, transfer of technology and the maintenance of the high trade levels and guaranteed prices for raw materials that had occurred during the war. After 1945, however, the United States showed little economic favour to Latin America. Indeed, American war orders and Lend-Lease aid were abruptly cancelled shortly after the end of the conflict. When Latin American governments subsequently implemented nationalistic economic policies that resulted in high tariff barriers that restricted trade, they encountered American criticism.[4] Moreover, American officials supported American businessmen in their exploitation of Latin American dependence on the US market by using their country's economic strength to bring down the prices of raw materials and primary products.

'To the Latin American countries economic development is a foremost objective of national policy', noted a state department report in 1948, which added: 'At international conferences, at United Nations meetings and whenever the opportunity arises, they have actively sought measures to promote economic development.'[5] Latin American governments drew particular attention to the Marshall Plan, the massive programme of American financial assistance designed to aid the economic recovery of Western Europe that had been launched in 1947. Despite the concession of a 'Point Four' programme of technical assistance offered later (in 1949) by Truman, they persistently complained that there was no counterpart of the Marshall Plan in Latin America and that they had been allocated an inferior status to Western Europe. 'We fought in the last war and were entirely forgotten and rejected in the division of the spoils', protested Brazilian President Getúlio Vargas in 1951.[6] Indeed, between 1945 and 1952 Belgium and Luxembourg received more direct financial aid from the United States than all the twenty nations of Latin America combined. Replying to charges that they were parsimonious and ungrateful to their wartime allies, American diplomats characteristically preached and urged the adoption of the values of self-help and private enterprise. Truman's secretary of state, George C. Marshall, explained in 1948 that the United States did not possess unlimited financial resources. Moreover, the role and power of the state were constrained in the economic sphere:

> My Government is prepared to increase the scale of assistance it has been giving to the economic development of the American republics. But it is beyond the capacity of the United States Government itself to finance more than a small portion of the vast development needed. The capital required through the years must come from private sources, both domestic and foreign.[7]

American officials considered Europe a priority for economic reconstruction on account of its perceived vulnerability to Communist expansion and because it had suffered so much more extensive damage and destruction than Latin America during the war. Moreover, the traditional American criticism of Latin Americans was reflected in the opinion that the economic difficulties of the region were linked with their alleged incompetence and inefficiency in political and economic management. The state department official George F. Kennan visited Latin America for the first time in 1950 and concluded pessimistically that: 'the shadow of a tremendous helplessness and impotence falls today over most of the Latin American world'. He simplistically singled out for blame the influence of Spanish fanaticism: 'The handicaps to progress are written in blood and in the tracings of geography; and in neither case are they readily susceptible of obliteration.'[8] In a similar vein Truman's secretary of state, Dean Acheson, attributed Latin American economic backwardness to 'Hispano-Indian culture – or lack of it [that] had been piling up its problems for centuries'.[9]

While carefully avoiding discussion of economic matters, American officials displayed much keener interest in grasping opportunities to assert their country's exclusive political and military leadership of the hemisphere. Following on from the Chapultepec Conference they agreed to strengthen inter-American relations by establishing a permanent military alliance. Indeed, disappointment over the role of the UN and growing conflict with the Soviet Union meant that the idea of a regional military alliance had found more favour among American officials. In 1947 at the Pan-American Conference held in Rio de Janeiro, the Inter-American Treaty for Reciprocal Assistance set up a regional system of collective security known as the Rio Treaty or Rio Pact. Article 3 of the treaty foreshadowed and served as a model for the 1949 North Atlantic Treaty Organization (NATO) by providing 'that an armed attack by any State against an American State shall be considered as an attack against all the American States'.[10] It was understood, however, that the response to an attack might not necessarily involve the use of armed force. Nor was a response necessarily automatic but would depend on a decision reached by a meeting of foreign ministers – and a two-thirds majority vote in favour. In effect, this was an important safeguard for the Latin American countries, because it put in place a procedure that would serve to constrain the United States from armed intervention on account of the requirement to consult with and secure the consent of a majority of the Latin American members. Nevertheless, the military role of the United States was acknowledged as crucial. Although the treaty was a pact rather than an alliance, it represented a commitment given by the United States to take primary responsibility for military action to protect the hemisphere. It thereby demonstrated that the Latin American countries recognized the fundamental importance of military collaboration with the United States for their own national security. 'The vital spirit of Pan American solidarity is implicit in the provisions of the treaty and there is every reason to believe that the treaty affords an adequate guarantee of the peace and security of this Hemisphere', summed up Truman's acting secretary of state, Robert Lovett.[11]

American political leadership was also enhanced during the following year at the Ninth Pan-American Conference in Bogotá, when the United States replaced the long-standing but informal Pan-American system based upon Special Conferences and the Pan-American Union with a new political institution still located in Washington but now consisting of a permanent headquarters and staff. This was to be known as the Organization of American States (OAS) and was created in accordance with articles 52–4 of the UN Charter that allowed member states to enter into separate regional organizations to deal with their local security problems. The Charter of the OAS affirmed the equality of its member nations. It also included a guarantee of the principle of non-intervention. 'No State or group of States', declared Article 15, 'has the right to intervene, directly or indirectly, for any reason whatever, in the internal or external affairs of any other State.'[12] The OAS gave the Latin American governments what they had long desired in the form of a permanent forum and machinery to debate and directly influence hemispheric issues. But the United States also stood to gain from the new institution. The OAS was valuable for American diplomacy because it provided a convenient tool that could be used to prevent external political influence and interference in the Western Hemisphere. Moreover, the compliance with the UN Charter meant that international re-affirmation of the Monroe Doctrine had also essentially been secured. 'We have preserved the Monroe Doctrine and the Inter-American system', remarked the chairman of the Senate Foreign Relations Committee, Senator Arthur Vandenberg of Michigan, and more to the point he added: 'We have retained a complete veto – exclusive in our own hands – over any decisions involving external activities.'[13]

Responding to crisis events in the Balkans, in March 1947 President Truman had proclaimed the Truman Doctrine in which he pledged support for 'free peoples who are resisting attempted subjugation by armed minorities or by outside pressures'.[14] In effect, the United States adopted the policy of 'containing' the perceived expansive tendencies of international Communism. Although the Western Hemisphere was judged to be quite different to the Balkans, the Middle East or the Philippines in not facing an immediate external Communist threat, American officials confidently assumed and anticipated that the countries of Latin America would play a supportive role in the emerging Cold War. In the process, the Rio Pact and the OAS became part of the evolving policy of the global containment of international Communism. For example, Latin American countries were expected to support the United States at the UN. They were also encouraged to break off diplomatic relations with the Soviet Union. Five countries did so between 1947 and 1952. Only Mexico, Argentina and Uruguay had relations with the Soviets in 1952. Moreover, national Communist parties suffered severe restrictions on their activities and were made illegal in several countries.

The Korean War, however, exposed a divergence of opinion over how to respond to the external Communist threat. Most Latin American governments initially joined the United States in approving the UN action condemning the North Korean invasion of South Korea in June 1950. But attitudes became more ambivalent when the war was widened after the military intervention of the People's Republic of China in November. Seeking hemispheric support for the war effort, the Truman Administration invited Latin American foreign ministers to a conference at Washington in March 1951. They were welcomed by the president, who noted that their purpose was 'to work out ways and means by which our united strength may be employed in the struggle for freedom throughout the world'.[15] Under the US Mutual Security Act of 1951, designed to promote the common defence of the hemisphere, twelve Latin American governments signed treaties with the United States for the provision of weapons and training. With the exception of a small token force from Colombia, however, they were unwilling to participate directly in the Korean War. The Brazilian government pointedly blamed American economic policy for the negative response. 'If [Washington] had elaborated a recovery plan for Latin America similar to the Marshall Plan for Europe', explained Brazilian Foreign Minister João Neves da Fontoura, 'Brazil's present situation would be different and our cooperation in the present emergency could probably be greater.'[16] Economic factors were influential, but the geopolitical reality was that, in contrast to the United States, Cold War battles in Europe or the Far East were not a pressing strategic concern of Latin American governments.

Resisting Communism in Guatemala

During an era in which anxiety over the 'red scare', the 'loss of China' to Communism and the Korean War resulted in public anti-Communist hysteria in the United States in the form of McCarthyism, it was not surprising that American officials were disturbed by any sign of alleged

Communist activity in Latin America. The talk of major land reform, greater power for labour unions and expropriation of foreign companies was not a new phenomenon and notably had been associated with the Mexican Revolution earlier in the twentieth century. It was, however, now simplistically and at times conveniently attributed not to internal nationalist political forces but to the pernicious influence of an international Communist conspiracy led and orchestrated by the Soviet Union. While American officials dismissed the prospect of Soviet military aggression in the Western Hemisphere as unrealistic, the much more sinister employment of covert political infiltration and subversion by local Communists and their sympathizers was believed to be spreading. In effect, the fascist danger of the 1930s and early 1940s was now replaced by the Communist threat.

In his report on his 1950 visit to Latin America, George Kennan warned: 'as things stand today, the activities of the communists represent our most serious problem in the area. They have progressed to a point where they must be regarded as an urgent, major problem.'[17] Nevertheless, he believed that presently only in Guatemala was there a real prospect of Communist political advance. Kennan took comfort in the historical fact that the negative view of Communism as an alien and anti-Christian ideology was so strong and ingrained in Latin American society that American diplomacy was able to persuade not only conservative but even some radical nationalist governments to put restrictions on the activities of their Communist parties and left-wing labour unions. This occurred, for example, in Costa Rica in 1953 where Communist activities were severely curtailed by President José Figueres Ferrer. 'Communism has no political appeal to individualistic, liberty-loving Latin Americans', the Costa Rican president had declared before assuming office.[18] 'The new government is anti-Communist and animated by a devotion to democratic procedure', noted an American journalist who approvingly added: 'It is a model other Latin American reformers could well follow.'[19]

A similar course of events took place in Bolivia where a self-styled 'revolutionary' party, known as the National Revolutionary Movement (*Movimento Nacional Revolucionario* or MNR), seized power in a violent uprising in 1952, but proceeded to modify its radical policies of economic nationalism and major land reform. The Bolivian Revolution, however, did not cause the same difficulties as the earlier Mexican Revolution because the MNR agreed to compensate the foreign-owned tin companies that suffered expropriation. In return, the United States consented to continue programmes of financial aid and to maintain substantial purchases of Bolivian tin, to the extent of having to stockpile large quantities. 'The economic respite US aid gave to Bolivia', concluded a state department assessment, 'encouraged the government to moderate its policies, particularly with regard to economic nationalism.'[20] During the decade of the 1950s Bolivia received more American financial aid than any other Latin American country.

The sum amounted to a third of the country's annual budget and was regarded in Washington as a most successful political and economic investment. Eisenhower's assistant secretary of state, Henry Holland, remarked in 1955 that American financial assistance had 'been of great assistance in maintaining economic and political stability . . . and aiding the Bolivian Government to counteract Communist pressures'.[21]

In general, however, officials in the Eisenhower Administration (1953–61) conveyed characteristic American attitudes of superiority in dismissing many Latin American political leaders as 'immature and impractical idealists', who 'not only are inadequately trained to conduct government business efficiently but also lack the disposition to combat extremists within their ranks, including communists'.[22] According to Eisenhower's secretary of state, John Foster Dulles, Latin Americans were 'people who have practically no capacity for self-government and indeed are like children'.[23] The sense of frustration felt by American officials was most evident in their policy towards Guatemala. In 1944 a left-wing political coalition had overthrown the dictatorship of Jorge Ubico Castañeda in that country and, inspired by the visionary and socialist ideas of President Juan José Arévalo, had inaugurated a period of radical economic and social reform known as the Guatemalan Revolution. In November 1950 President Jacobo Arbenz Guzmán won the presidential election and in 1952 proceeded to go further than his predecessor in implementing schemes of major agrarian reform based on the expropriation of uncultivated land for redistribution to peasant families. The expropriation included land owned by the Boston-based United Fruit Company (UFCO), a major exporter of bananas. While the Guatemalan government offered UFCO $1 million in compensation, the American company claimed that the value of the land in question was at least $16 million. Except among the landed elite, there was little sympathy for UFCO in Guatemala where the company had established itself in 1899 and was believed to own 550,000 acres of land of which it was estimated that no more than 15 per cent was currently under cultivation. UFCO was popularly and unflatteringly known as 'the Octopus' (*el pulpo*) and regarded as the supreme symbol of American imperialism.[24]

The dispute had ramifications far beyond Guatemala because American officials regarded the agrarian reform measure as having been instigated by local Communists who were reported to have infiltrated into influential positions in the government and labour unions. 'American interests in Guatemala are being hard pressed by extremist labor demands, sparked by Communist leaders and by the open partisanship of the Government', noted a state department report in 1951, which added: 'The United Fruit Company is continually being subjected to harassing work stoppages and extreme demands and threats backed by Government pressure.'[25] Moreover, UFCO had direct influence among government officials in Washington because several senior members of the Eisenhower Administration, notably

Secretary of State John Foster Dulles and his brother, CIA Director Allen Dulles, had previously worked for an international law firm, Sullivan and Cromwell, that still retained contracts with the company. A skilful lobbying exercise was mounted by UFCO in the United States, which not only outlined the view that the company was suffering excessively harsh and unfair treatment in Guatemala but also more importantly contributed to the Cold War mindset of the Eisenhower Administration and also of American politicians, who became convinced that Arbenz was being unduly influenced if not manipulated by Communists. In the US Senate, Allan Ellender of Louisiana denounced the activities of 'fanatical and determined' Communists who have 'cunningly devised to identify themselves as the champions of the social justice and nationalist aspects of the Guatemalan Revolution'.[26] The particular concerns and economic interests of UFCO, however, became a secondary consideration as a growing anxiety emerged in Washington over the prospect that a Soviet satellite state was about to be created in Central America. Such a development would pose a serious strategic threat to American security because of its geographical proximity to Mexico and the Panama Canal and would also register a major setback for the United States in the Cold War with the Soviet Union.

The Eisenhower Administration responded to the perceived Communist danger by placing increasing diplomatic and economic pressure on President Arbenz to remove alleged Communists from their positions in the government and labour unions. To convey Eisenhower's views, the abrasive and strongly anti-Communist John Peurifoy was appointed as the new American ambassador to Guatemala. After a lengthy private meeting with Arbenz in December 1953, Peurifoy informed the state department that their suspicions of the president's ideological leanings and alarm over Communist subversion of the government were entirely justified: 'I came away definitely convinced that if President [Arbenz] is not a Communist, he will certainly do until one comes along, and that normal approaches will not work in Guatemala.'[27] In March 1954 John Foster Dulles went to the Tenth Inter-American Conference at Caracas determined to gain Latin American support for a resolution condemning foreign intervention in the form of international Communism. It was evident, however, that what Dulles wanted was not discussion but an explicit Latin American endorsement of American armed intervention to punish Arbenz. The Guatemalan foreign minister, Guillermo Toriello Garrido, defiantly argued that the US government:

> wanted to find a ready expedient to maintain the economic dependence of the American Republics and suppress the legitimate desires of their people, cataloguing as 'Communist' every manifestation of nationalism or economic independence, and desire for social progress, and intellectual curiosity, and any interest in progressive or liberal reforms.[28]

A 'Declaration of Solidarity' critical of the 'aggressive character' of International Communism was passed at Caracas.[29] Contrary to Dulles's wishes, however, it made no specific mention of Guatemala. Moreover, while Guatemala was the only delegation to vote against the resolution, it was not isolated in its opposition because Mexico and Argentina were also notable abstainers in the vote.

The failure to secure Latin American approval or support was disappointing, but did not deter the Eisenhower Administration. Even before the meeting in Caracas, the Central Intelligence Agency (CIA) had been assigned the task of preparing a covert military operation, codenamed 'Operation PBSUCCESS', to bring down the government of President Arbenz. A small army of Guatemalan political exiles was duly recruited, equipped and organized in Honduras and Nicaragua. Meanwhile, Arbenz refused to be deflected from implementing his agrarian reforms. He also sought to strengthen his own military forces, but was denied weapons from the United States. When the Guatemalan president looked to alternative suppliers and succeeded in purchasing weapons and ammunition from Czechoslovakian sources in 1954, John Foster Dulles ominously warned at a press conference that 'a government in which Communist influence is very strong has come into a position to dominate militarily the Central American area'.[30] The implication was that a clear danger to American and hemispheric national security now existed. 'The threat of Communist imperialism is no longer academic, it has arrived', declared the *Washington Post* in an editorial entitled 'Communist Beachhead'.[31]

The decision was duly taken in Washington to implement the covert plan to overthrow Arbenz. Consequently, in June the CIA directed its small army of around 150 Guatemalan exiles commanded by Colonel Carlos Castillo Armas to prepare to invade Guatemala from Honduras. While the rebels would be given air support by bombers supplied by the CIA and flown by privately contracted American pilots, no American troops were to be involved in the fighting on the ground. Meanwhile, CIA agents would take control of Guatemalan radio communications and broadcast anti-Arbenz propaganda. The actual invasion began on 18 June. Ten days later Arbenz resigned. The CIA had been very effective in transmitting radio broadcasts to the Guatemalan people that portrayed the advancing rebel army as a large invasion force. For Arbenz, however, the crucial factor was his inability to count on the loyalty of the Guatemalan army. 'If you don't resign,' a trusted aide informed him, 'the Army will march on the capital to depose you.'[32] Without any major battle being fought, Arbenz decided to resign and was replaced by Castillo Armas, who was strongly anti-Communist and, most of all, the choice of the United States. The significant role of the CIA in the coup was widely suspected but was not revealed at the time. Instead, John Foster Dulles denied American involvement and publicly declared that the coup was internally motivated. He also disingenuously claimed that the Guatemalan people had determined events and that the country's future would now be directed by 'loyal' leaders 'who have not treasonably become the agents of an alien despotism which sought to use Guatemala for its own evil ends'.[33] The same message was faithfully conveyed in an editorial in the *New York Times* that was entitled 'Red Defeat in Guatemala' and triumphantly described the course of events as 'the first successful anti-Communist revolt since the last war'.[34]

The new government of Castillo Armas brought an end to the 1944 Guatemala Revolution by carrying out the policies that the Eisenhower Administration had wanted Arbenz to follow. It arrested suspected Communists, renegotiated UFCO's financial contracts, reversed the policies of agrarian reform, and restricted the activities of labour unions. After a visit to Guatemala in 1955, Vice-President Richard Nixon reported to a meeting of the national security council that Castillo Armas was 'a good man with good intentions'. Nixon confidently believed that: 'We [the United States] had good possibilities of succeeding in Guatemala and of holding up to the world the picture of our success.'[35] Castillo Armas, however, was soon overthrown by assassination in 1957 and Guatemala subsequently became a byword for civil unrest and a series of brutal military governments, a development for which American policy could not escape some of the moral responsibility. The 1954 coup would also have an important influence on future behaviour at a critical time. Ernesto 'Che' Guevara, who would later become Fidel Castro's most famous fellow guerrilla fighter, was living in Guatemala in 1954 and regarded the example of Arbenz's lack of control over the army and his subsequent abject surrender as an example of how not to respond to an armed incursion.

'By the middle of 1954 Latin America was free, for the time being at least, of any fixed outposts of Communism', proudly remarked President Eisenhower.[36] Latin American governments, however, were generally dismayed by America's use of armed force in the guise of a covert operation to overthrow a legally elected government and suppress radical reforms. In effect, the Guatemalan episode marked a reversion to the policy of unilateral interventionism and thereby the definitive end of the 'Good Neighbor Policy' launched by Herbert Hoover and Franklin Roosevelt. What the Guatemalan coup and its aftermath also demonstrated was that, in its desire for political stability, public order and resistance to Communism, the United States was prepared to destabilize elected governments. Furthermore, it continued to cooperate with and, indeed, to give material support to the most reactionary dictators in Latin America. While outwardly in favour of democratic governments, the United States often found it easier and preferable to work with right-wing authoritarian regimes and those political and especially military leaders who shared America's anti-Communist ethos. Prominent examples of leaders who were given American approval and backing were Fulgencio Batista in Cuba, the Somoza family in Nicaragua, Marcos Pérez Jiménez in Venezuela, Manuel Odría in Peru, and Alfredo Stroessner in Paraguay. 'It is better to have a strong regime in power than a liberal government if it is indulgent and relaxed and penetrated by Communists', summed up George Kennan after his visit to Latin America in 1950.[37] As events in Guatemala demonstrated, this attitude meant that the United States could become a major obstacle to the achievement of social and economic progress. Moreover, not only did American officials appear to give open support to brutal dictatorships but they also were accused of actively colluding with their huge business corporations such as UFCO to exploit and plunder the rich resources of the hemisphere.

Alliance For Progress

The fall of Arbenz briefly provoked a few minor demonstrations organized mainly by students and labour unions in Latin America. Latent anti-American sentiment, however, emerged at its most virulent during Vice-President Richard Nixon's 'goodwill' tour of Latin America in May 1958. Nixon's visit started peacefully in Buenos Aires with his attendance at the inauguration of the Argentine president, Arturo Frondizi. In Lima, however, he was confronted by student riots. In Caracas his life was endangered when a howling mob attacked his motorcade. 'There is considerable evidence that the demonstrations in the various countries visited by the Vice President followed a pattern and were Communist inspired and staged', reported Deputy Under Secretary of State Robert D. Murphy.[38] Despite the attribution that the actions against Nixon were the work of Communists, the Eisenhower Administration was more taken aback by the depth of anti-American hostility that had been so openly displayed. Indeed, Nixon had completed what had been regarded as a successful goodwill visit to Latin America as recently as 1955. CIA Director Allen Dulles considered the reception accorded to the Vice-President in 1958 to be a 'shock' that 'brought South American problems to our attention as nothing else could have done'.[39] In the opinion of the influential columnist, Walter Lippmann, the mission represented a 'diplomatic Pearl Harbor'.[40] A reassessment of Latin American policy took place, in which Eisenhower decided to try and remedy the previous attitude of neglect by making a personal visit to several countries in February–March 1960 'to provide a dramatic stimulus to establish closer United States relations'.[41] At the same time the provision of financial aid for the region was considerably increased. In what was a marked departure from traditional self-help policies, emphasis was placed not only on assisting economic development but also on fighting poverty by allocating funds mainly in the form of loans to promote social reform and improve standards of living. In April 1959 a new federal agency, the Inter-American Development Bank (IADB) was created for this purpose and provided with initial resources of $1 billion.[42]

The political importance of implementing policies of financial aid was boosted by the rise to power of Fidel Castro Ruz in Cuba in 1959 and the serious challenge that the radicalism of the Cuban Revolution subsequently presented to American democracy and the capitalist system. This coincided with the election in 1960 of a new Democratic president, John F. Kennedy, who promised a 'New Frontier' for the American people. A task force set up to advise the president-elect on policy for the region reported to him 'that the greatest single task of American diplomacy in Latin America is to divorce the inevitable and necessary Latin American social transformation from connection with and prevent its capture by overseas Communist power politics'.[43] The new president was especially concerned about the extent of economic backwardness in Latin America and confided to an aide, Richard Goodwin, his anxiety that 'the whole place could blow up on us'.[44] While Kennedy undertook to continue Eisenhower's policy of financial aid for Latin America, he also sought to expand and make it his own personal programme in the form of the Alliance For Progress (La Alianza para el Progreso). Moreover, Kennedy had a genuine personal interest in Latin America and wanted to stage a news event that would draw the attention of the American public to the importance of the region. Consequently, he chose to announce his policy of a 'Ten-Year Plan for the Americas' before an invited audience of distinguished Latin American diplomats in the White House. In a well-received speech on 13 March 1961 he described the scheme as 'a vast cooperative effort, unparalleled in magnitude and nobility of purpose, to satisfy the basic needs of the American people for homes, work and land, health and schools'.[45]

As with so many presidential initiatives involving Latin America, the programme was proclaimed unilaterally and its contents very much reflected traditional American values and sense of democratic mission. But it was not to be imposed. In a style reminiscent of Franklin Roosevelt and the 'Good Neighbor Policy', the new president stressed that this was to be a joint, cooperative effort and that the United States undertook to listen to the ideas and requests for aid from Latin America itself. A conference of hemispheric leaders, including Che Guevara representing Cuba, subsequently met at Punta del Este, Uruguay, in August 1961 in order to discuss the plan in more detail. In the resulting Charter of Punta del Este the United States agreed to a commitment to provide the nations of Latin America, though excluding Cuba, the substantial sum of $20 billion in aid over a period of ten years. The stated aim was 'to accelerate the economic and social development of the participating countries of Latin America, so that they may achieve maximum levels of well-being, with equal opportunities for all, in democratic societies adapted to their own needs and desires'.[46] The scheme essentially represented a belated Marshall Plan and was similarly politically motivated in seeking to contain the advance of Communism in a strategically important region of the world that was visibly suffering from extreme poverty and destitution. Moreover, by firmly linking the United States with movements for democratic reform and social justice, the Kennedy Administration was confident that it would successfully counter the challenge of the Cuban Revolution and prevent the occurrence of 'another Cuba' in the hemisphere. 'Just as the Marshall Plan was the United States answer to Josef Stalin', asserted the *New York Times*, 'so the Kennedy Plan is the United States answer to Fidel Castro.'[47]

Despite the large and unprecedented financial commitment made by the United States, the economic goals of the Alliance as stated by President Kennedy proved to be far too optimistic and over ambitious. Only one year after the meeting at Punta del Este an American journalist remarked that 'few great projects in recent memory have been so hopefully launched and so quickly scorned as the Alliance For Progress'.[48] The ensuing decade demonstrated that Latin America could not be easily remade in the American image according to a set plan and a fixed schedule. Too much was expected in too short a space of time and, in marked contrast to the success of the Marshall Plan in Western Europe, the actual performance proved to be acutely disappointing. The American ambassador to Brazil, Lincoln Gordon, who was also a distinguished economist, identified one of the main differences between the European and Latin American experiences when he explained that 'development is a far more difficult undertaking than economic recovery'.[49]

Ironically, while American officials were concerned at the prospect of radical nationalist political leaders and movements emerging in Latin America in imitation of the Cuban Revolution, a major reason for the lack of success of the Alliance was the existence of considerable internal resistance within Latin America from elite and conservative elements whose self-interests and privileges were adversely affected by radical programmes of land redistribution, the extension of democratic reforms and the prospect of having to pay higher personal income taxes to fund programmes of social welfare. The Kennedy Administration wanted and, as it turned out, mistakenly expected a definite political swing in the direction of democratic government. In fact, the decade of the 1960s experienced right-wing military coups in several Latin American countries including Argentina and Brazil. Moreover, there was also criticism from Latin Americans that the programme possessed inherent flaws for which they were not to blame. They pointed out that too many strings were attached to American aid and that the scheme was not as generous as it seemed at first sight. Instead of being seen as a major effort at social, economic and political change, the Alliance For Progress appeared more like a conventional foreign aid programme which was criticized for seeking to put American business interests first. As early as 1962 the US diplomat Arturo Morales-Carrion had reported that to Latin Americans the Alliance 'still looks "foreign" and "imported", it still looks as a "Made in USA" product'.[50] The statistics made disappointing reading. At the end of the decade it was widely acknowledged that, in terms of economic development since 1961, Latin America had arguably fallen further behind the United States and the developed world. One of the most publicized targets of the Alliance was to achieve an annual economic growth rate of not less than 2.5 per cent. During the decade of the 1960s, however, the annual rate of growth in Latin America remained stuck at 1.5 per cent and was outstripped by the population explosion that averaged an annual increase of around 3 per cent. At the same time unemployment actually grew from 18 million to 25 million.

Although the architects of the Alliance For Progress within the Kennedy Administration sincerely wished to improve inter-American relations, it was evident that American strategic priorities not only remained with Europe but also became increasingly preoccupied with South-east Asia and the escalating war in Vietnam. This was further underscored after Kennedy's assassination on 22 November 1963 and the elevation of Lyndon Johnson to the presidency. In contrast to his predecessor, Johnson was not one of the original architects of the Alliance. Moreover, he also showed a much more limited personal interest than Kennedy in Latin American affairs. Under the 'Mann Doctrine', named after Assistant Secretary of State Tom Mann, the Johnson Administration (1963–9) declared that its Latin American policy would first and foremost stress an anti-Communist approach. This meant that it intended to be pragmatic in its dealings with governments in the region and would no longer put pressure on authoritarian regimes to implement democratic reforms.

At the same time as Administration officials gave progressively less attention to the Alliance, the US Congress adopted a more sceptical view of funding programmes of foreign aid. Latin American issues diminished in political significance as congressmen became preoccupied with the growing inflationary pressures upon the American economy, domestic racial tensions especially in American cities and the damaging political impact of the Vietnam War. Consequently, in 1967 Congress refused Johnson's request for additional funds for the Alliance. When he launched the programme in 1961, Kennedy had thought in terms of a decade of successful implementation and achievement. By the close of the 1960s, however, it was evident, in the words of President Eduardo Frei Montalva of Chile, that the Alliance For Progress had 'lost its way'.[51] President Kennedy's younger brother, Senator Edward M. Kennedy, summed up in 1970 that the programme 'has been a major economic disappointment . . . a social failure . . . a political failure'.[52]

The Cuban Revolution

The Alliance For Progress was the economic aspect of an American strategy that was designed to counter the perceived threat of Communism in the

Western Hemisphere and especially the new revolutionary regime established in Cuba in 1959 under the leadership of the charismatic Fidel Castro. As it had so often been in the past, Cuba, once again, became a major issue not only in American foreign policy but also in American political debate. This was exemplified in the 1960 presidential election contest between the Republican candidate, Richard Nixon, and the Democratic candidate, John F. Kennedy. Both candidates competed with each other in alerting the American public to the danger posed by the new government in Cuba. 'In 1952 the Republicans ran on a program of rolling back the Iron Curtain in Eastern Europe', declared Kennedy, and he added: 'Today the Iron Curtain is 90 miles off the coast of the United States.' Nixon replied by condemning Kennedy's 'defeatist talk' and insisted that 'Cuba is not lost'.[53]

The debate between Nixon and Kennedy showed that the American public was uncertain in its attitude towards Fidel Castro. On the one hand, there was the image presented in the media of a brave Cuban patriot fighting against and ultimately overthrowing the reactionary and corrupt regime of Fulgencio Batista. This view owed much to the admiring articles published in 1957 by the *New York Times* reporter Herbert L. Matthews, which had been a journalistic scoop in revealing that 'Fidel Castro, the rebel leader of Cuba's youth, is alive and fighting hard and successfully in the rugged, almost impenetrable fastnesses of the Sierra Maestra'.[54] When Castro talked about replacing a dictator with an honest government, he sounded like a middle-class liberal. But he was also an admirer of José Martí who pledged to bring about major land reform and substantial improvement in the working conditions and standard of living for Cuba's peasants and workers. The puzzle for American diplomats and politicians was to decide whether he was a Communist or a radical nationalist. The answer to this question would determine the extent to which Cuba could avoid becoming involved in Cold War politics. On his brief visit to the United States in April 1959 Castro met Vice-President Nixon. After the meeting Nixon reported rather patronizingly that Castro 'has those indefinable qualities which make him a leader of men', but that he was 'either incredibly naive about communism or under communist discipline – my guess is the former.'[55] A state department analysis in June agreed that Castro's 'temperament and inexperience ill fit him to administer the government'. While the report believed that 'the Communists probably do not now control Castro', it warned that the Cuban Communist Party had shown 'great skill . . . in identifying itself with the Castro revolution' and was steadily increasing its influence within the regime.[56]

Castro was proud of the fact that, in contrast to events in 1898, his guerrilla movement had overthrown an oppressive regime without the military intervention of the United States. Indeed, officials in the Eisenhower Administration were certainly irritated by Castro's frequent condemnation of American imperialism and his proclaimed determination to break with the past and bring an end to Cuba's humiliating political and economic dependence on the United States. 'We no longer live in times', Castro told the American ambassador in Havana, 'when one had to worry when the American Ambassador visited the [Cuban] Prime Minister.'[57] This defiantly independent attitude was unsympathetically interpreted in Washington as a broad and calculated challenge to American pre-eminence in the hemisphere. Instead of adopting an accommodating attitude like the leaders of the Bolivian Revolution, Castro chose to copy the example of the earlier Mexican Revolution and present an alternative model of economic development to American free-enterprise capitalism. Relations grew increasingly unfriendly when he expropriated American banks and utility companies and signed a trade agreement with the Soviet Union. In turn the Eisenhower Administration imposed punitive economic sanctions, including the suspension of imports of Cuban sugar. Castro proceeded to negotiate the sale of 4 million tons of sugar to the Soviet Union and the People's Republic of China.

Evidently, neither side was willing to compromise or accommodate the other. In fact, the increasing hostility of the United States was useful in helping Castro to demonstrate his nationalist credentials and to win popular support in Cuba for his revolutionary reforms. Eisenhower eventually broke off diplomatic relations in January 1961. He considered Castro a pro-Communist and 'a madman' and earlier, in March 1960, had authorized the CIA to prepare a covert operation to overthrow him.[58] The president envisaged an operation along the same lines as that successfully undertaken in Guatemala in 1954. In similar fashion an army of political exiles would be recruited, trained at a secret Central American location and then provided with logistic support in an invasion to overthrow the government. In the case of Cuba the basic CIA plan was to make an amphibious landing to establish a secure beachhead that would provide a rallying point for a general uprising against Castro. At an appropriate time a provisional government of Cuban exiles would be flown in from Florida and accorded official diplomatic recognition by the United States.

During the summer of 1960 a few hundred anti-Castro Cuban exiles were recruited by the CIA and taken first to the Panama Canal Zone and then to Guatemala and later Nicaragua for training. The actual military effort 'to give Castro the Guatemala treatment' was code named 'Operation Zapata' and was not ready for execution until after Eisenhower had given up his presidential office to Kennedy in January 1961. Following the hard-line views that he had expressed in his presidential debates with Nixon and conscious of current Communist pressure in Berlin and South-east Asia, the new president saw Cuba as a crucial battleground in the Cold War against the Soviet Union. While endorsing Eisenhower's decision to overthrow Castro, Kennedy was well aware that the proposed covert operation was inherently risky and that its success was by no means guaranteed. He was worried, therefore, that this would lead the CIA to develop the type of large amphibious and airborne assault that had been launched in Europe during the Second World War. As a result the landing site was moved from the city of Trinidad to the much more remote Zapata region on the southern coast of Cuba. At the same time as giving his approval to the operation, Kennedy ordered reductions in size and scale so that it would appear as an infiltration of guerrillas in support of an internal insurgency. He also insisted that American military personnel must not directly take part in any actual combat activity. This would enable his administration to maintain plausible deniability of any participation in the operation.

Once the training was completed in Guatemala and Nicaragua, the operation involved transporting and landing a force (Brigade 2506) of over 1,400 men on 17 April 1961 at the location known as the Bay of Pigs (Bahía de Cochinos or Playa Girón). More than six years earlier in Guatemala, news of invasion had virtually paralysed Arbenz and persuaded him to resign and seek exile. But Castro and Che Guevara had learned the lesson of 1954. In contrast to Arbenz, Castro maintained effective personal control over the army and acted decisively by dispatching all available troops, tanks and airplanes to the invasion area. He also ordered the immediate arrest of suspected opponents of his regime throughout the island. In calling for forceful resistance against the invaders Castro appealed not to Communist ideology but directly to Cuban nationalism and long-standing anti-American feeling. He urged: 'Forward Cubans! Answer with steel and with fire the barbarians who despise us and want to make us return to slavery.'[59] Consequently, instead of gaining a secure beachhead and provoking armed uprisings in the rest of the island as planned, the small invading army was quickly isolated and overwhelmed within two days by forces loyal to Castro. Twelve hundred men surrendered and became prisoners.[60]

Despondency reigned at the White House in Washington. 'It was a long and grim day – the longest and grimmest the New Frontier had known', recalled the presidential adviser, Arthur Schlesinger.[61] If threatened with complete disaster, the anti-Castro brigade had expected to be saved by timely and decisive American military intervention. But Kennedy refused to order air-strikes from the aircraft carrier *Essex*, which was standing by for just such a contingency. Over-ambitious and poorly planned, Operation Zapata ended in disastrous failure. Though the CIA was widely blamed for its faulty planning and ill-conceived advice, Kennedy immediately accepted full responsibility for the disaster. With the benefit of hindsight, he asked one of his aides: 'All my life I've known better than to depend on the experts. How could I have been so stupid, to let them go ahead?'[62]

In the immediate aftermath of the disaster, the US ambassador to the UN, Adlai Stevenson, reported by telegram that the 'atmosphere in UN, among both our friends and neutrals is highly unsatisfactory and extremely dangerous to US position throughout world'.[63] While Kennedy was humiliated by the setback, Castro jubilantly claimed a great victory for the Cuban Revolution over American imperialism. As a result the Cuban leader's personal prestige was enormously enhanced not only in Cuba but also in Latin America and throughout the world. The failure of Operation Zapata also strengthened the growing bond between Cuba and the Soviet Union. The Soviet leader, Nikita Khrushchev, pledged his support for Castro and declared that the Soviet Union 'will not abandon the Cuban people'.[64] Castro replied by affirming for the first time in public his personal adherence to the ideology of Marxism-Leninism and aligning Cuba with the Communist nations. While the rest of Latin America generally applauded Castro's defiant stand against American bullying and violation of international law, they watched with dismay as the politics of the Cold War were fastened upon the Western Hemisphere. Cuba became a satellite of the Soviet Union and a base for 'exporting revolution' in the form of organizing and launching guerrilla operations designed to overthrow governments on the mainland of Central and South America. 'We have demonstrated', Che Guevara jubilantly declared, 'that a small group of men who are determined, supported by the people, and not afraid of death . . . can overcome a regular army.'[65]

The Kennedy Administration responded by seeking to isolate Castro both politically and economically. The policy was not just confined to the Western Hemisphere but was intended to have world-wide application. After some initial reluctance, the Latin American nations narrowly voted to approve American proposals to expel Cuba from the OAS in January 1962. But agreement to impose mandatory collective economic sanctions was not forthcoming. The argument that carried most weight in favour of political isolation was the fact that Cuba had openly adopted Marxism-Leninism as its state ideology and joined the Soviet bloc in the Cold War, developments that were regarded as 'incompatible with the principles and standards that govern the regional system'.[66] 'The Castro regime has extended the global battle to Latin America', Kennedy's secretary of state, Dean Rusk, informed the OAS and he warned: 'It has supplied Communism with a bridgehead in the Americas.'[67]

Even those Latin American countries that sympathized with Cuba were alarmed by Castro's desire to obtain substantial military assistance from the Soviet Union. Castro argued that a military build-up was necessary to defend Cuba against the threat of an imminent American invasion. It was, however, Khrushchev's secret attempt to construct offensive missile sites on the island in 1962 that brought the very real prospect of a nuclear war occurring in the hemisphere. In the ensuing 'Missile Crisis' of October 1962, Kennedy publicly stated that the whole hemisphere was in danger because the purpose of the missile sites 'can be none other than to provide a nuclear strike capability against the Western Hemisphere'.[68] Nevertheless, he treated the issue purely as a confrontation between the United States and the Soviet Union and, consequently, preferred to deal directly with Khrushchev. It was only after he had made the decision to place a US naval quarantine around Cuba that Kennedy invoked the 1947 Rio Treaty and sought the endorsement of the OAS to approve the use of armed force. An affirmative vote was forthcoming from the Latin American countries, but there was not unqualified support for Kennedy's technically illegal action. Bolivia, Brazil and Mexico notably abstained in one of the votes in order to show their opposition. In fact, a majority vote in the OAS for punitive economic sanctions against Cuba was delayed until 1964. This occurred not as a result of American prompting but after the revelation in November 1963 from the Venezuelan government that its army had discovered a secret cache of Cuban weapons. Venezuela formally complained to the OAS that the discovery demonstrated that Castro was planning to use violence to disrupt the forthcoming Venezuelan elections. A majority of the Latin American nations, with the notable exception of Mexico, subsequently backed an OAS resolution sponsored by Venezuela to isolate Cuba both politically and economically.

As part of the 1962 Cuban Missile Crisis accord with Khrushchev, Kennedy gave a secret undertaking not to mount an armed invasion of Cuba to overthrow Castro in return for the supervised withdrawal of Soviet offensive missiles from the island.[69] However, while the United States apparently consented to the existence of a Communist state in the Western Hemisphere, it continued to strive for the political and economic isolation of the Castro regime. In addition, 'Operation Mongoose', which had been authorized by Kennedy in November 1961 and placed under the direction of the CIA counter-insurgency expert General Edward Lansdale, was given extra funds to pursue a strategy of covert operations involving paramilitary sabotage, subversion and even assassination attempts, including the use of exploding cigars and poisonous ball-point pens, to destabilize the Castro regime in Cuba. Like Operation Zapata, Operation Mongoose was unsuccessful because Castro and the Cuban Revolution enjoyed genuine public support in Cuba. Furthermore, Castro shrewdly used evidence of American covert operations to appeal to Cuban nationalism and anti-Americanism while at the same time justifying an increase in his security forces and a strengthening of his personal control of the political system. In April 1963, Kennedy's national security adviser, McGeorge Bundy, acknowledged that Operation Mongoose should be closed down because 'such activity is not worth the effort expended on it'.[70]

On the other hand, American policy in the form of the economic embargo on trade and investment was successful in severely damaging the Cuban economy. For the Soviet Union this meant that the pledge of support for Castro was financially very costly and proved to be an enduring economic liability. During the 1960s the Cuban economy was only saved from collapse by generous Soviet financial subsidies, especially in the form of supplies of oil and industrial equipment, and an agreement to purchase more than 50 per cent of Cuba's exports. Although the Soviets had successfully established a beachhead in Cuba, their first in the Western Hemisphere, they used the island as a propaganda showpiece and centre of operations for the gathering of intelligence information rather than a fortress or base for offensive military operations. The alarmist American predictions of rapid and relentless Communist advance throughout the Central American–Caribbean region proved to be incorrect. Indeed, no serious attempt was made to integrate Cuba into the Warsaw Pact or formally join a Soviet system of world-wide military alliances. This cautious policy was explained by two facts: the Soviets did not want to fight a war over Cuba and they recognized the Western Hemisphere as a well-established American sphere of influence. By contrast, the Soviet Union was a remote power that had a history of minimal political and economic contact with the region. Only Argentina, Mexico and Uruguay maintained diplomatic relations with Moscow throughout the 1950s. Trade was also relatively very modest. In comparison to products from the West, the Soviet Union and its European satellites had little to offer in terms of quality and price, while their desire for Latin American grain, coffee, wool and minerals resulted in a trade balance that was strongly in favour of Latin America. Furthermore, Marxism-Leninism was regarded as an alien ideology and its appeal was blunted by the fact that the strongly Catholic societies of Latin America had an innate aversion to Communism. Much to the relief of American officials, the Cuban example of armed struggle and enacting a socialist revolution was not successfully copied elsewhere in the hemisphere during the 1960s. Indeed, the failure of Cuba's attempts to 'export revolution' to the mainland was most vividly illustrated by the capture and death of Che Guevara in Bolivia in 1967.

The Johnson Doctrine

The defeat of the Communist guerrilla movement in Bolivia was also a reflection of the substantial efforts undertaken by the United States to build up Latin American internal security and police forces and provide equipment and instruction for use in counter-insurgency techniques. Indeed, American diplomacy placed considerable stress on the value of military assistance programmes and covert operations in containing the spread of Communism in the hemisphere. 'The US', remarked President Kennedy in 1962, 'should give considerably greater emphasis to police assistance programs in appropriate less developed countries where there is an actual or potential threat of internal subversion or insurgency.'[71] A particularly close relationship was established with the Brazilian military. Not only was financial aid considerably increased, but personal relations were greatly strengthened by the appointment in 1962 of Colonel Vernon Walters as

US defence attaché in Rio de Janeiro. Walters had served as a liaison officer and interpreter for the Brazilian Expeditionary Force that had fought in Italy during the Second World War and personally knew a number of senior Brazilian military commanders. The relationship between the US Embassy and the Brazilian military was so friendly that American complicity was suspected in the military coup that overthrew the radical government of President João Goulart in April 1964. 'Our embassy did have far ranging contacts,' admitted US Ambassador Lincoln Gordon, 'but we were not participants in the planning of action against Goulart.'[72] On the other hand, the Johnson Administration had secretly prepared a contingency plan codenamed 'Operation Brother Sam' that involved mobilizing a US naval task force off-shore with instructions to intervene in Brazil to protect American citizens should the military coup fail.

In fact, the Brazilian president was not a political favourite of either Kennedy or Johnson. A protégé of Getúlio Vargas and known for his close associations with labour unions, Goulart had long aroused the suspicion of American officials that he was a pro-Communist. 'A significant consequence of Goulart's political opportunism', a state department assessment informed Kennedy, 'is the favor and patronage which he has shown to Communists and suspected Communists throughout his career, in return for their political support.'[73] After becoming president in 1961, Goulart formally renewed Brazil's diplomatic relations with the Soviet Union and was critical of American efforts to expel Cuba from the OAS. The disquiet of the Brazilian military was expressed by General Humberto de Alencar Castelo Branco, who feared that Goulart's policies would 'submit the nation to Moscow Communism'.[74] The Johnson Administration was therefore delighted to learn of Goulart's fall from power in 1964. Even though Goulart was still known to be in Brazil and the exact constitutional position was uncertain, Johnson soon telegraphed his 'warmest good wishes' to the new interim Brazilian president.[75] No objection was made as the Brazilian military installed themselves in government and, proclaiming a war on 'corruption and communism', proceeded ruthlessly to suppress any signs of political opposition.

The first Latin American foreign policy crisis of Johnson's administration had actually occurred some months earlier in Panama. The CIA had predicted the development because 'Fidel Castro, working closely with the Panamanian Communist party, had been sending guns, money, and agents into Panama'.[76] The president accordingly refused to make concessions to the Panamanian government when it broke off diplomatic relations after disturbances in the Panama Canal Zone in January 1964 in which four Americans and twenty-four Panamanians were killed.[77] Johnson appreciated the Panamanian desire for 'a fresh look' at the treaty arrangements over the canal, but he was insistent that: 'Decisions had to be reached on the merits of the case, not in response to rioting in Panama or to attempts by the Panamanian government to gain popular support by putting pressure on us.'[78]

A similar determination not to be seen to be yielding to pressure was evident in Johnson's attitude to events in the Dominican Republic in 1965. In fact, on this occasion the perceived imperatives of Cold War politics resulted in unilateral American military intervention and a return to the policy of sending in the marines even though this indicated a reversal of Franklin Roosevelt's 1934 pledge of non-intervention. In the same way that he was determined not to 'lose' South Vietnam to Communism, Lyndon Johnson would not allow 'another Cuba' in the hemisphere. In April 1965 when political chaos erupted into violence in Santo Domingo, the capital of the Dominican Republic, he suspected that a pro-Castro Communist conspiracy was responsible. More than 20,000 American troops were dispatched to restore order, the first overt military intervention by the United States in Latin America since Nicaragua in the late 1920s. 'The last thing I wanted – and the last thing the American people wanted – was another Cuba on our doorstep', the president explained.[79]

The fighting in the Dominican Republic was a continuation of an internal political struggle that had resulted from the assassination of President Rafael Leonidas Trujillo y Molina in May 1961, an action that had brought an end to three decades during which the Trujillo family had ruled the country as virtually their personal property. The radical political leader and poet Juan Bosch was elected president and assumed office in February 1963, but a military coup in September forced him to seek exile in Puerto Rico. During his short period as president, Bosch had introduced a new constitution and sought political and agrarian reform. The Kennedy Administration, however, regarded him as a weak leader. There was also suspicion that some members of his government were sympathetic to Communist ideas. American officials were not, therefore, displeased by his overthrow in 1963. The US ambassador in the Dominican Republic, John Bartlow Martin, summed this up by saying that 'during his seven months in office he [Bosch] accomplished nothing, that he made fatal political mistakes, that he had no idea of what "being President" means, that he was a divider, not a builder'.[80] Nevertheless, Martin acknowledged that Bosch had inaugurated a period of honest government and brought the prospect of real reform to a society that had suffered for so long under the oppressive dictatorship of the Trujillo family. The rebel military faction that sought to seize power in 1965 was called the 'constitutionalists' and claimed that it wished to restore the 1963 Constitution and secure the reinstatement of Bosch as president.

Lyndon Johnson, however, ignored this internal political aspect of the crisis and instead highlighted the external Communist threat. By doing so, he provoked a heated debate within the United States because only a very small number of Communists were ever actually identified among the rebel forces. In fact, Johnson was accused of seeking to maintain the conservative Dominican political elite in power by deliberately exaggerating the threat of 'another Cuba' and reacting with excessive military force. In keeping with his criticism that the US government was tragically afflicted with 'the arrogance of power', Senator William Fulbright of Arkansas condemned the action as not only illegal but also 'a grievous misreading of the temper of contemporary Latin American politics'.[81] Critics in Latin America also pointed out that Johnson had not consulted the OAS prior to his decision to send in troops and that his unilateral intervention signified the return of the 'Roosevelt Corollary' which they now scathingly called the 'Johnson Doctrine'.

On the other hand, Johnson made it clear that he had no intention of establishing an American protectorate in the dollar diplomacy style of previous presidents. If somewhat belatedly, he brought the issue to the OAS and, despite considerable misgivings being expressed from some members of the Council, secured agreement for the dispatch of an OAS military presence in the form of token contingents of troops from six Latin American nations to supervise peace arrangements. In effect, the affirmative vote signified retrospective OAS approval of Johnson's armed intervention. American troops were withdrawn from the Dominican Republic within six months and a staunch anti-Communist and pro-American politician, Joaquín Balaguer, defeated Juan Bosch in the 1966 presidential election. Some years earlier in 1961 President Kennedy had privately expressed his 'admiration' for Balaguer and hoped that he 'will endure as one of the great figures of his country's history and an important figure in the history of this hemisphere'.[82] Once in power in 1966, Balaguer embarked on a systematic campaign to suppress Bosch's supporters. At the same time he consolidated his own personal control of the Dominican political system that would last for the rest of the twentieth century. In the United States, as the issue became less politically contentious and the controversy subsided, the apparent 'success' of the 1965 intervention was interpreted as a reaffirmation of American pre-eminence in the Central American–Caribbean region and to some extent a compensation for the earlier disaster at the Bay of Pigs. To Latin Americans, however, it was further evidence that any suspected involvement in Cold War politics on the side of the Soviet Union or Cuba would court severe American displeasure. The Dominican intervention also showed the limitations of the OAS as a means of restraining the power of the United States in the Western Hemisphere.

The threat of Allende

When Richard Nixon became president in 1969 he unveiled a global diplomatic strategy that concentrated on relations with the Soviet Union, Western

Europe, Communist China and Japan. The biggest priority was placed on the relaxation of tensions with the Soviet Union, a policy that came to be known as détente. Extricating the United States from the Vietnam War and resolving the Middle East crisis were other major concerns of the new administration. By contrast, affairs in the rest of the world, including Latin America, were accorded far less significance and only attracted close American interest and active involvement when they directly interacted with Cold War politics, an uncommon occurrence during the period of détente. The notable exception was in Chile where the Nixon Administration (1969–74) was concerned that the rise of anti-Americanism and Communism in that country would spread not only throughout neighbouring nations of South America but to the rest of Latin America and the wider world.

The seminal event in Chile occurred when Salvador Allende Gossens won a narrow presidential victory in 1970. A declared Marxist and leader of the Socialist Party, Allende had already been an unsuccessful presidential candidate in 1952, 1958 and 1964. In 1970 he represented a broad left-wing coalition called the Alliance of Popular Unity (Unidad Popular or UP). Openly modelled upon the Cuban Revolution, his platform promised a radical programme to transform Chile into a socialist state with particular stress on major agrarian reform and the achievement of economic independence by the expropriation of foreign-owned companies, especially in banking and mining. The election was closely fought and ended in victory for Allende who polled 36 per cent of the popular vote and was just 1.2 per cent ahead of the next candidate, Jorge Alessandri.

President Nixon and his national security adviser, Henry Kissinger, were surprised by the unanticipated election of a Marxist and the prospect of Communist government being legally established for the first time in a South American country. The development was perplexing because Kissinger's diplomatic world revolved around an East–West axis in which Latin America was peripheral. This was illustrated in his celebrated comments to Chilean Ambassador Gabriel Valdés at a meeting in the Oval Office of the White House in June 1969:

> You come here speaking of Latin America, but this is not important. Nothing important can come from the South. History has never been produced in the South. The axis of history starts in Moscow, goes to Bonn, crosses over to Washington, and then goes to Tokyo. What happens in the South is of no importance.[83]

Kissinger's bravado, however, disguised his very real concern over developments in Chile. He later pointed out the geopolitical threat to the whole hemisphere of 'a red sandwich' cutting across South America in an axis running from Santiago in Chile to Havana:

> Allende's election was a challenge to our national interests. We did not find it easy to reconcile ourselves to a second Communist state in the Western Hemisphere. We were persuaded that it would soon be inciting anti-American policies, attacking hemispheric solidarity, making common cause with Cuba, and sooner or later establishing close relations with the Soviet Union.[84]

Allende's victory in the election of September 1970, however, was not completely final because he had failed to win an outright majority of the popular vote. According to the Chilean Constitution, he could not formally become president until he had secured a vote of confirmation by the Chilean Congress within fifty days of the first election. Since the presidential contest had been so close, American officials believed that the result might yet be reversed in the Chilean Congress. Consequently, the Nixon Administration decided to interfere covertly in Chilean politics and provide funds for the printing and distribution of anti-Allende political propaganda in the form of pamphlets, newspaper articles, radio and television programmes. Money would also be used to bribe members of the Chilean Congress to vote against Allende's confirmation and to favour the election of an alternative candidate who was acceptable to the United States. The policy of American covert interference in Chilean politics was not new and had been regularly employed by the CIA, sometimes with financial support from US corporations such as International Telephone and Telegraph Company throughout the 1960s and as recently as the 1970 presidential election. It was estimated that the CIA had spent more than $1 million in that election.[85] The strategy to prevent Allende's confirmation was later named 'Track I' to distinguish it from a separate operation known as 'Track II'. Track II arose directly from a private meeting on 15 September between President Nixon and CIA Director Richard Helms at which Nixon instructed Helms to 'save Chile' from Communism by provoking an internal military coup that would prevent Allende from taking office.[86] The Track II operation was so secret that neither the state department, the American ambassador in Chile nor his diplomatic staff were informed about it.

Track II proved to be counter-productive. When CIA meddling contributed to a bungled kidnapping attempt in which a leading Chilean general, René Schneider, was assassinated, the Chilean military resolved to abstain from any interference in the political process of electing the president. On 3 November 1970 the Chilean Congress duly confirmed Allende as president. In office, Allende proceeded to implement his radical electoral platform. A particularly controversial battle erupted with American business interests over the expropriation of the big American-owned copper companies, Kennecott and Anaconda. It was initially estimated that the companies would receive more than $300 million from the Chilean government for their assets, but Allende declared that the companies had made so much excess profit in the past that they did not merit any financial compensation at all. On behalf of Kennecott and Anaconda, the state department protested that Chile's action of minimizing compensation was unprecedented, retrospective and was a departure from 'accepted standards of international law'.[87]

Even more worrying for the Nixon Administration was Allende's foreign policy and especially his desire for close and friendly relations with Fidel Castro. Under Allende, Chile resumed full diplomatic relations with Cuba and called on the OAS to end its policy of economic sanctions against the Castro regime. Moreover, Castro was invited to make a state visit to Chile in November 1971 and a statue of Che Guevara was erected in Santiago de Chile. Allende also established diplomatic relations with several Communist countries, including the People's Republic of China, North Korea, North Vietnam, Albania and the German Democratic Republic. In December 1972 he travelled to the UN in New York and in the General Assembly delivered a speech condemning imperialism and the power of international corporations upon the nations of the Third World. Complaining of attempts 'to strangle our economy', Allende stated: 'We are the victims of a new form of imperialism, one that is more subtle, more cunning, and for that reason, more terrifyingly effective [than in the past].'[88] Like Castro in 1959, Allende was pointedly not invited to visit the White House for talks with the president. Instead, he was treated to an informal meeting with the American ambassador to the UN, George Bush, Snr. A very different reception awaited Allende in the Soviet Union. From New York he travelled on to Moscow where he was personally received at the airport by the Soviet leader, Leonid Brezhnev. On his journey back to Chile, Allende made a brief stop in Havana to return Castro's earlier visit to Chile. 'He used the excursion to burnish his anti-American credentials and vent his usual anti-American themes', laconically commented Henry Kissinger.[89]

At his meeting with CIA Director Helms on 15 September, Nixon had expressed his wish to make the Chilean economy 'scream'.[90] To achieve this outcome he approved the application of economic pressure that consisted of reducing American financial aid, both governmental and private, and denying Chile access to international loans from institutions such as the World Bank and the Inter-American Development Bank. The resulting shortage of foreign capital was not total and was merely one factor that contributed to the growing economic difficulties caused by Allende's ambitious attempts to impose what amounted virtually to a command economy. By 1973 a massive budget deficit was predicted, agricultural and industrial production were in decline, while inflation had climbed from an annual rate of 163 per cent in the previous year to more than 300 per cent. National strikes by shopkeepers, truckers and copper miners caused further economic damage and added to the atmosphere of growing political uncertainty and tension within the country.

In September 1973 General Augusto Pinochet Ugarte seized power in a military coup during which Allende committed suicide. The new military government proudly declared that Chile had been saved from Communism. Like the overthrow of Goulart in Brazil in 1964, American complicity in the coup was widely suspected but could not be proved. The American ambassador in Chile, Nathaniel Davis, admitted that he had been given prior intelligence of the coup but stated that he 'did not engage in coup plotting' and was 'unaware of any of my US colleagues having done so, including the personnel of the CIA station, the attaché office, and the Military Advisory Group'.[91] The Nixon Administration was undoubtedly hostile to Allende, but internal Chilean political factors were decisive in explaining the decision of the Chilean military to stage a coup. While Allende's policies undeniably had popular support in Chile, they had also aroused considerable political controversy and hostility. On a number of occasions senior army generals had privately warned him that the growing scale of political and economic difficulties posed a danger to Chile's national security. 'If the armed forces had not been predisposed to oppose the UP government', explained Allende's foreign minister, Clodomiro Almeyda Medina, 'the Pentagon's call for a military uprising would have gone unheeded.'[92] Among the president's admirers, his violent death gained him the image of a martyr who had sacrificed his life for his country and was also a victim of American imperialism.

For Nixon and Kissinger, the coup had removed the geopolitical threat that they believed Allende had posed. They welcomed the new regime and quickly restored full economic relations. But the personal reputations of Nixon and Kissinger were severely damaged by their lack of any public criticism of the brutal and repressive policies subsequently pursued by Pinochet in Chile. 'The Chilean junta', acknowledged Kissinger, 'probably continued authoritarian practices for too long', but he believed that it 'was being judged with exceptional severity while it faced near-civil-war conditions.'[93] Although American diplomatic interest in Chilean affairs gradually diminished once the military regime consolidated its position in power, the political controversy in the United States continued over the exact role of the Nixon Administration in the 1973 coup. The debate was further stimulated by damaging revelations arising from the findings of the 'Church Committee', the investigation in 1975 by the US Senate Select Committee on Intelligence, chaired by Senator Frank Church of Idaho. While the Committee reported that there was 'no hard evidence of direct US assistance to the coup, despite frequent allegations of such aid',[94] it confirmed, and was highly critical of, the Nixon Administration's use of covert methods, including bribery, and the adoption of the Track II strategy. The Committee's investigations also covered the conduct of previous presidential administrations and disclosed that the CIA had organized eight assassination attempts against Fidel Castro during the period from 1960 to 1965. Beguiled by the perceived success of the 1954 Guatemala coup, successive presidents had been tempted to resort to covert operations to achieve their foreign policy aims in Latin America. In so doing, the Church Committee argued that the United States had betrayed its traditional sense of moral purpose and idealism. As a result, it believed that American prestige and influence in the Western Hemisphere had declined to its lowest point for some decades.

7

END OF THE TWENTIETH CENTURY (1974–2000)

The Panama Canal treaties

The policy pursued by the Nixon Administration of destabilizing the Allende regime in Chile occurred at a time when the United States appeared to be losing its political and economic pre-eminence in the Western Hemisphere. This was visibly demonstrated by the continued survival of the Castro regime in Cuba and the desire of Latin American governments to diversify and extend their diplomatic and economic relations to include Communist nations and the Third World. For the people of the United States there was also a sense of a broader global decline that was reflected in the failure to win the Vietnam War and the growing economic challenge of nations such as West Germany and Japan. Moreover, the massive rise in energy prices caused by the 'oil-shock' of 1973 underscored America's reliance on foreign imports of petroleum and stimulated greater awareness of the importance of securing access to supplies from Latin American countries such as Mexico and Venezuela. In response to criticism that the United States was neglecting the region, the Nixon Administration talked about creating a 'new partnership' or 'new dialogue' with the nations of Latin America. 'The time has come to infuse the Western Hemisphere relationships with a new spirit', stated Kissinger at a meeting of foreign ministers in Tlatelolco, Mexico City, and he added: 'Today – together – we can begin giving expression to our common aspirations and start shaping our common future.'[1] Kissinger's subsequent cancellation of scheduled trips to Latin America in order to deal with more urgent business in the Middle East drew the criticism of some observers that his slogans were merely empty posturing designed to conciliate domestic political criticism. Nevertheless, the US government did become more actively involved in hemispheric issues, in particular the negotiation of new arrangements concerning the future of the Panama Canal.

The canal question basically revolved around differing interpretations of the 1903 Treaty, especially the extent of the sovereign rights exercised by the United States over the Canal Zone. There was also a long-standing sense of grievance among Panamanians arising from their conviction that the terms of the original treaty had been too favourable to the United States. On occasion, Panamanian resentment had erupted into violent anti-American riots as in 1959 and 1964. In order to conciliate Panamanian opinion and fearful of possible sabotage against the operation of the canal, the Johnson Administration entered into discussions to establish a revision of the existing treaty arrangements. Progress was stalled, however, not only by Johnson's awareness that the waterway was declining in its relative economic importance for the United States but most of all by his increasing preoccupation with the war in Vietnam. Panamanian impatience steadily increased. The Panamanian political leader or 'Maximum Chief', General Omar Torrijos Herrera, astutely gained external diplomatic support from his neighbours and Third World countries and, deliberately bypassing the OAS, raised the issue at the UN. A special meeting of the UN Security Council was held in Panama City in March 1973 at which Torrijos made a powerful and well-received speech stating that the United States had established 'a colony in the heart of my country' and that such an anomaly was unjust and unacceptable in an age of decolonization.[2] A resolution was overwhelmingly passed calling for a renegotiation of the canal treaty between the United States and Panama. Although the American delegation conspicuously exercised its power of veto to defeat the UN resolution, both Nixon and his successor, Gerald Ford, recognized that Torrijos had effectively out-manoeuvred the United States in the court of world opinion. It was clear that the canal issue could not be dismissed as unimportant and that discussions should be reopened with the Panamanian government.

Implicit in the subtext of the ensuing negotiations was American willingness to fix a definite date for the ending of American control over the canal and also the confirmation of Panamanian sovereignty over the US Canal Zone. But the prospect of giving up what was popularly perceived as 'American' territory was controversial and provoked a right-wing political backlash in the United States. In the battle for the Republican presidential nomination in 1976, the former governor of California, Ronald Reagan, was severely critical of what he described as the weak policy of the Ford Administration (1974–7). 'When it comes to the canal, we bought it, we paid for it, it's ours, and we should tell Torrijos and company that we are going to keep it', declared Reagan.[3] The demagogic outburst politicized the canal issue and led President Ford to deny that he had any intention of giving up American control over the operation of the canal. The political controversy effectively suspended talks on revising the canal treaty until after the 1976 presidential election.

The election to the presidency in 1976 of a Democrat and a Washington 'outsider', James Earl 'Jimmy' Carter, raised the prospect of radical changes in American foreign policy, including a new emphasis upon closer relations between the United States and Latin America. Instead of viewing the world strictly in terms of bipolar Cold War politics, Carter insisted on the inclusion of a North–South perspective in which there would be a constructive dialogue between the 'developed' and 'developing' nations. In his policy towards the 'developing' countries of Latin America, Carter particularly wanted to improve relations with Panama and finally resolve the long-standing controversy over the status of the Canal Zone which, he believed, had not only been demeaning to the people of Panama but had also severely damaged the image of the United States throughout the hemisphere. During the interregnum period before he assumed the presidency, Carter was given the final copy of the Linowitz Report, which had been prepared by the privately funded Commission on US–Latin American Relations, under the chairmanship of the former American ambassador to the OAS, Sol Linowitz. The Report singled out the canal as a matter for urgent diplomatic action.[4] After studying the Report, Carter told the press that the canal question would be given high priority in his administration. It was considered especially important to act quickly. 'Our view', noted the president's national security adviser, Zbigniew Brzezinski, 'was that if the new administration did not move rapidly on the Panama issue, capitalizing on the new President's mandate, the problem would become unmanageable and sour our relations with Latin America.'[5]

The negotiations that followed were not without their particular difficulties, but two canal treaties were drawn up and formally signed with great public fanfare by Carter and Torrijos in Washington in September 1977. The first treaty stated the arrangements by which the United States and Panama would manage the canal in joint partnership until it was handed over to Panama on 31 December 1999. The second treaty stipulated the terms for the operation and defence of the canal after that date. While the treaties were speedily ratified in Panama where Torrijos possessed considerable control over the political system, the same process was not so straightforward in the United States. 'The [canal] question demonstrated the increasingly close relationship between American domestic politics and the conduct of foreign affairs', observed Carter's secretary of state, Cyrus Vance.[6] Vance identified a real political problem, but it was hardly new and had applied just as much to Grant's attempt to annex the Dominican Republic a century earlier. In the case of the Panama Canal treaties Vance argued that, unlike Louisiana or Alaska, the United States had never actually purchased the Canal Zone and did not, therefore, possess sovereign rights. Nevertheless, the nationalist sentiments expressed by Ronald Reagan in 1976 were still very influential. For example, Senator Paul Laxalt of Nevada, who led the Republican opposition in the US Senate, criticized the administration for 'backing down' under pressure and argued that the United States was abandoning 'a vital strategic and economic asset'.[7]

To sway the vote in favour of ratifying the treaties, Carter found that he had to make significant concessions to his political opponents. In order to allay apprehension that American shipping might be denied use of the canal at some date in the future, a reservation was added to the second treaty reserving for the United States the right to intervene militarily to defend or reopen the canal after it had passed to Panamanian control in 1999. Torrijos protested that the reservation implied a return to the policy of dollar diplomacy but was conciliated by the explanation that the United States did not claim a right of interference in Panamanian domestic political affairs. The treaties were eventually ratified by the US Senate in April 1978 though only narrowly, by 68 to 32 votes, just one vote more than the two-thirds necessary for ratification. Although the ratification process had been extremely divisive and had taken much longer than he had either wanted or anticipated, President Carter believed that he had successfully addressed an awkward issue that had damaged relations with Panama for too long and had threatened to disturb the efficient operation of the canal. Moreover, he considered that the vote in favour of ratification had great significance for American foreign policy:

> These treaties can mark the beginning of a new era in our relations not only with Panama but with all the rest of the world. They symbolize our determination to deal with the developing world, the small nations of the world, on the basis of mutual respect and partnership.[8]

Relations with Cuba

In campaigning for the presidency in 1976, Jimmy Carter had announced his desire for a reassessment of the relationship between the United States and Cuba as part of his policy to improve relations not only with Latin America but also between the 'developed' and 'developing' nations of the world. During the late 1960s the images of Castro and the Cuban Revolution had been positively enhanced by their success in achieving full employment and impressive advances in education and health care. Indeed, the strategy of isolating Cuba in the Western Hemisphere had clearly begun to unravel during the Nixon Administration when Argentina and Peru re-established diplomatic relations with the Castro regime in 1972. The desire for trade with Cuba's expanding economy also resulted in the OAS lifting economic sanctions in 1975. While the United States chose to maintain its own policy of a strict economic embargo, President Ford agreed to a relaxation of restrictions on Cuban diplomats travelling within the United States. The prospect of further conciliatory measures was ruled out, however, by what Ford regarded as Fidel Castro's provocative decision to dispatch Cuban troops overseas in support of pro-Marxist forces in Angola in South-west Africa. Nevertheless, at his confirmation hearings as secretary of state in January 1977, Cyrus Vance made the significant remark that 'if Cuba is willing to live within the international system, then we ought to seek ways to find whether we can eliminate the impediments which exist between us and try to move toward normalization'.[9] A symbolic step in this direction was taken with the opening on 1 September 1977 of Cuban and US interests sections in Washington and Havana respectively. Castro also agreed to the release of more than 3,000 'counter-revolutionaries' or 'political' prisoners and allowed them the option of emigrating to the United States.

However, the expansion of Cuba's military involvement in Africa in 1978 to include sending troops to Ethiopia in the Horn of Africa and to Zaire made it very difficult to achieve any further progress to 'normalize' relations. Brzezinski scathingly referred to 'the Soviet-sponsored deployment of the Cuban military'[10] and regarded Cuba as a surrogate of the Soviet Union fighting its battles in Africa. There was also the report that Soviet MiG jet airplanes had been introduced into the Cuban Air Force and that a Soviet combat brigade of 2,500 men was permanently stationed on the island. Both reports underscored issues of superpower rivalry and placed Cuba once again firmly within the context of Cold War politics rather than as part of the policies aimed at improving relations with Latin America or the dialogue between the North–South nations. At the same time, other international tensions arising from the controversy over the SALT II treaty to limit strategic weapons and especially the Soviet invasion of Afghanistan in December 1979 created additional impediments to the improvement in relations between the United States and Cuba.

Human rights

Another very public and highly controversial aspect of Carter's foreign policy was his affirmation of the obligation to respect human rights in his inaugural presidential address: 'Because we are free, we can never be indifferent to the fate of freedom elsewhere. Our moral sense dictates a clear-cut preference for those societies which share with us an abiding respect for individual human rights.'[11] Though the emphasis was on the new concept of 'human rights', Carter was essentially building on the work of critics such as the Church Committee whose investigations had underscored the moral failings of recent American foreign policy. In the process, Carter sought to rekindle America's unique historical and self-appointed mission to promote the spread of freedom and democracy. The high priority that he gave to the issue, however, raised controversy in Latin America because violations of human rights, including torture, summary executions, disappearances and the violent activities of military and police forces referred to as 'death squads', were a frequent and well-publicized occurrence in that region especially during the 1970s.

Moreover, in contrast to the Soviet Union or countries in the Middle East or Asia, the United States believed that it could directly influence the behaviour of Latin American governments on the issue of respect for human rights. Although this would inevitably lead to some form of direct American interference in the domestic affairs of Latin American states, Carter was like Woodrow Wilson in believing that there was a moral imperative to act. Consequently, in marked contrast to its two Republican predecessors, the Carter Administration refused to condone violations of human rights on the grounds that they were a regrettable but necessary evil in the war against Communism and terrorism. 'Justice that is summary undermines the future it seeks to promote', Cyrus Vance told the OAS, and he added: 'It produces only more violence, more victims, and more terrorism.'[12]

In the aftermath of the Vietnam War, Watergate and the damning report of the Church Committee, the US Congress was very willing to participate in the making of a more ethically based foreign policy. It followed up Vance's comments by voting to reduce American military aid to repressive governments, starting with Argentina in 1977. In fact, the reduction of military aid was counter-productive in the short term because it exerted little visible impact on the policies of authoritarian regimes. Indeed, the policy brought stinging criticism from the governments of Argentina, Brazil and Chile of American interference in their internal political affairs. They also complained that Carter unfairly adopted double standards by not putting the same pressure on Communist countries where human rights were routinely violated. Indeed, the governments of Argentina, Brazil, El Salvador and Guatemala felt so aggrieved that they retaliated by suspending their existing military assistance agreements with the United States. They turned instead to Western Europe and Israel for supplies of weapons and military equipment.

Carter and Nicaragua

Another example of the decline of American pre-eminence in the hemisphere was Carter's evident inability to direct events in Central America. Civil unrest in that region was increased during the 1970s by severe natural disasters such as the 1972 Managua earthquake and a series of world economic shocks, especially the dramatic rise in the cost of imports of oil and the steep fall in the prices for local export commodities such as coffee, sugar and bananas. Economic adversity promoted the growth of political discontent, exemplified by the emergence of 'national liberation fronts' based on guerrilla movements, which operated in the countryside and both imitated and drew inspiration from the success of Fidel Castro and the Cuban Revolution. The leading movements in Central America were the Farabundo Martí National Liberation Front (FMLN) in El Salvador and the Sandinista National Liberation Front (FSLN or 'Sandinistas') in

Nicaragua named after the Nicaraguan national hero, Sandino. The FSLN was established in 1961 and steadily grew during the late 1970s from a tiny force in the countryside to a powerful national political movement dedicated to the overthrow of the Somoza family who had dominated Nicaragua since the 1930s.

'The world's greediest ruler', considered the columnist Jack Anderson, 'is Anastasio Somoza D., the pot-bellied potentate who rules Nicaragua as if it were his private estate.'[13] Anastasio Somoza had been elected president in 1967 but acted like a dictator. The Carter Administration was privately very critical of Somoza's repressive rule and believed that political, economic and social discontent was so serious in Nicaragua that he could not hold on to power for very much longer. However, it did not want to see him replaced by the pro-Marxist and anti-American Sandinistas. Even though he was aware of Carter's critical views, Somoza was unrepentant and determined to remain president. Moreover, the well-funded 'Nicaragua lobby' in Washington dutifully pointed out that he was a staunch anti-Communist, a long-standing friend of the United States, and that his father had provided military bases for the operations to overthrow Arbenz in Guatemala in 1954 and for the Bay of Pigs in 1961. Moreover, the views of pro-Somoza congressmen gained added value at a time when the Carter Administration was struggling to secure ratification of the Panama Canal treaties. For political and strategic reasons, Carter was, therefore, understandably ambivalent in his public attitude towards Somoza. He privately hoped that a democratic group committed to social and economic reform and with respect for human rights would emerge as a party of government and an alternative political force to Somoza and the Sandinistas.

The president's lack of a coherent policy was exposed by events in Nicaragua where political opposition was routinely and savagely repressed. In January 1978 Somoza's leading critic, the newspaper editor Pedro Joaquín Chamorro, was assassinated in the capital. However, it was only when the Sandinistas gained military victories, occupied the important provincial capital of León and were on the point of launching what appeared to be a final military offensive in June 1979 that American policy belatedly sought to bring about Somoza's resignation and replacement. To achieve a peaceful transition of power, Carter characteristically ruled out unilateral American military action and favoured an inter-American multilateral approach. He requested a special meeting of OAS foreign ministers at which Secretary of State Vance alluded to Cuban interference in Nicaraguan internal affairs and called for the dispatch of an OAS peacekeeping force to bring about a ceasefire in Nicaragua. Vance's proposal was roundly rejected and regarded as an American ploy to prevent the Sandinistas from ever gaining power. Instead, a resolution was passed calling on Somoza to resign. The meeting was a humiliation for President Carter and illustrated not only the failure of his Nicaraguan policy but also, for once, the inability of the United States to manage and manipulate the OAS.

Aware that not only pro-Communist Cuba but democratic countries such as Costa Rica and Venezuela were openly backing the Sandinistas, Carter concluded that Somoza must resign in order for a peaceful transition of government to take place. But Carter still hoped to determine the course of political events. The American ambassador in Nicaragua, Lawrence Pezzullo, was instructed to convey personally to Somoza what amounted to an ultimatum. 'We think', the ambassador diplomatically told Somoza, 'that without a statesmanlike act on your part, we are going to be caught in something which is going down.'[14] In July 1979 Somoza duly resigned and left the country.[15] The Sandinistas came to power as the dominant group in a 'Government of National Reconstruction'. Determined to avoid what he perceived as the mistakes of the past, Carter favoured an open-minded pragmatic approach to political developments in Nicaragua. Most of all, he did not want to develop an adversarial relationship with the Sandinistas that would result in a repetition of the break with Castro's Cuba in 1959–61. Consequently, he agreed not only to recognize the new regime but also to give financial aid to it. The Sandinistas, however, were determined not to appear as dependent upon the United States. They refused to abandon their proclaimed intention of implementing a Nicaraguan revolution that would transform the country into a socialist society. Moreover, despite stating that they would pursue a non-aligned foreign policy and not become entangled in Cold War politics, they clearly wished to have friendly relations with the Soviet Union and with Cuba. Trade agreements were concluded with the Soviet Union, and military advisory missions from Eastern Europe were invited to Nicaragua. The Sandinista leader, Daniel Ortega Saavedra, visited Cuba and the Soviet Union in 1985. The Sandinistas also expanded their guerrilla army of 6,000 soldiers into powerful military and police forces eventually exceeding 100,000. Furthermore, they expressed their support for the FMLN in El Salvador to the extent of providing a conduit for weapons and training from Cuba. In the United States there was growing criticism of Carter's policies. As the 1980 presidential election approached, his critics added the 'loss of Nicaragua' to the list of his alleged foreign policy disasters that included the Iranian embassy hostage crisis and the unopposed Soviet invasion of Afghanistan.

Despite his fresh ideas and good intentions, Carter's Latin American policies appeared as ineffective and indecisive. The Panama Canal treaties had been successfully ratified but at considerable political cost. Little progress had been made in normalizing relations with Cuba, while Cuban military forces had been noticeably expanded in Africa. The stress on human rights caused controversy and angered some of America's long-standing military friends in the region. In Nicaragua Carter had seemingly prevaricated for too long and thereby facilitated the rise to power of a pro-Marxist revolutionary movement which, once in office, proceeded to consolidate relations with the Soviet Union and Cuba while giving aid and encouragement to the neighbouring pro-Marxist revolutionary movement in El Salvador. The American president looked a decidedly ineffectual and somewhat forlorn figure when his call for a boycott of the 1980 Moscow Olympic Games as a protest against the Soviet invasion of Afghanistan met with a lukewarm response from most Latin American governments. A prominent critic of Carter's Latin American policies was the Georgetown University professor Jeane Kirkpatrick, who summed up the Carter record:

> American policies have not only proved incapable of dealing with the problems of Soviet/Cuban expansion in the area, they have positively contributed to them and to the alienation of major nations, the growth of neutralism, the destabilization of friendly governments, the spread of Cuban influence, and the decline of US power in the region.[16]

Reagan and the Central American Crisis

Jimmy Carter's apparent tolerance of the rise of a pro-Marxist government in Nicaragua was one of the foreign policy issues that contributed to his defeat by the Republican candidate, Ronald Reagan, in the presidential election of November 1980. During the electoral campaign Reagan criticized Carter's policy of stressing human rights as divisive and mistaken in its application to Latin America. Carter appeared to acknowledge the validity of the criticism when, even before he left the presidency in January 1981, he responded to news of a major guerrilla offensive in El Salvador by agreeing to an emergency measure to resume military aid for the government of that country. Military funding had been suspended in 1977 as a result of the Salvadoran government's patchy record on human rights.

The ideas underpinning the Latin American policy of the new Reagan Administration (1981–9) were considerably influenced by the writings of Jeane J. Kirkpatrick and also of the conservative scholars in the 'Report of the Committee of Santa Fe' published in 1980. Kirkpatrick emphasized the view that the Carter Administration had adopted double standards in unfairly singling out particular dictators for violating human rights while ignoring others with similar records. In her analysis, the policy had actually undermined US national security because it had weakened these governments and, by encouraging their enemies, made them more vulnerable to Communist subversion. Kirkpatrick contended that right-wing 'authoritarian' governments in Latin America were not the same as left-wing 'totalitarian' regimes. While acknowledging their deficiencies, she maintained that authoritarian governments were preferable and worthy of support because they were friendly to the United States and anti-Communist. They were also favourable to capitalism and contained elements of democratic political behaviour.[17] For party political reasons relating to the 1980 presidential election Kirkpatrick's analysis was treated as original, but it essentially articulated a policy that had often been followed by American presidents in their Latin American policies since the 1920s.

Providing a stark contrast to the liberal tone of the Linowitz Report, the Santa Fe Report alarmingly declared that the Caribbean was 'becoming a Marxist-Leninist Lake' and warned that: 'Never before has the [American] Republic been in such jeopardy from its exposed southern flank.'[18] The main thrust of the report was its recommendation that, in defence of its national security, the United States must challenge and reverse the alleged recent advance of Soviet influence in the Western Hemisphere. This would be achieved by rejecting the policies of accommodation associated with Carter and demonstrating instead a determination to confront and, where necessary, use American military power to defeat the threat of international Communism. 'Only the United States', ominously summed up the Santa Fe Report, 'can . . . protect the independent nations from communist conquest.'[19]

President Reagan was deeply distrustful of Communism and determined to confront and defeat what he described as the 'evil empire' of the Soviet Union. While endorsing the ideas expressed by Kirkpatrick and the Santa Fe Report, his administration was actually very selective in applying their recommendations to Latin America. There was a desire to contain Cuba and to improve relations with neighbouring Mexico, but relatively little attention was given to the countries of South America. Just like the Eisenhower Administration during the 1950s, most priority was given to Central America where local revolutionary movements were regarded as instruments of Soviet expansionism. The Reagan Administration referred to the region as America's 'backyard' and saw the struggle taking place there as an East–West confrontation that would play a significant part in the global crusade to roll back International Communism. Central America, observed Reagan, 'is simply too close, and the strategic stakes are too high, for us to ignore the danger of governments seizing power there with ideological and military ties with the Soviet Union'.[20]

The biggest concerns were El Salvador and Nicaragua. In El Salvador the danger of 'another Cuba' was the main worry. The conflict in that country was attributed not to internal factors but to deliberate Communist interference. As usual, Fidel Castro and Cuba loomed large. 'There could not be the slightest doubt', declared Reagan's secretary of state, Alexander Haig, 'that Cuba was at once the source of supply and the catechist of the Salvadoran insurgency.'[21] While endorsing the government in power, led for most of the 1980s by the Christian Democrat José Napoleón Duarte, the Reagan Administration dropped Carter's emphasis on achieving internal political and economic reforms and respect for human rights. The immediate priority now became the total military destruction of the FMLN. In 1981 $25 million in new military assistance was given to El Salvador, the largest amount that country had received from the United States since 1946. From 1981 to 1984 the armed forces were increased in size from 12,000 to 50,000. Modernizing and equipping the Salvadoran military was seen as the best way to defeat the guerrillas and maintain public order. 'Though this was not a point likely to be credited by many people outside of that country', argued Haig, 'the military was the guarantor of a democratic solution in El Salvador.'[22]

The policy of stressing a military solution did not deliver the quick victory that was desired. In fact, the FMLN were never actually militarily defeated and continued to survive as a serious fighting force in the countryside. Reagan's policy, however, was successful to the extent that it prevented the guerrillas from achieving the same military success as the Sandinistas in Nicaragua. Nevertheless, it was also highly controversial because the support given to the military and right-wing elements worsened existing internal tensions and impeded political reforms in El Salvador. Criticism was provoked not only in the United States but also in Latin America and Western Europe as civil unrest and violence in El Salvador continued unabated throughout the decade of the 1980s resulting in extensive economic destruction, violations of human rights, and massive civilian casualties, including an estimated one million people forced to become refugees. A substantial number of those displaced people ironically chose to migrate and seek their economic salvation in the United States.

In Nicaragua Carter's policy of seeking political accommodation with the Sandinistas was changed by Reagan to one of outright hostility in which both overt and covert measures were employed in an attempt to overthrow a regime that was viewed as an instrument of Soviet expansion and whose leader, Daniel Ortega, was regarded as identical to Fidel Castro. The confrontational policy of the Reagan Administration, however, was constrained by the fact that the US Congress, American public opinion and even senior members of the administration and the armed services were sharply divided over the issue of Nicaragua. In particular, anxiety over the 'Vietnam syndrome', the nightmare scenario of being sucked into 'another Vietnam [War]' ruled out the deployment of American combat troops. As a result the Reagan Administration sought to destabilize the Sandinista regime by promoting internal civil disorder while at the same time applying external economic pressure. The CIA under Director William Casey secretly organized and financed an army of Nicaraguan exiles, many of whom were anti-Sandinistas and former officers of Somoza's National Guard. This force, numbering initially around 500 and rising to 15,000, called itself the 'Nicaraguan Democratic Force', but became more popularly known as the counter-revolutionaries or 'Contras'.

Casey's purpose was not to create an invasion force on the lines of the 1954 Operation PBSUCCESS in Guatemala or Operation Zapata against Cuba in 1961 but was more like President Kennedy's Operation Mongoose in seeking primarily to inflict internal economic disruption and thereby damage both the national and international image of the Sandinistas as a credible government. 'It was hoped', remarked a CIA official, David MacMichael, in 1985, 'that the Nicaraguan government would clamp down on civil liberties within Nicaragua itself, arresting its opposition, demonstrating its allegedly totalitarian nature and thus increase domestic dissent within the country.'[23] From their bases in neighbouring Honduras and Costa Rica, the Contras launched 'low-intensity' military operations inside Nicaragua aimed at blowing up bridges, mining harbours, carrying out industrial sabotage and destroying agricultural crops. The Contras, however, remained dependent upon continuing American financial backing. Heavily outnumbered by the Sandinista army, they never acquired or held any actual territory in Nicaragua and, on account of their previous links with the hated Somoza regime and currently with the CIA, attracted insignificant popular support in the countryside. While they gained little tangible military success, the Contras did damage the local economy and compelled the Sandinistas to maintain large military forces and divert scarce resources to fighting the 'Contra War'.

The Reagan Administration also sought to weaken the Sandinistas by applying economic pressure in the form of reducing the quota for imports of Nicaraguan sugar into the United States by 90 per cent in 1983 and extending commercial restrictions to what amounted to a total trade embargo in 1985. In addition, American economic aid was reduced and attempts were made to implement an international credit squeeze on the country. From late 1981 to 1984 Nicaragua received only $50 million in loans from the Inter-American Development Bank and the World Bank. In the previous two years, the sum from the same sources had been $284 million. There was also the use of psychological warfare as exemplified in the regular staging of war games and large-scale military manoeuvres in neighbouring Honduras, sometimes lasting for several months, to convey the impression that preparations were well-developed for an invasion. By contrast, Soviet military aid to the Sandinistas was limited in terms of quantity and quality.

Furthermore, a diplomatic campaign was undertaken by the Reagan Administration with the purpose of isolating the Sandinistas. American officials stressed the close links that the Sandinistas had cultivated with the Soviet Union and Cuba. Nicaragua was likened to Cuba and described as a totalitarian state that ruthlessly violated human rights and imposed a strict censorship of the media. The Sandinistas, declared Ronald Reagan, were 'a Marxist-Leninist clique that broke the hearts of the freedom-loving people of their country by imposing a brutal dictatorship'.[24] The Reagan Administration also sought to cultivate support for its policy of isolating

Nicaragua by offering economic inducements to other countries in the Central American–Caribbean region. The aid programme was announced in 1982 and known as the Caribbean Basin Initiative.

Reagan supported the Contras in Nicaragua and admiringly complimented them as courageous 'freedom-fighters' who were engaged in the struggle to liberate their country from Communist control and thereby were helping to implement what was popularly called the 'Reagan Doctrine'. But opposing views were just as fervently held. Several Latin American political leaders considered Reagan to be too ideological and too confrontational. They believed that the 'Central American Crisis' would never be resolved by military means alone and that a peaceful diplomatic approach was preferable. In January 1983 the foreign ministers of Mexico, Panama, Venezuela and Colombia held a meeting on Contadora Island, off the coast of Panama, to discuss means of assisting a negotiated peace settlement for the region. One of the main suggestions to emerge from what became known as 'the Contadora Group' was an arrangement in which the Sandinistas would agree not to aid the guerrilla movement in El Salvador and in return the United States would end its support for the Contras. The Reagan Administration was placed in a dilemma because it was not willing to enter into negotiations with the Sandinistas. To admit this publicly, however, would be politically and diplomatically damaging in terms of both American and international public opinion. Consequently, Reagan appeared to welcome the formation of the Contadora Group, but later withdrew his support when formal proposals were made, even though these were approved by the Sandinistas. Reagan's secretary of state, George Shultz, disingenuously dismissed the action of the Sandinistas as a 'political ploy'. 'This draft, if accepted', he contended, 'could spell an end to US military assistance to El Salvador, Honduras, and the Contras, while the verification and monitoring weaknesses of the text would allow Nicaragua to avoid compliance.'[25]

The diplomatic approach recommended by the Contadora group was welcomed and even supplemented in the United States by the activities of what quickly became the largest anti-war mobilization of the public since the Vietnam War during the 1960s. Influential sections of the media, religious organizations, peace groups and human rights groups were prominent in presenting a positive view of the Sandinistas that pictured them as committed radical nationalists who were attempting to alleviate the problems of poverty and deprivation in their country caused by centuries of internal and external oppression. It was also pointed out that, under the Sandinistas, Nicaragua had not become formally aligned with the Soviet Union and that it had established friendly diplomatic and economic relations with the democratic governments of Western Europe and Japan. Indeed, the Sandinistas were applauded for agreeing to hold national elections in 1984. Moreover, they had proved to be accommodating to world opinion and had invited international observers to monitor those elections. In 1984 more than 400 observers from around 40 countries confirmed that the elections had been fairly conducted. The Reagan Administration, however, chose to dismiss the elections as fraudulent and meaningless.

In fact, it was Reagan rather than the Sandinistas whose reputation as a champion of democracy had suffered major damage in 1982 when the American press first revealed that the Administration was conducting a 'secret war' in Nicaragua. The perception that the president was deliberately withholding information from the public raised memories of the controversial use of executive power during the Vietnam War and the Watergate crisis. The US Congress acted to assert its role in the making of foreign policy. In December 1982 the House of Representatives passed an amendment to the annual defence appropriations bill to limit funds going to the Contras. Named after its sponsor, the Democratic Congressman from Massachusetts and chairman of the House Intelligence Committee Edward P. Boland, the Boland Amendment prohibited agencies of the federal government connected with intelligence activities from using congressional funds for the specific purpose of attempting to overthrow the government of Nicaragua. 'I can certainly say', stated Boland, 'that the committee certainly does understand its obligations to rein in activities which can get out of control or which could threaten to involve this nation or its allies in a war.'[26] The Amendment expired after one year, in December 1983.

The legality of Reagan's policy was openly questioned in early 1984 when Congressional Hearings learned that the CIA had been secretly mining Nicaraguan harbours. When the information was released to the press, the Sandinistas denounced American terrorism and complained to the International Court of Justice in The Hague.[27] Meanwhile, a majority of the UN Security Council voted in favour of a resolution condemning American acts of military aggression. In October 1984 in the US Congress a second Boland Amendment was passed to prevent the intelligence agencies of the federal government from supporting the Contras. The passage of a second Amendment indicated the extent of congressional opposition to Reagan's Central American policy. The critics, however, were considerably disarmed, while supporters were greatly encouraged by Reagan's landslide victory over his Democratic opponent, Walter Mondale, in the 1984 presidential election. Congress subsequently proved amenable to passing special appropriations to aid the Contras with the proviso that the money be spent only on 'humanitarian' and 'non-lethal' activities. The Reagan Administration, however, was determined to maintain the Contras as a credible fighting force and, in order to circumvent the restrictions of the Boland Amendment, it resorted to covert methods. This resulted in the Iran-Contra Affair in which it was learned in November 1986 that, in violation of federal law, the national security council aide Lieutenant Colonel Oliver North had secretly directed the financial proceeds of arms sales to Iran to be used to provide weapons for the Contras from 1984 to 1986.

Although Reagan ultimately served out his full term of office, the Iran-Contra Affair raised the possibility of his resignation or impeachment. Moreover, the scandal brought Reagan and his Central American policy into serious disrepute and provided an opportunity for a renewal of Latin American diplomatic mediation to resolve the crisis. In response to the initiative of Costa Rican President Oscar Arias Sánchez, the presidents of the Central American nations, including Nicaragua, met in San José, Costa Rica, in August 1987 and signed the Esquipulas II Accord or Arias Peace Plan.[28] The Accord called on governments in the region to negotiate directly with guerrilla movements to end all fighting. Amnesties would be granted and, in what was a significant addition to the Contadora proposals, free elections would be organized as a first step to political and economic reform. Although the Reagan Administration reluctantly accepted the Accord, it still sought to persuade the US Congress to continue funding the Contras. But Congress favoured the Esquipulas Accord and would only vote money to the Contras on condition that it was used specifically for 'humanitarian' purposes such as the provision of food and medical supplies. Deprived of American material support, the Contras were compelled to agree to a ceasefire in 1988. In return, the Sandinista government offered a general amnesty and affirmed its support for the Esquipulas Accord. President Arias was awarded the Nobel Peace Prize for his contribution to the peace settlement. The Arias Peace Plan was also notably the first major Latin American peace initiative to be accepted by the United States since the ABC mediation in Wilson's dispute with Mexico in 1914.

In January 1989 as Reagan left office after serving two presidential terms, it seemed that the Sandinistas had finally triumphed. Elections took place in Nicaragua ahead of schedule in February 1990. The Sandinistas were confident of victory but, as the party of government, they found themselves blamed for the prevailing economic recession, hyperinflation and the severe decline in the standard of living of workers and peasants. Consequently, they unexpectedly lost the election to a new anti-Sandinista political coalition known as the National Opposition Union (UNO) whose electoral campaign received financial aid from American sources. In the presidential election, the UNO candidate was Violeta Barrios de Chamorro, whose husband had led the opposition to Somoza and had been assassinated in 1978. She won 54.7 per cent of the popular vote to Daniel Ortega's 40.8 per cent. The new president immediately turned to the United States and requested economic aid. President George Bush, Snr, complied by releasing emergency funds and lifting the trade embargo. At the same time arrangements were made for the demobilization, under UN supervision, of the remaining Contra forces. Under the Esquipulas Accord a negotiated ending to the war in El Salvador was also achieved in January 1992.

These events, however, did not attract very much public notice in the United States where the end of the Cold War with the Soviet Union meant that the region suddenly lost the strategic and geopolitical significance that it had been given by American officials during the 1980s.

South Atlantic War

The East–West fixation of the Reagan Administration so evident in the Central American Crisis was also demonstrated in its response to events occurring much further away in the South Atlantic. In April 1982 Argentina launched an unexpected military invasion of the Falkland Islands in the South Atlantic and seized possession of territory that had been under the colonial control of Great Britain since 1833. Great Britain sent a military task force of more than 100 ships to retake the islands, the first armed intervention by a European power in the hemisphere since the Venezuela incident of 1902. The outbreak of the South Atlantic War came as a surprise to the Reagan Administration and posed an awkward choice as to which side to favour in the conflict. During Carter's presidency the United States had been particularly critical of the Argentine military government on account of its notorious violation of human rights during the so-called 'dirty war' against its political opponents. However, in accordance with Jeane Kirkpatrick's ideas on authoritarian regimes, the Reagan Administration had sought to cultivate friendly relations with the Argentine military government and especially with General Leopoldo Galtieri who had become president in December 1981. Argentine support for Reagan's anti-Communist crusade extended even to the provision of Argentine military instructors to train the Contras in Honduras. On the other hand, Great Britain was America's closest ally in NATO and the British prime minister, Margaret Thatcher, had many admirers in the Reagan Administration on account of her remarkable personality and forthright anti-Communist views.

Although it voted in favour of the British-sponsored UN Security Council Resolution 502 condemning Argentine aggression and calling for Argentine withdrawal from the islands, the United States initially adopted an even-handed approach and offered mediation to secure a peaceful end to the crisis. 'While my sympathy was with the British', remarked Secretary of State Haig, 'I believed that the most practical expression of that sympathy would be impartial United States mediation in the dispute.'[29] Haig engaged in frantic and highly visible shuttle diplomacy between Washington, London and Buenos Aires, but his claim to be even-handed could not disguise the fact that the Administration pursued a policy that sympathized with Great Britain by being openly critical of Argentine aggression. This was made apparent when the United States imposed economic sanctions on Argentina. The British task force was also secretly supplied with American military equipment and valuable intelligence information on the location of enemy forces. The Argentine invasion force was defeated in June and Great Britain recaptured the islands.

The South Atlantic War illustrated the predisposition of the United States during the Cold War to look at events in an East–West perspective and to attach much greater importance to its European allies than its Latin American neighbours. Drawing a direct analogy with the Second World War and the Cold War, Haig considered that the South Atlantic War 'was caused by the original miscalculation on the part of the Argentinian military junta that a Western democracy was too soft, too decadent, to defend itself'. In his opinion 'the West was given a great victory by Great Britain'.[30] While Latin American governments were opposed in principle to Argentina's use of force to resolve a territorial dispute, they were alarmed by America's evident pleasure at the British military triumph and support for what was essentially a reassertion of British colonialism. They were also disturbed at the ineffectiveness of the inter-American system in dealing with a regional dispute involving armed conflict with an external power. Blame was placed on the uncooperative attitude of the United States and especially its abstention in votes taken by the OAS urging a cessation of hostilities and expressing criticism of Great Britain for its use of excessive military force. By stating that Security Council Resolution 520 calling for Argentine withdrawal should be implemented, the United States demonstrated an unaccustomed preference for action by the UN rather than the OAS.

Grenada

In 1983 the small Caribbean island of Grenada briefly became a central issue in the Cold War. A former British colony, Grenada had gained its independence in 1974. Its political system, however, was transformed in 1979 when the pro-Marxist New Jewel Movement led by Maurice Bishop seized power, replaced the army and police forces with the 'People's Revolutionary Army' and pursued a foreign policy that was openly critical of the United States and stressed the cultivation of close links with Cuba and the Soviet Union. 'No country has the right to tell us what to do or how to run our country or who to be friendly with', defiantly declared Bishop and he added, 'we are not in anybody's backyard, and we are definitely not for sale.'[31] While the Carter Administration chose to avoid a confrontation with the new government, Ronald Reagan considered Grenada to be a Cuban satellite and broke off diplomatic relations. In 1983 civil disorder erupted as a result of an internal coup in which Bishop was murdered. On 21 October, fearing the spread of unrest to their islands, six neighbouring Caribbean governments representing the Organization of Eastern Caribbean States (OECS) requested American armed intervention to restore peace in Grenada.

The request from the OECS was also given more urgency by reports that the disorder threatened the safety of resident American foreign nationals, most of whom were medical students studying at the St George's medical school. The memory of the recent humiliating hostage crisis in Tehran, Iran, when Americans had been held captive for 444 days, made this a possibility that was taken very seriously. 'We had to respond positively', argued Secretary of State Shultz, because 'Americans were in serious danger of being killed or taken hostage.'[32] In addition, there was the knowledge that Cuban engineers were currently constructing a new airport runway which, it was suspected, would be used by the Soviets as a strategic airbase for military operations in the region. The value of projecting American power and credibility worldwide also became a significant consideration when news reached Washington on 23 October of a suicide bomb attack on the US embassy compound in Lebanon killing more than 200 American marines. Two days later 1,900 American troops invaded Grenada in 'Operation Urgent Fury'. American control of the island was enforced after three days of fighting. A government acceptable to the United States was installed in office. One of its first actions was to terminate the foreign policy of aligning with the Soviet Union and Cuba.

Operation Urgent Fury was the first instance of direct American military intervention in Latin America since the Dominican Republic in 1965. The action in 1983 was just as controversial. The UN Security Council voted 11 to 1 to condemn the invasion and called for the withdrawal of all foreign troops from the island. The United States, however, used its veto to defeat the resolution. Latin American nations were displeased that the OAS had been deliberately bypassed. Like Johnson in 1965, Reagan argued that armed intervention was necessary to defeat a Communist design to establish a military base in the Caribbean in order to undermine democracy throughout the Western Hemisphere. The Reagan Administration also contended that the operation was not an 'invasion' but a 'rescue mission' intended to forestall a potential hostage crisis. Nor was it unilateral armed intervention because it was carried out in response to a request from the OECS, whose members had also agreed to contribute troops to the peacekeeping forces. Critics contended that the request from the OECS came after the decision to send troops had already been taken. They described the intervention as a blatant example of the 'Big Stick' that was not only illegal but unnecessary. It was also argued that the improvements to the runway were meant to aid the local tourist industry and had no military purpose. Moreover, the safety of the American students on the island was placed more at risk by the aggressive actions of the invading forces.

The exact reason for the intervention remained uncertain, but criticism in the United States was effectively disarmed by the fact that it was executed rapidly and successfully with relatively few casualties. Moreover, the intervention in Grenada showed Reagan's determination to follow the advice of the Santa Fe Report and reassert American pre-eminence in the hemisphere by acting decisively in local conflicts and removing Marxist influence by military force if necessary. In effect, a salutary warning was being delivered to the Sandinistas in Nicaragua and the FMLN in El Salvador. 'There were many signals sent by the Grenada operation', noted Secretary of State George Shultz, and he added: 'In many different parts of the world, people began to get the message: Ronald Reagan is capable of action beyond rhetoric.'[33]

Debt Crisis

Preoccupation with the Central American crisis meant that the Reagan Administration neglected the growing problem of external debt that was adversely affecting most of Latin America. During the 1970s there had been an unusual surplus in international capital liquidity resulting from the recycling of the 'petrodollars' that mainly arose from the new-found wealth of the oil-exporting nations of the Middle East. Like the heady days of the 1820s when Latin America was first opened up to foreign investors, it had never seemed so easy to borrow money. Instead of having to enter into lengthy negotiations with governments and international lending agencies, Latin American countries were able to contract large external loans at relatively low interest rates from private commercial banks. The loans helped to pay for the rising cost of oil imports, boost productivity, and fund ambitious programmes of economic development. The result was a substantial increase in the total external debt of Latin America from $27 billion in 1970 to $340 billion in 1984. The servicing of the debt became extremely difficult at the beginning of the 1980s as a result of a sudden world economic recession that brought a big rise in international interest rates combined with a sharp fall in the income earned from exports, especially commodities and agricultural products. In 1984 the cost for Latin America of servicing the external debt was estimated to be nearly 50 per cent of the annual income derived from exports. Ironically, for its own domestic political reasons the Reagan Administration contributed to this adverse development by adopting a 'strong dollar' policy that pushed up the international exchange value of the US dollar and directly influenced the rise in world interest rates.

The 'Debt Crisis' came to the world's attention in August 1982 when Mexico revealed that it was defaulting on repayments of the interest on its external debt that currently amounted to $80 billion. The Mexican action was unexpected and posed a threat to the stability of some leading American commercial banks that were known to be heavily involved in the overseas loans business. There was also concern that the default might provoke a severe financial crisis leading to civil unrest in Mexico that would spread to the region along the border with the United States. Consequently, the Reagan Administration reacted quickly and made available emergency loans to Mexico and later assisted in negotiations with other governments and international financial institutions led by the International Monetary Fund (IMF) to arrange a satisfactory rescheduling of Mexico's debt repayments.

The debt problem, however, was not just confined to Mexico; it extended beyond Latin America to most of the countries in the Third World. Nevertheless, so great was the amount of debt owed by Latin American countries that the crisis was often misleadingly referred to as the 'Latin American Debt Crisis'. Admittedly, the biggest single debtor nation was Brazil, whose massive external debt in 1982 was estimated in excess of $100 billion. In November 1982 Brazil followed Mexico's example and announced a suspension of payments to foreign creditors. The Reagan Administration did not want to become involved in another short-term emergency rescue package as had been the case with Mexico. Despite the fact that US private banks, led by Citicorp, Chase Manhattan and Bank of America, had willingly lent much of the money in the first place, a belief persisted in Washington that the Latin American governments had been reckless and profligate in their borrowing and that they must face up to the consequences. Furthermore, American officials stressed that the crisis was an economic and not a political issue and that each debtor nation should negotiate directly with the IMF.

In the ensuing negotiations the IMF agreed to provide short-term finance so that debt payments could be rescheduled, but insisted in return that governments undertook to carry out policies of economic 'adjustment'. In practice, this invariably required tight fiscal discipline in the form of reducing budget deficits, cutting back on money supply, maintaining high domestic interest rates in real terms, privatizing state enterprises and earning more foreign exchange income by stimulating exports while at the same time restricting imports. The implementation of these austerity measures enabled debt servicing to be maintained, but insufficient amounts of new borrowing resulted in an annual net outflow of capital to creditor countries that was estimated at 4 to 5 per cent of the region's gross national product. In effect, the arrangements with the IMF severely stunted economic growth and imposed declining standards of living on the region to such an extent that conditions were likened to the Great Depression of the 1930s. In terms of overall Latin American economic development, the 1980s became known as 'the lost decade'. During the same period, however, the international banks, mostly American and British, rebuilt their capital reserves, made provisions for financial losses and sharply reduced the scale of their business with Latin America in preference to other areas of the world.

In international crises Latin America historically looked to the United States for support and leadership. As part of its strategy to isolate the Sandinistas in Nicaragua, the Reagan Administration was prepared to give financial aid and preferential commercial terms to the countries of Central America and the Caribbean in the form of the Caribbean Basin Initiative. But there was no sign of a similar aid programme for the rest of Latin America. Instead, the Latin American governments felt compelled to resort to regional cooperation and held conferences at Quito, Ecuador, in January 1984 and at Cartagena, Colombia, in June 1984 to which the United States was not invited. Colombian President Belisario Betancur Cuartas conveyed the prevailing mood of anxiety at the opening of the Cartagena Conference: 'Latin America's foreign debt service has become so burdensome that it threatens the very stability of the international monetary system and the survival of the democratic process in various countries.'[34] The seven governments attending the meeting at Cartagena included Argentina, Brazil, Colombia, Ecuador, Mexico, Peru and Venezuela. They owed around $286 billion of the region's estimated $340 billion foreign debt.

As usual, however, Latin American unity was not forthcoming. Agreement on collective action could not be easily achieved because each nation was reluctant to divulge full information on its economic circumstances to others. It was also widely believed that better and, perhaps preferential terms could be gained in separate bilateral negotiations with the IMF. A radical tone, however, was adopted in July 1985 when President Alan García Pérez of Peru declared publicly that his country's foreign debt repayments would in future be limited to no more than 10 per cent of its earnings from annual exports. García later stated in a keynote speech before the General Assembly of the UN in September 1985 that the foreign debt had become so huge that it could never be paid off because 'the effort to service it on time will keep our democracies trapped in misery and violence'. 'Thus', he argued, 'we are faced with a dramatic choice: it is either debt or democracy.'[35] A more strident voice calling for drastic action came from Fidel Castro, who organized an international conference on the Debt Crisis in Havana in July 1985 in which he urged debtor nations to form a cartel and suspend all debt repayments. 'We are caught up in the Third World War, an economic war', declared Castro, and he added: 'It is an undeclared war, over the extortionate interest rates of debt.'[36]

The possibility of collective action by the debtor nations presented a political challenge that prompted a constructive response from the Reagan Administration. At the annual meeting of the IMF in South Korea in October 1985 the American delegation unveiled the Baker Plan, named after Reagan's secretary of the treasury, James A. Baker. With the aim of stimulating economic growth, the Plan proposed that the World Bank make available $20 billion in new loans over a period of three years to the developing countries, most of whom were located in Latin America. But austerity policies were still expected in return. The financial arrangements of the Baker Plan helped to alleviate the current shortage of loans, but were merely a short-term emergency solution. The Debt Crisis continued and was illuminated once again in 1987 when Brazil declared a unilateral moratorium on its repayments.

The election of George Bush, Snr, in 1988 brought a new president to the White House who was more willing than his predecessor to endorse fresh initiatives designed to deal with the issues of hemispheric debt relief and trade. This was exemplified by the Brady Plan, named after Bush's secretary of the treasury, Nicholas Brady, which was proposed in 1990 and was intended primarily to help Mexico. In contrast to the Baker Plan, the new measure emphasized debt reduction by the elimination of arrears and, in effect, represented a tacit acknowledgment that the debt would never be repaid in full. The Brady Plan was implemented at a time when revival in the world economy was already helping to diminish the severity of the austerity measures imposed by the Debt Crisis. As international trade and investment recovered during the second half of the decade of the 1980s, interest rates fell and more private capital became available for loans. The export earnings of the Latin American countries steadily increased so that the inflows of capital into the region actually exceeded outflows in 1991. Though Latin America and the majority of its people remained relatively poor in comparison to the First World, the revival of the international banking system, in which US banks predominated, meant that the Debt Crisis had essentially come to an end.

North American Free Trade Agreement

As part of their arrangements with the IMF, the Latin American countries had sought to boost exports, especially of staple goods, in order to increase their earnings of foreign exchange. This resulted in a boom in Latin American exports to the United States so that Latin American trade with that country reversed the downward trend of the 1970s and steadily increased during the 1980s. Consequently, support noticeably grew for hemispheric economic integration. Despite a long history of awkward relations, Mexico was particularly keen to expand its economic contacts with the United States because that country was its single most important trading partner and supplier of capital investment and the transfer of technology. In 1990 Mexican President Carlos Salinas de Gortari announced his aim of negotiating a free trade agreement with the United States on the lines of an arrangement that the latter had signed with Canada in the previous year. The Bush Administration (1989–93) welcomed the Mexican president's proposal as a means of supplementing the talks on reducing barriers to international trade that were being discussed under the Uruguay Round of the General Agreement on Trade and Tariffs (GATT).

Indeed, Bush recognized the political value of the United States developing closer economic relations and especially the lifting of trade barriers with all the countries of the hemisphere. The 'Enterprise for the Americas

Initiative' (EAI) was launched in June 1990 in which Bush envisaged a free trade area covering all of the Americas and extending from Alaska to Tierra del Fuego. The EAI was likened to the Alliance For Progress and was well received in Latin America as an expression of Bush's intention to focus on hemispheric economic issues. But the idea of commercial union once again provoked contentious political debate within the United States. Criticism was most concentrated on the proposed extension of the existing free trade agreement with Canada to include Mexico in what would become the North American Free Trade Agreement (NAFTA). 'NAFTA', considered Secretary of State James A. Baker, 'would be a boon to the American economy, create hundreds of thousands of jobs, and generate tens of billions in additional output.'[37] Advocates of the scheme also stressed the importance of promoting economic stability and development in Mexico, a nation of vital strategic importance to the United States. In addition, they highlighted the significance of creating a major trading bloc in which internal tariff and investment barriers would be eliminated and which would be able to compete with the global economic challenge of Japan and the European Union. On the other hand, labour unions argued that free-trade agreements would result in the inevitable relocation of American jobs and factories to Mexico where employers would be attracted by lower wages and costs. House Majority Whip David Bonior of Missouri warned: 'What we are exporting to Mexico is our factories – and our jobs. Rather than reversing this trend, NAFTA rolls out the red carpet for multinationals who want to move to Mexico. That's why NAFTA must be defeated.'[38] Both the Bush and Clinton administrations declared that the American economy would benefit greatly from NAFTA and strongly supported the measure. The NAFTA treaty was signed in October 1992 and was eventually ratified by the US Congress in November 1993.

Latin American governments regarded NAFTA as the first step towards what would become a hemispheric free trade area to be known as the 'Free Trade Area of the Americas' (FTAA). After the bitter political controversy generated in the US Congress over NAFTA, however, the new American president, Bill Clinton, would not publicly endorse the proposal to admit the next applicant, Chile. Clinton duly attended the meeting of all hemispheric leaders, excepting Fidel Castro, at the Miami Summit of the Americas in December 1994, but he showed equal if not more personal interest in hosting the Asia-Pacific Economic Cooperation Forum where it was pointed out that American trade with Asia was currently double that with Latin America. While the United States sought increasing economic cooperation with Latin America, it still refused to give priority to the region. By default, Latin Americans attempted to protect themselves from the increasing globalization of the world economy by consolidating their own sub-regional agreements such as the Andean Pact, the Central American Common Market and, most notably, in 1991 the customs union known as Mercosur (or

Mercosul) consisting of Brazil, Argentina, Paraguay and Uruguay. This organization stimulated the development of internal markets and gave a stronger bargaining position in negotiations with the large trading blocs of the world such as the European Union and NAFTA.

After the Cold War

During the 1970s and for much of the 1980s American pre-eminence in the Western Hemisphere appeared to be in relative decline. One illustration was the confidence that the Latin American countries demonstrated in seeking to act independently of the United States. This was exemplified by the diplomatic actions of General Torrijos in using the UN as a means of securing a revision of the Canal Treaty. The Contadora Group was similarly exasperated by American policy and independently sought to find a resolution of the Central American Crisis. On the other hand, the prestige and power of the United States were visibly increased by the electoral defeat of the Sandinistas in 1990 and especially by the events in Europe bringing a dramatic end to the Cold War leading to the disintegration of the Soviet Union in 1991. A historical watershed occurred. Not only did Soviet political, military and economic involvement in the region markedly decline, but Western European countries also turned their attention away from Latin America and took a greater interest in economic developments and opportunities in the ex-Communist states of Eastern Europe.

The most prominent feature of the Soviet decision to disengage from Latin America was the severing of the close relationship with Fidel Castro that had lasted for three decades. For Cuba this meant the withdrawal of generous financial subsidies estimated at $5 billion per year. Faced with the loss of its Soviet patron and experiencing serious economic hardship, Cuba decided to abandon its formerly high-profile support for pro-Marxist liberation movements seeking revolution in Central America and Africa. A number of Latin American leaders saw an opportunity for a constructive response and proposed to readmit Cuba to the OAS. The US government, however, remained implacably hostile and viewed the end of the Cuban–Soviet alliance not as an opening for constructive negotiations to normalize relations but as an opportunity to apply further political and economic pressure on Cuba and bring about a change of regime. President Bush compared Castro to Stalin and stated that 'there cannot be and will not be a normal dialogue with Cuba as long as this dictatorship is in power'.[39] Anti-Castro organizations led by the Cuban American National Foundation (CANF) lobbied the US Congress and were influential in securing the passage of the Torricelli Act in 1992 and the Helms-Burton Act in 1996, both of which sought to tighten the existing economic embargo. Despite international criticism of their restrictive policy and, in contradiction of their support for the principle of lifting trade barriers, both the Bush and Clinton administrations gave more weight to domestic political factors and remained committed to maintaining a punitive policy towards Cuba. 'I don't think that there's any prospect of lifting those [economic] sanctions as long as Fidel Castro is there', summed up Vice-President Richard Cheney in 2001.[40]

While Cuba still remained an important issue of domestic political debate, the collapse of International Communism and the end of the East–West conflict meant that Central America notably lost its significance in American national security policy. During the 1990s the focus of American diplomatic activity was firmly fixed on Europe, the Middle East and Asia. Programmes of economic and military aid for Latin America were correspondingly reduced or even withdrawn. New issues emerged, however, that pointed to the desirability of a closer and cooperative relationship between the United States and the countries of Latin America. The development of hemispheric trade was considered particularly valuable not only for American business but also as a means of promoting Latin American economic growth and political stability to help alleviate the difficulties affecting the United States that were caused by the increase in narcotics trafficking and illegal immigration.

Narcotics control

During the second half of the twentieth century drug (narcotics) dependence and drug-related crime and violence became an increasingly salient feature of American society. In fact, the United States was the world's biggest importer of illegal narcotics such as cocaine, marijuana and heroin. In response the US government developed a policy of narcotics control which sought to prevent drugs from reaching the country by interdiction in transit, especially along the Mexican border with the United States, and also by destroying and eradicating the sources of supply in the producing countries.[41] The main suppliers were located in Turkey and South-east Asia, but Latin America was also implicated because the coca leaf had long been a traditional cash crop in Bolivia and Peru, while countries such as Mexico and Colombia provided staging posts for the re-export of coca leaves in the form of cocaine to the United States. The task of interdicting narcotics lay primarily with the Drug Enforcement Agency (DEA), which had been established within the Department of Justice in 1972.

The production and trafficking in narcotics greatly expanded in Latin America during the 1980s as a result of growing demand in the United States and also the pressure of the Debt Crisis for ways of earning more foreign exchange. Narcotics became organized like big business, with an enormous financial turnover. Colombia was one of the Latin American countries that was most affected. In 2000 it was estimated that Colombia was producing 70 per cent of the world's coca and that 300,000 people were involved in its cultivation. A notable development was the rise of organized criminal drug cartels, the most notorious of which were located in Cali and Medellín. To protect their activities, cartels used bribery, corruption and intimidation, including even the assassination of prominent politicians. The cartels also sought political representation and, notably, contributed funds to the successful presidential campaign of Ernesto Samper in Colombia in 1994. In some cases, they even established links with left-wing political movements especially in Colombia and Peru. According to Congressman Charles B. Rangel of New York, 'sophisticated, well-financed narco-trafficking organizations' with their 'combinations of cocaine, money, and violence are attempting to suppress the development of democracy in America'.[42]

The strategy of eradicating the production of narcotics at its Latin American sources required close cooperation between the United States and the local governments. Since its inception in 1972 the DEA provided training and equipment, including weapons, ships, helicopters and radar for Latin American police forces and para-military activities. In addition, DEA agents were sent to Latin America to act as advisers. From the 1960s onwards financial aid programmes were also established to educate and provide incentives for local farmers and peasants to switch production from narcotics to foodstuffs and staple goods. During the 1980s and 1990s the Reagan, Bush and Clinton administrations continued and expanded these policies but, like their predecessors, found that success was elusive so long as the demand for narcotics in the United States constantly remained high and offered opportunities to make lucrative financial profits.

In fact, the trafficking of narcotics from Latin America to the United States arguably increased rather than decreased. In most of Latin America the production and use of narcotics had long been tolerated and was not seen as a major social problem. Moreover, if drugs were destroyed in one particular place, production simply moved elsewhere. The policies of narcotics control also highlighted many of the historical problems of inter-American relations, especially the preference of the United States for unilateral rather than multilateral action. Consequently, DEA agents were often regarded as foreigners whose forceful and often insensitive behaviour, especially the destruction of crops and disruption of peasant communities, did much to upset rather than cultivate a cooperative working relationship with local officials and people. Latin American governments were also irritated by American insistence on the extradition to the United States of Latin American nationals for alleged criminal activities. The practice introduced in 1986 of annually 'certifying' governments for their compliance with American policies of narcotics control was also controversial. In April 1988 the US Senate criticized the Mexican government for its failure to control narcotics trafficking. The Mexican foreign ministry indignantly replied: 'No one can take upon themselves the right to certify the conduct of other societies or governments.'[43]

In one individual case, the personal involvement in narcotics trafficking of a leading Latin American political figure provided a justification for American military intervention. In 1983 Manuel Antonio Noriega had taken command of the Panamanian National Guard, which he renamed the Panamanian Defence Force, and from this position of military power ruled Panama as a virtual dictator. Noriega aided the Reagan Administration in its covert operations against the Sandinistas, but at the same time he allowed Panama to become a leading trans-shipment point for drugs destined for the United States and also a centre for money laundering the vast profits made from the trade in narcotics. In 1988 the US Department of Justice named Noriega in indictments for narcotics trafficking. Noriega defiantly organized large rallies demonstrating that he could command a high degree of public support in Panama. In a mission to apprehend Noriega and bring him before an American court, President George Bush, Snr, ordered 25,000 American troops to enter Panama on 20 December 1989. 'Operation Just Cause' was the largest deployment of American troops in combat since the Vietnam War. Bush explained that its purpose was 'to safeguard the lives of Americans, to defend democracy in Panama, to combat drug trafficking and to protect the integrity of the Panama Canal Treaties'.[44] Noriega sought political asylum but eventually surrendered five days after the beginning of the invasion. He was arrested, extradited to Miami and put on trial in the United States and convicted in 1992.

Democracy and human rights

The decision to intervene in Panama in 1989 aroused widespread criticism in Latin America. In the OAS it was described as an act of aggression and was condemned by a vote of 20 to 1. To register the extent of its disapproval the Peruvian government broke off diplomatic relations with the United States. Resolutions were passed in the UN Security Council and the General Assembly condemning the action as a violation of international law. In its defence, the Bush Administration maintained that Noriega had to be brought to trial on account of accusations that he was personally involved in narcotics trafficking. Bush also argued that the operation had been motivated by a desire to protect democracy. Noriega's rule was known to be brutal and oppressive. But American criticism had been conveniently muted so long as Noriega was a valued ally in the struggle to defeat the Sandinistas. After Noriega was indicted for narcotics trafficking in 1988, the Reagan Administration finally attempted to replace him by imposing economic sanctions and giving financial backing to the political opposition. When elections were held in April 1989 and his political opponent, Guillermo Endara, appeared on the point of winning the presidency, Noriega simply annulled the elections. Consequently, the Bush Administration explained that the forced removal of Noriega was necessary to enable a democratically elected civilian president to take office. 'The United States', remarked Secretary of state Baker, 'was simply enforcing the will of the Panamanians by restoring the legitimately elected government to authority.'[45]

A similar problem of dealing with unconstitutional action confronted President Bill Clinton in Haiti. From 1957 to 1986 Haiti had been ruthlessly dominated and plundered first by François Duvalier and then by his son, Jean-Claude Duvalier. A Roman Catholic priest, Jean-Bertrand Aristide, was elected president in 1990 with a majority of the popular vote in an election that was acknowledged as fairly conducted. Aristide, however, was overthrown in a military coup organized by General Raoul Cédras in September 1991 and sought political exile in the United States. Under diplomatic pressure from the United States and economic sanctions issued by the OAS and the UN, General Cédras agreed to Aristide's return to serve out his original term of office, but then reneged on the arrangement. The continuation of economic sanctions wreaked devastation on the Haitian economy and stimulated the flight to the United States of thousands of Haitians in boats, a number of which were sunk at sea with considerable loss of life. American military intervention occurred in Haiti in October 1994. The mission was called 'Operation Uphold Democracy' to reflect its proclaimed aim of restoring President Aristide to office. Despite the emphasis on political idealism, it was evident that the Clinton Administration had an ulterior motive in installing a democratic government in Haiti. Political order and economic stability were important but not just to promote democracy. They were also regarded as a necessary means of halting the flow of illegal migrants to the United States.

Migration

The migration of Haitians was part of a growing political and administrative problem for the US government caused by the relentless rise in the number of illegal ('undocumented') migrants during the last quarter of the twentieth century. The migration of Latin Americans to the United States, largely in search of economic opportunity and betterment, had a long history and was traditionally linked to the movement of Mexicans back and forwards across the US–Mexican border in response to the rise and fall of the American business cycle. For example, immigration was sharply reduced during the Great Depression of the 1930s, but rose rapidly when the American economy recovered at the beginning of the Second World War. American governments sought to manage this movement by encouraging the recruitment of temporary contract labour in the 1942 Bracero Accord. During the operation of the Accord from 1942 to 1964, more than 4 million *braceros* (labourers) officially entered the United States. For the same period, however, it was estimated that a similar number of Mexicans crossed the border as undocumented workers. After 1964 the Bracero

Accord was replaced by granting visas to legal immigrants. A series of legislative measures was passed to prohibit the employment of undocumented immigrants and to restrict entry to the United States by guarding and policing the American side of the border. Programmes of economic aid were also devised, one of which developed into the NAFTA agreement, to help reduce the number of migrant workers by creating alternative employment opportunities in Mexico.

From the 1970s onwards the largest source of legal and illegal immigration into the United States from Latin America was not from Mexico but from the countries of Central America and the Caribbean Islands. It was estimated that more than 80 per cent of immigrants from Latin America originated from this region. Migration was still motivated mainly by population pressure and economic factors but the impact of political repression and violence associated with the Central American Crisis was also increasingly influential. This resulted in greater numbers of migrants originating from El Salvador, Guatemala and Nicaragua. By the 1990s it was estimated that one-sixth of the population of El Salvador had settled in the United States.

The historic need for workers in the American economy meant that immigrants were readily accepted and absorbed within American society. The numbers were substantial. During the 1980s the United States received around 800,000 legal immigrants every year from all over the world. Demands for restriction on immigration, however, emerged during periods of economic recession when immigrants were seen as pushing down wages and taking jobs from native workers and causing an intolerable financial burden on local welfare services. At times, the number of aliens entering the country from Latin America was perceived by the public as overwhelming, though official estimates for the decade of the 1990s stated that only around 200,000 to 400,000 entered annually and that the total population of illegal aliens in the United States was between 2 and 4 million. Nevertheless, the attempted migration to South Florida of more than 100,000 Cubans and 25,000 Haitians in hundreds of makeshift rafts and small boats became an issue of significant political controversy in the 1980 presidential election between Jimmy Carter and Ronald Reagan. The debate between the candidates concentrated not on the plight of the boat people but on Carter's alleged weakness and ineptitude in dealing with the governments of Cuba and Haiti.

The evident concern of the American public to restrict illegal immigration resulted in the passage in 1986 of the Immigration Reform and Control Act (IRCA). In addition, there was the difficult political problem caused by granting automatic 'political refugee' status to immigrants from Cuba and Nicaragua on the grounds that they were fleeing from Communist states. While this led to Nicaraguan migrants being given preferential treatment and being allowed to remain in the United States, many Salvadorans were classified as 'economic migrants' to be detained and deported. The US navy instituted a policy of naval blockade to prevent Haitian 'boat people' from even reaching the United States so that the question of their immigrant status did not arise. Haitian boats were therefore intercepted on the high seas, passengers were taken for detention in the US naval base in Guantánamo and later repatriated to Haiti.

Immigration was not only an awkward political and administrative problem for American governments but its national composition also posed significant demographic consequences for the United States. Between 1970 and 1980 statistics from the US Census Bureau revealed that the population of Latin American ('Hispanic' or 'Latino') origin in the United States increased by around 60 per cent. From 1980 to 1990 the number rose by more than 50 per cent to a total of over 22 million people. Hispanics made up around 6 per cent of the US population in 1990 and 9 per cent in 1990. If the same trend of rising population continues, this percentage is estimated to grow to nearly 25 per cent in 2050. In some localities in the United States, especially the South-east and South-west, the Hispanic proportion of the population was estimated to have already reached 50 per cent by the late 1990s and will form a majority early in the twenty-first century. These areas not only have large numbers of Spanish speakers but they also possess a growing Spanish-language media exemplified in radio, television, newspapers and books. The Hispanic influence is also highly visible in social and cultural institutions such as schools, small businesses and religious organizations. For the last two centuries the large majority of the people inhabiting the United States and dominating the political system have been white Anglo-Saxons. They have been distant from their neighbours in Latin America and have pursued foreign policy goals that have often been different and divergent. But the contrast between 'Ariel' and 'Caliban' that José Enrique Rodó pointed out in 1900 is no longer valid in 2000. The distant relationship has steadily been eroded. Indeed, the intermingling of populations to include significant numbers of Hispanics, who have and will continue to become US citizens with full political rights, has been a recent and fascinating historical development. The closer relationship that has developed and is still evolving will have significant implications for the future Latin American diplomacy of the United States.

NOTES

1 INDEPENDENCE (1776–1830)

1 Other important colonial empires in the New World were established by the French and Dutch.

2 This study will use collective terms such as the 'United States', 'Latin America', 'American', 'Latin American' and 'Spanish-American'. Even though they are broad generalizations and contain ambiguities and deficiencies, they are convenient to use and will be familiar terms for English-language readers to understand.

3 One study found only a single descriptive work on the British colonies that was written and published in the Spanish language prior to 1776. See José de Onís, *The United States as seen by Spanish American writers* (New York: Gordian Press, 1975), p. 13.

4 For an analysis of the economic relationship see Peggy K. Liss, *Atlantic empires: the network of trade and revolution, 1713–1826* (Baltimore, MD: Johns Hopkins University Press, 1983).

5 The Declaration of Independence, 4 July 1776, quoted in Henry Steele Commager (ed.), *Documents of American history* (2 vols) (New York: Crofts, 1944), I, p. 100.

6 Floridablanca to Aranda, 13 January 1778, quoted in Thomas E. Chávez, *Spain and the independence of the United States: an intrinsic gift* (Albuquerque, NM: University of New Mexico Press, 2002), p. 76.

7 Quoted in Simon Schama, *Citizens* (New York: Knopf, 1989), p. 49.

8 Washington's Farewell Address, 17 September 1796, quoted in Commager, *Documents*, I, p. 174.

9 Carlos Martínez de Irujo to Pedro Cevallos, 18 November 1801, quoted in Sylvia L. Hilton, 'Movilidad y expansión en la construcción política de los Estados Unidos: "essos errantes colonos" en las frontreras españolas del Misisipí (1776–1803)', *Revista complutense de historia de américa*, 28 (2002), p. 69.

10 Quoted in Arthur P. Whitaker, *The United States and the independence of Latin America, 1800–1830* (Baltimore, MD: Johns Hopkins Press, 1941), p. 43. Whitaker's work is rather dated, but it is still the most informative study on this topic. For a general discussion that includes the European powers see D. A. G. Waddell, 'International politics and Latin American independence', in Leslie Bethell (ed.), *The independence of Latin America* (Cambridge: Cambridge University Press, 1987), pp. 195–226.

11 Quoted in Whitaker, *US and independence*, p. 82.

12 John Quincy Adams to Richard Anderson, 27 May 1823, in William R. Manning, *Diplomatic correspondence of the United States concerning the independence of the*

Latin-American Nations (3 vols) (New York: Oxford University Press, 1925), I, p. 193.

13 John Quincy Adams to George Campbell, 3 June 1819, in Manning, *Diplomatic correspondence*, I, p. 107.

14 Quoted in Whitaker, *US and independence*, p. 209.

15 No-Transfer Resolution, 15 January 1811, quoted in J. Lloyd Mecham, *A survey of United States–Latin American relations* (Boston, MA: Houghton Mifflin, 1965), p. 27.

16 Robert Smith to Joel R. Poinsett, 28 June 1810, quoted in Manning, *Diplomatic correspondence*, I, pp. 6–7.

17 Aguirre to Pueyrredón, 17 August 1817, quoted in Whitaker, *US and independence*, p. 236.

18 Jefferson to Humboldt, 1813, quoted in Whitaker, *US and independence*, p. 188, n. 30.

19 Speech dated 20 January 1816, quoted in Whitaker, *US and independence*, p. 183.

20 Article in *North American Review*, April 1821, quoted in Whitaker, *US and independence*, p. 336.

21 For an informative discussion of the treaty see Philip C. Brooks, *Diplomacy and the borderlands: The Adams–Onís treaty of 1819* (Berkeley, CA: University of California Press, 1939). An excellent study of Adams is William Earl Weeks, *John Quincy Adams and American global empire* (Lexington, KY: University Press of Kentucky, 1992).

22 Bolívar to Santander, 20 December 1819, quoted in Harold A. Bierck Jr., *Selected writings of Bolívar* (New York: Colonial Press, 1951), p. 213.

23 Miller to Poinsett, 27 April 1819, quoted in Whitaker, *US and independence*, p. 271.

24 Rebello to Carvalho e Melo, 5 June 1824, quoted in Stanley E. Hilton, 'The United States and Brazilian independence' in A. J. R. Russell-Wood (ed.), *From colony to nation* (Baltimore, MD: Johns Hopkins University Press, 1975), p. 125.

25 Ricketts to Canning, 18 February 1826, in Charles K. Webster (ed.), *Britain and the independence of Latin America, 1812–1830. Select documents from the foreign office archives* (2 vols) (London: Oxford University Press, 1938), I, p. 529.

26 Rush to Rodney and Graham, 18 July 1817, in Manning *Diplomatic correspondence*, I, p. 43.

27 Quoted in R. A. Humphreys, *Tradition and revolt in Latin America and other essays* (London: Weidenfeld and Nicolson, 1969), p. 139.

28 Bland to John Quincy Adams, 2 November 1818, in Manning, *Diplomatic correspondence*, I, p. 434.

29 Charles F. Adams (ed.), *Memoirs of John Quincy Adams* (12 vols) (Philadelphia, PA: Lippincott, 1874–7), V, p. 325.

30 See Dexter Perkins, *The Monroe doctrine, 1823–1826* (Cambridge, MA: Harvard University Press, 1927), p. 48.

31 Monroe's message to the House of Representatives, 8 March 1822, in Manning, *Diplomatic correspondence*, I, p. 147.

32 Letter dated 20 June 1823, quoted in Samuel F. Bemis, *The Latin-American policy of the United States: an historical introduction* (New York: Norton, 1967), p. 62.

33 Monroe's Message to the US Congress, 2 December 1823, quoted in Commager, *Documents*, I, p. 236.

34 Imperial Russia also posed a territorial threat by claiming possession of territory extending from Alaska along the Pacific coastline to Bodega Bay, located just north of San Francisco. In addition, British possession of Canada was

affected, so Great Britain joined the United States in successfully resisting the Russian claim.

35 The standard work on the Monroe Doctrine remains Dexter Perkins, *The Monroe doctrine, 1823–1826* (Cambridge MA: Harvard University Press, 1927). On its later evolution see the essays in Donald M. Dozer (ed.), *The Monroe doctrine: its modern significance* (New York: Knopf, 1965).
36 Quoted in Commager, *Documents*, I, p. 236.
37 Perkins, *Monroe Doctrine*, p. 168.
38 Rebello to John Quincy Adams, 28 January 1825, quoted in Manning, *Diplomatic correspondence,* II, p. 808.
39 Rodney to Monroe, 10 February 1824, quoted in Paul B. Goodwin, Jr., 'Initiating United States relations with Argentina', in T. Ray Shurbutt (ed.), *United States–Latin American relations, 1800–1850* (Tuscaloosa, AL: University of Alabama Press, 1991), p. 103.
40 Canning to Granville, 21 November 1825, quoted in Humphreys, *Tradition and revolt*, p. 153.
41 The United States was not alone in being excluded from the initial invitations to the conference. Brazil and Haiti were also not invited. Great Britain, however, was invited to send an observer. A perceptive treatment of the diplomacy of this period can be found in Ron Seckinger, *The Brazilian monarchy and the South American republics, 1822–1831: diplomacy and state building* (Baton Rouge, LA: Louisiana State University Press, 1984).
42 Message of President Adams, 26 December 1825, quoted in Commager, *Documents*, I, p. 245.
43 March 1826, quoted in Whitaker, *US and independence*, p. 579, n. 34.
44 Vaughan to Canning, 16 March 1826, quoted in Webster, *Britain and independence*, II, p. 543.

2 TERRITORIAL EXPANSIONISM (1830–79)

1 On US diplomatic relations with Latin America during the first half of the nineteenth century see John J. Johnson, *A hemisphere apart: the foundations of United States policy toward Latin America* (Baltimore, MD: Johns Hopkins University Press, 1990) and the chapters dealing with individual Latin American countries in T. Ray Shurbutt (ed.), *United States–Latin American relations, 1800–1850: the formative generations* (Tuscaloosa, AL: University of Alabama Press, 1991).
2 Quoted in John Lynch, *The Spanish-American revolutions 1808–1826* (New York: Norton, 1986), p. 294.
3 James C. Pickett to John C. Calhoun, 3 March 1845, quoted in Shurbutt, *US–Latin American relations*, p. 63.
4 Henry Clay to John M. Forbes, 3 January 1828, quoted in Shurbutt, *US–Latin American relations*, p. 106.
5 Buchanan to William Harris, 30 March 1846, quoted in Shurbutt, *US–Latin American relations*, p. 118.
6 Howden to Palmerston, 26 May 1847, National Archives, London, FO (Foreign Office) Correspondence, 6/133.
7 The British also later occupied the Bay Islands off the coast of Honduras and established a protectorate over the Mosquito Indians on the mainland of Central America.
8 8 February 1830, *Hansard, Parliamentary Debates*, new series, 22, p. 223.
9 Charles Francis Adams (ed.), *Memoirs of John Quincy Adams* (12 vols) (Philadelphia, PA: Lippincott, 1874–7), V, p. 325.

10 Quoted in William F. Sater, *Chile and the United States: empires in conflict* (Athens, GA: University of Georgia Press, 1990), p. 17.
11 Adams, *Memoirs*, VI, p. 25.
12 Daniel P. Kidder and James C. Fletcher, *Brazil and Brazilians portrayed in historical and descriptive sketches* (Philadelphia, PA: Childs and Peterson, 1857), p. 195.
13 Letter dated 16 May 1854, quoted in Richard Graham, *Britain and the onset of modernization in Brazil, 1850–1914* (Cambridge: Cambridge University Press, 1968), p. 73.
14 John W. Foster, *Diplomatic memoirs* (2 vols) (New York: Houghton Mifflin, 1909), I, p. 5.
15 Quoted in Lester D. Langley, *The Americas in the age of revolution, 1750–1850* (New Haven, CT: Yale University Press, 1996), p. 226. An excellent study on the emergence of Texas is David J. Weber, *The Mexican frontier, 1821–1846: the American southwest under Mexico* (Albuquerque, NM: University of New Mexico Press, 1982). On diplomatic aspects see David M. Pletcher, *The diplomacy of annexation: Texas, Oregon, and the Mexican War* (Columbia, MO: University of Missouri Press,, 1973). American racist attitudes are examined in Reginald Horsman, *Race and manifest destiny: the origins of American racial anglo-saxonism* (Cambridge MA: Harvard University Press, 1981).
16 Quoted in Pletcher, *Diplomacy of annexation*, p. 74.
17 Quoted in Charles H. Brown, *Agents of manifest destiny: the lives and times of the filibusters* (Chapel Hill, NC: University of North Carolina Press, 1980), p. 16. O'Sullivan first used the term in an article in the *Democratic Review* (July–August 1845). On Manifest Destiny see Frederick Merk, *Manifest destiny and mission: a reinterpretation* (New York: Vintage, 1963). A readable account of the filibusters is Brown, *Agents of manifest destiny.* See also Robert E. May, *Manifest destiny's underworld: filibustering in antebellum America* (Chapel Hill, NC: University of North Carolina Press, 2002).
18 Polk's First Annual Message to Congress, 2 December 1845, quoted in Henry Steele Commager (ed.), *Documents of American history* (2 vols) (New York: Crofts, 1944), I, p. 310.
19 In a Special Message to Congress on 29 April 1848 Polk extended his territorial definition to include Central America when he affirmed that the United States would not accept the transfer of Yucatán to a European power. Yucatán was in a state of civil turmoil known as 'the Caste War' and was seeking to secede from the Mexican Union.
20 Almonte to Calhoun, 6 March 1845, quoted in K. Jack Bauer, *The Mexican War, 1846–1848* (Lincoln, NE: University of Nebraska Press, 1974), p. 16.
21 *New York Sun*, 20 November 1847, quoted in Merk, *Manifest destiny*, p. 122.
22 Quoted in Merk, *Manifest destiny*, p. 120.
23 *National Intelligencer* (Washington DC), 21 October 1847, quoted in Merk, *Manifest destiny*, p. 165. A brief debate took place in 1848 over a similar proposal to annex the Mexican province of Yucatán.
24 'Central American–Caribbean' will be used as a convenient term to refer to the geographical area that broadly approximated to the Viceroyalty of New Spain and includes Mexico, the Central American nations as far as Panama, and the Caribbean island nations.
25 Jefferson to Monroe, 24 October 1823, quoted in Louis A. Pérez, Jr., *Cuba and the United States: ties of singular intimacy* (Athens, GA: University of Georgia Press, 1990), p. 39.
26 Adams to Hugh Nelson, 28 April 1823, US Congress, 32nd Congress, 1st Session, House Doc. no. 121, p. 7.
27 Puerto Rico also remained part of the Spanish empire until 1898.

28 Marcy to Shepard, 15 April 1855, quoted in Lars Schoultz, *Beneath the United States: a history of US policy toward Latin America* (Cambridge MA: Harvard University Press, 1998), p. 55.
29 Clayton to Letcher, 18 September 1849, quoted in E. Taylor Parks, *Colombia and the United States, 1765–1934* (Durham, NC: Duke University Press, 1935), pp. 214–15.
30 Quoted in James Dunkerley, *Americana: the Americas in the world, around 1850* (London: Verso, 2000), p. 605.
31 *New York Evening Post*, 1 December 1855, quoted in Brown, *Agents of manifest destiny*, p. 309.
32 *Harper's Weekly*, 13 October 1860, quoted in Brown, *Agents of manifest destiny*, p. 456.
33 Memorandum dated 17 November, 1868. FO 55/248.
34 Bunch to Hammond, 17 February 1869, FO 55/248. Secretary of State Seward also entered into diplomatic negotiations to purchase the Danish West Indies from Denmark and the island of Saint Barthólemy from Sweden. A treaty was signed with Denmark, but was shelved in the US Senate.
35 Quoted in Jackson Crowell, 'The United States and a Central American Canal, 1869–1877', *Hispanic American Historical Review* 49 (1969), p. 51.
36 William Harris to Buchanan, 16 June 1847, quoted in Shurbutt, *US–Latin American relations*, p. 119.
37 Quoted in Sater, *Chile and the United States*, p. 21.
38 Seward to Bigelow, no. 30, 6 November 1865, quoted in Stephen J. Valone, '"Weakness offers temptation": William H. Seward and the reassertion of the Monroe doctrine', *Diplomatic History* 19 (1995), p. 587. Seward was especially concerned by reports that Austria was preparing to send troops to Mexico.
39 Quoted in Dexter Perkins, *The Monroe doctrine, 1826–1867* (Baltimore, MD: Johns Hopkins University Press, 1933), p. 312.
40 Speech dated 21 December 1870, quoted in Charles S. Campbell, *The transformation of American foreign relations, 1865–1900* (New York: Harper & Row, 1976), p. 52.
41 James D. Richardson (ed.), *A compilation of the messages and papers of the presidents, 1789–1897* (10 vols) (Washington DC: GPO, 1896–9), V, p. 4016.
42 Palmerston to Clarendon, 31 December 1857, quoted in Kenneth Bourne, *Britain and the balance of power in North America, 1815–1908* (Berkeley, CA: University of California Press, 1967), p. 16.
43 Webb to Seward, 7 August 1866, Department of State, *Foreign relations of the United States* (1866), II, p. 320.
44 Seward to Webb, 17 June 1867, Department of State, *Foreign relations of the United States* (1867), II, p. 255.

3 PAN-AMERICANISM (1879–1900)

1 US diplomatic relations with individual countries are expertly covered in Thomas M. Leonard (ed.), *United States–Latin American relations, 1850–1903: establishing a relationship* (Tuscaloosa, AL: University of Alabama Press, 1999).
2 *New York Herald*, July 1879.
3 Charles R. Williams (ed.), *Diary and letters of Rutherford Birchard Hayes* (5 vols) (Columbus, OH: Ohio State Archaeological and Historical Society, 1922–6), III, p. 589.
4 The Special Message is reprinted in 'Background documents relating to the Panama Canal', 95th Congress, 1st Session, Committee on Foreign Relations US Senate, November 1977, p. 51.

5 *The Times* (London), 20 March 1880.
6 Ferdinand de Lesseps, 'The Interoceanic Canal', *North American Review* 130 (1880), p. 77.
7 Construction work continued until 1889 and the French company went into bankruptcy in 1892. The scheme that had been launched with so much fanfare at Paris in 1879 was ruined just over a decade later by a combination of mismanagement, financial corruption and the inability to overcome major engineering and climatic difficulties.
8 See Blaine to Lowell, no. 187, 24 June 1881, Department of State, *Foreign relations of the United States* (1881), pp. 537–40.
9 Granville to Hoppin, 10 November 1881, FO 55/282.
10 Blaine to Morton, no. 30, 5 September 1881, Department of State, *Foreign relations of the United States* (1881), p. 427. On Blaine and Latin America see David Healy, *James G. Blaine and Latin America* (Columbia, MO: University of Missouri Press, 2001). The foreign policy of the Garfield and Arthur Administrations is expertly analysed in David M. Pletcher, *The awkward years: American foreign relations under Garfield and Arthur* (Columbia, MO: University of Missouri Press, 1962).
11 These remarks were made before a congressional inquiry in 1882 and are quoted in Perry Belmont, *An American democrat* (New York: Columbia UP, 1940), pp. 258–60. The theme of rivalry between the United States and Great Britain over Latin America is examined in Joseph Smith, *Illusions of conflict: Anglo-American diplomacy toward Latin America, 1865–1896* (Pittsburgh, PA: University of Pittsburgh Press, 1979).
12 When he was Speaker of the House of Representatives in 1876 Blaine was accused of using his office to assist railroad interests. While he survived the scandal known as the 'Mulligan Letters', suspicions of bribery and corruption plagued his later political career.
13 Blaine to Trescot, 1 December 1881, quoted in Pletcher, *The awkward years*, pp. 74–5.
14 Spenser St John to Granville, no. 26, 26 March, 1882, FO 61/339.
15 James G. Blaine, *Political discussions* (Norwich, CN: Henry Bill, 1887), p. 419.
16 The influential study stressing the importance of economic factors on American expansion is Walter LaFeber, *The new empire: an interpretation of American expansion, 1860–1898* (Ithaca, NY: Cornell University Press, 1963). David M. Pletcher, *The diplomacy of trade and investment: American economic expansion in the hemisphere, 1865–1900* (Columbia, MO: University of Missouri Press, 1998) is a balanced work that places more emphasis on the importance of political issues. A perceptive overview is Robert L. Beisner, *From the old diplomacy to the new, 1865–1900* (Arlington Heights, IL: Harlan Davidson, 1975) which is still one of the best overviews of American foreign policy at the end of the nineteenth century.
17 James D. Richardson, *A compilation of the messages and papers of the presidents, 1789–1897* (10 vols) (Washington DC: Government Printing Office, 1896–9), VIII, p. 251.
18 Quoted in *New York Herald*, 29 July 1885.
19 The idea of resolving hemispheric problems by inviting the parties concerned to a conference in Washington was the natural corollary to the role that the United States was seeking to assume as leader and protector of its hemispheric sisters. In 1866 the US Congress had attempted to bring the belligerents in the Pacific War and the War of the Triple Alliance to discuss peace terms in Washington. The idea of a fully representative inter-American conference under US auspices found concrete expression in 1881 when Blaine proposed this as a means of resolving the War of the Pacific. Frelinghuysen reversed Blaine's policy in 1882.

20 Congressional Record, 50th Congress, 1st Session, p. 1656, appendix, p. 308.
21 Congressional Record, 50th Congress, 1st Session, p. 1658, appendix, p. 308.
22 See *South American Journal* (London), 27 July 1889.
23 The Dominican Republic stated that a treaty signed in 1884 during the Arthur Administration had settled its commercial relations with the United States. The treaty, however, was still awaiting ratification by the US Senate. In the circumstances, attendance at the Washington conference was therefore regarded as futile.
24 See Alva Curtis Wilgus, 'James G. Blaine and the Pan American movement', *Hispanic American Historical Review* 5 (1922), p. 692.
25 Anonymous article by Curtis in *Frank Leslie's Illustrated Newspaper* (New York), 8 June 1889.
26 *Boston Journal*, 26 July 1889.
27 *Rio News*, 14 October 1889.
28 On the relationship between Argentina and the United States see Thomas F. McGann, *Argentina, the United States, and the Inter-American System, 1880–1914* (Cambridge, MA: Harvard University Press, 1957).
29 See International American Conference, 1889–90, *Minutes of the Conference* (Washington DC: Government Printing Office, 1890) pp. 293–334.
30 It was quite a while before arrangements for a follow-up meeting were made. The idea was revived in 1899 on the initiative of President William McKinley. The Second Pan-American Conference met in Mexico City in 1901. Regular meetings were then scheduled, resulting in conferences at Rio de Janeiro in 1906 and Buenos Aires in 1910.
31 Letter dated 11 July 1890, quoted in Ida M. Tarbell, *The tariff in our times* (New York: Macmillan, 1911), p. 205.
32 Reciprocity treaties were not limited to Latin American countries and were also concluded with Germany and Austria-Hungary.
33 Curtis to John W. Foster, 20 December 1892, quoted in 2nd Annual Report of the Bureau of American Republics, 1892, 52nd Congress, 2nd Session, Senate executive document no. 84, p. 20.
34 See minute on Pauncefote to Kimberley, 21 August 1894, FO 5/2238. Julian Pauncefort was the British ambassador at Washington and Kimberley was the British Foreign Minister.
35 West to Salisbury, no. 189, 17 July 1885, FO 5/1910.
36 International American Conference, *Minutes*, p. 324.
37 Memorandum by Pauncefote, 15 February 1890, FO 5/2085.
38 Richardson, *Messages and papers*, IX, p. 185.
39 *The Times* (London), 27 October 1891.
40 Gresham to Overmeyer, 25 July 1894, Library of Congress, Walter Q. Gresham Papers.
41 20 December 1889, *Congressional Record*, 51st Congress, 1st Session, p. 315.
42 *New York Sun*, 20 December 1889.
43 Gresham to Bayard, 21 January 1894, Library of Congress, Walter Q. Gresham Papers.
44 See dispatch of Thomas L. Thompson dated 12 October 1895, quoted in 54th Congress, 1st Session, House document no. 377, part 1, p. 92.
45 Report of the secretary of the navy, 17 November 1894, 53rd Congress, 3rd Session, House Document no. 1, p. 23.
46 On Scruggs's diplomatic activities see John A. S. Grenville and George B. Young, *Politics, strategy, and American diplomacy: studies in foreign policy, 1873–1917* (New Haven, CT: Yale University Press, 1966).
47 Olney to Bayard, no. 804, 20 July 1895, Department of State, *Foreign relations of the United States* (1895), p. 558.

48 Quoted in Charles C. Tansill, *The foreign policy of Thomas F. Bayard, 1885–1897* (New York: Fordham University Press, 1940), p. 209.
49 See Festus P. Summers (ed.), *The cabinet diary of William L. Wilson, 1896–97* (Chapel Hill, NC: University of North Carolina Press, 1957), p. 5.
50 Cleveland's Message to Congress, 17 December 1895, quoted in James W. Gantenbein (ed.), *The evolution of our Latin-American policy: a documentary record* (New York: Octagon, 1950), p. 356.
51 Pauncefote to Salisbury, 20 December 1895, quoted in R. A. Humphreys, *Tradition and revolt in Latin America and other essays* (London: Weidenfeld & Nicolson, 1969), p. 207.
52 Quoted in Charles S. Campbell, *The transformation of American foreign relations, 1865–1900* (New York: Harper & Row, 1976), p. 149.
53 Letter dated 26 April 1898, quoted in Philip S. Foner, *The Spanish–Cuban–American War and the birth of American imperialism, 1895–1902* (2 vols) (New York: Monthly Review Press, 1972), I, p. 181.
54 *Chicago Tribune*, 29 November 1896, quoted in Marcus M. Wilkerson, *Public opinion and the Spanish–American War: a study in war propaganda* (Baton Rouge, LA: Louisiana State University Press, 1932), p. 48.
55 Roosevelt to Dibblee, 16 February 1898, quoted in Elting E. Morison (ed.), *The letters of Theodore Roosevelt* (8 vols) (Cambridge, MA: Harvard University Press, 1951–4), I, p. 775.
56 *New York Journal*, 18 February 1898.
57 McKinley's War Message dated 11 April 1898, quoted in Henry Steele Commager (ed.), *Documents of American history* (2 vols) (New York: Crofts, 1944), II, p. 185.
58 Joint Resolutions, 13 April 1898, Congressional Record, 55th Congress 2nd Session, 3814–15.
59 Teller Amendment, 20 April 1898, quoted in Commager, *Documents*, II, p. 186.
60 American diplomacy prior to the war is carefully examined in John L. Offner, *An unwanted war: the diplomacy of the United States and Spain over Cuba, 1895–1898* (Chapel Hill, NC: University of North Carolina Press, 1992). An older but informative study of diplomatic relations is Ernest R. May, *Imperial democracy: the emergence of America as a great power* (New York: Harcourt, Brace and World, 1961). On military aspects of the war see David F. Trask, *The war with Spain in 1898* (New York: Macmillan, 1981) and Joseph Smith, *The Spanish–American War: conflict in the Caribbean and the Pacific, 1895–1902* (New York: Longman, 1994). An excellent survey of the considerable historical literature on this subject is Louis A. Pérez Jr., *The war of 1898: the United States and Cuba in history and historiography* (Chapel Hill, NC: University of North Carolina Press, 1998).
61 Statement reported in the American press on 2 January 1898, quoted in Louis A. Pérez, Jr., *Cuba between empires, 1878–1902* (Pittsburgh, PA: University of Pittsburgh Press, 1983), p. 167.
62 Letter dated 12 November 1889, quoted in Pérez, *Cuba between empires*, p. 95. Cuban historians have argued that American military intervention was designed not to liberate Cuba from Spanish tyranny but to forestall and prevent an imminent insurgent victory that would lead to the emergence of a 'free' and independent Cuba. Consequently, the important Cuban military contribution to victory was deliberately downplayed and ignored so that the war became 'the Spanish–American War' rather than the 'Cuban–Spanish–American War'. 'Filipino' is also included by some historians in the descriptive title of the war because American troops were engaged in fighting in the Philippines until that conflict was formally declared closed by President Theodore Roosevelt in 1902.

For a work by an American historian that stresses the 'Cuban' contribution to the 1898 war see Foner, *Spanish–Cuban–American War*.

63 George Kennan, *Campaigning in Cuba* (Port Washington, NY: Kennikat Press, 1971), p. 92.

64 Quoted in *New York Tribune*, 19 December 1898. American views of Cubans were also influenced by gender. See Kristin L. Hoganson, *Fighting for American manhood: how gender politics provoked the Spanish–American and Philippine–American wars* (New Haven, CT: Yale University Press, 1998). The same topic is also discussed in Michael H. Hunt, *Ideology and US foreign policy* (New Haven, CT: Yale University Press, 1987).

65 Quoted in Louis A. Pérez, Jr., *Cuba under the Platt amendment, 1902–1934* (Pittsburgh, PA: Pittsburgh University Press, 1986), p. 33.

66 General Demetrio Castillo, 12 September 1898, quoted in Ada Ferrer, *Insurgent Cuba: race, nation, and revolution, 1868–1898* (Chapel Hill, NC: University of North Carolina Press, 1999), p. 192.

67 1901 Platt Amendment, quoted in Commager, *Documents*, II, p. 209.

68 See Pérez, *Cuba under Platt amendment*, p. 39.

69 Wood to Theodore Roosevelt, 28 October 1901, quoted in David F. Healy, *The United States in Cuba, 1898–1902: generals, politicians, and the search for policy* (Madison, WI: University of Wisconsin Press, 1963), p. 178.

4 DOLLAR DIPLOMACY (1900–28)

1 Archibald C. Coolidge, *The United States as a world power* (New York: Macmillan, 1908), p. 132.

2 Speech dated 4 May 1911, quoted in David Healey, *Drive to hegemony: the United States in the Caribbean, 1898–1917* (Madison, WI: University of Wisconsin Press, 1988), p. 146. On dollar diplomacy and the Caribbean region see Dana G. Munro, *Intervention and dollar diplomacy in the Caribbean, 1900–1921* (Princeton, NJ: Princeton University Press, 1964) and Healey, *Drive to hegemony*. A thoughtful overview of the topic is Emily S. Rosenberg, 'Revisiting dollar diplomacy: narratives of money and manliness', *Diplomatic History* 22 (1998), pp. 155–76.

3 Speech dated 6 October 1909, quoted in Louis A. Pérez, Jr., *Cuba under the Platt amendment, 1902–1934* (Pittsburgh, PA: University of Pittsburgh Press, 1986), p. 111.

4 For further reading see Lester D. Langley and Thomas Schoonover, *The banana men: American mercenaries and entrepreneurs in Central America, 1880–1930* (Lexington, KY: University of Kentucky Press, 1995) and Emily S. Rosenberg, *Financial missionaries to the world: the politics and culture of dollar diplomacy, 1900–1930* (Cambridge, MA: Harvard University Press, 1999).

5 See Robert H. Holden and Eric Zolov (eds), *Latin America and the United States: a documentary history* (New York: Oxford University Press, 2000), p. 78.

6 From 'To Roosevelt', quoted in Alberto Prieto-Calixto, 'Rubén Darío and literary anti-Americanism/anti-Imperialism', in David Sheinin (ed.), *Beyond the ideal: Pan Americanism in inter-American affairs* (Westport, CT: Greenwood Press, 2000), p. 64.

7 From 'Argentina', quoted in Gabriela Nouzeilles and Graciela Montaldo (eds), *The Argentina reader: history, culture, politics* (Durham, NC: Duke University Press, 2002), p. 207.

8 Roosevelt to Cleveland, 26 December 1902, quoted in Nancy Mitchell, *The danger of dreams: German and American imperialism in Latin America* (Chapel

Hill, NC: University of North Carolina Press, 1999), p. 105. On Roosevelt's diplomacy see Richard H. Collin, *Theodore Roosevelt's Caribbean: the Panama canal, the Monroe doctrine and the Latin American context* (Baton Rouge, LA: Louisiana State University Press, 1990).

9 Letter by Drago to Mérou, 29 December 1902, quoted in Henry Steele Commager (ed.), *Documents of American history* (2 vols) (New York: Crofts, 1944, 3rd edn), II, p. 205.

10 Roosevelt's Annual Message to Congress, 6 December, 1904, quoted in Commager, *Documents*, II, p. 213.

11 Roosevelt's Special Message to Congress, 15 February, 1905, quoted in Holden and Zolov, *Latin America and the United States*, p. 104. Roosevelt preferred to resort to diplomacy rather than force in cases of disputes between nations in the Central American–Caribbean region. With the cooperation of the Mexican government, he sponsored a conference of Central American nations in Washington in 1907 that resulted in agreement to establish a Court of Justice to which disputes would be submitted in future.

12 Huntington Wilson to Taft, 30 August 1912, quoted in Walter V. and Marie V. Scholes, *The foreign policies of the Taft Administration* (Columbia, MO: University of Missouri Press, 1970), p. 65.

13 Roosevelt to Hay, 19 August 1903, quoted in Elting E. Morison (ed.), *The letters of Theodore Roosevelt* (8 vols) (Cambridge: Harvard University Press, 1951), III, pp. 566–7.

14 See Walter LaFeber, *The Panama canal: the crisis in historical perspective* (New York: Oxford University Press, 1989), pp. 33–4.

15 1906 Hearings of the Senate Interoceanic Canals Committee, quoted in John Major, *Prize possession: the United States and the Panama canal, 1903–1979* (Cambridge: Cambridge University Press, 1993), p. 69.

16 James F. Vivian, 'The "taking" of the Panama Canal Zone: myth and reality', *Diplomatic History* 4 (1980), pp. 95–100. Good studies of canal diplomacy are Major, *Prize possession*, and LaFeber, *Panama canal.*

17 Quoted in Richard L. Lael, *Arrogant diplomacy: US policy toward Colombia, 1903–1922* (Wilmington, DE: Scholarly Resources, 1987), p. 27.

18 In 1921 the Harding Administration concluded a treaty of conciliation with Colombia in which the latter received from the US government compensation of $25 million.

19 See the article by the African American journalist James Weldon Johnson, 'Self-determining Haiti, III: government of, by and for the National City Bank', *The Nation*, 11 September 1920. A very perceptive analysis of US cultural attitudes towards Haiti is Mary A. Renda, *Taking Haiti: military occupation and the culture of US imperialism, 1915–1940* (Chapel Hill, NC: University of North Carolina Press, 2001).

20 Speech dated 12 January 1912, quoted in Pérez, *Cuba under Platt amendment*, p. 112.

21 Quoted in João Frank da Costa, *Joaquim Nabuco e a política exterior do Brasil* (Rio de Janeiro: Gráfica, 1968), p. 224.

22 See minute dated 22 October 1908 on Eddy to Root, no. 18, 16 September 1908. National Archives, Records of the Department of State. Record Group 59, NF 15865/1. On approximation see Joseph Smith, *Unequal giants: diplomatic relations between the United States and Brazil, 1889–1930* (Pittsburgh: University of Pittsburgh Press, 1991).

23 Wilson's Mobile Address, 27 October 1913, quoted in Commager, *Documents*, II, pp. 269–70. Wilson's policy towards Latin America is explored in Mark T.

Gilderhus, *Pan American visions: Woodrow Wilson in the Western Hemisphere* (Tuscon, AZ: University of Arizona Press, 1986).

24 Speech by Wilson dated 25 October 1913, quoted in Arthur S. Link (ed.), *The papers of Woodrow Wilson* (Princeton, NJ: Princeton UP, 1966–), XXVIII, p. 441.

25 Quoted in Robert E. Quirk, *An affair of honor: Woodrow Wilson and the occupation of Veracruz* (Lexington, KY: University of Kentucky Press, 1962), p. 2.

26 Quoted in Quirk, *Affair of honor*, p. 53.

27 Fletcher to Polk, 3 December 1918, quoted in Robert Freeman Smith, *The United States and revolutionary nationalism in Mexico, 1916–1932* (Chicago, IL: University of Chicago Press, 1972), p. 93.

28 Bryan to Wilson, 17 December 1914. Record Group 59, Decimal File 1910–29, 763.72119/35.

29 State Department memorandum dated 17 November 1914, quoted in Emily S. Rosenberg, *World War I and the growth of United States predominance in Latin America* (New York: Garland, 1987), pp. 9–10.

30 William McAdoo, *Crowded years* (Boston, MA: Houghton Mifflin, 1931), p. 351.

31 The comments of Samuel Hale Pearson, quoted in *Proceedings of the First Pan American financial conference* (Washington DC: Government Printing Office, 1915), p. 92.

32 Robertson to Grey, no. 19, 23 April 1915, FO 371/2294.

33 This proposal was the work of Wilson's aide, Colonel Edward House, and sought to reaffirm the Monroe Doctrine by seeking a Pan-American treaty that would guarantee the political independence and territory integrity of all the American nations. The concept was typically vague and idealistic. While Argentina and Brazil expressed approval in principle, Chile was opposed.

34 Domício to Muller, no. 6, 24 February 1917, Rio de Janeiro, Arquivo Histórico do Itamaraty 234/2/7.

35 Quoted in Percy A. Martin, *Latin America and the war* (Baltimore, MD: Johns Hopkins Press, 1925), p. 529. For an overview of the diplomatic context see Emily S. Rosenberg, *World War I and the growth of United States predominance in Latin America* (New York: Garland, 1987).

36 Brazilian consul-general at New York, Hélio Lobo, 8 April 1923, quoted in Stanley E. Hilton, 'Brazil and the post-Versailles world: elite images and foreign policy strategy, 1919–1929', *Journal of Latin American Studies* 12 (1980), p. 352.

37 See Gordon Connell-Smith, *The Inter-American system* (London: Oxford University Press, 1966), p. 56.

38 See minutes on Alston to Tyrell, telegram no. 42, 15 September 1927, FO 371/11965.

39 Tilley to Curzon, no. 62, 22 February, 1923, FO 371/8431.

40 Hughes to Harding, 28 November 1922, quoted in Kenneth J. Grieb, *The Latin American policy of Warren G. Harding* (Fort Worth, TX: Texas Christian University Press, 1976), p. 180. While Hughes had a low opinion of Latin American governments and showed no great interest in their affairs, he did, however, believe that American diplomats dealing with Latin American affairs should be able to speak Spanish. See Grieb, *The Latin American policy of Warren G. Harding*, p. 11.

41 For further reading on American diplomacy towards Latin America see Grieb, *Latin American policy of Warren G. Harding* and Joseph S. Tulchin, *The aftermath of war after World War I and US policy toward Latin America* (New York: New York University Press, 1971).

42 *New York Times*, 9 September 1922, quoted in Grieb, *Latin American policy of Warren G. Harding*, p. 178.

43 Letter dated 21 October 1927, quoted in Alan McPherson, *Yankee no! Anti-Americanism in US–Latin American relations* (Cambridge MA: Harvard University Press, 2003). p. 16.
44 Letter dated 20 July 1927, quoted in Andrew J. Bacevich Jr., 'The American electoral mission in Nicaragua, 1927–28', *Diplomatic History* 4 (1980), p. 244.
45 Quoted in Bacevich, 'The American electoral mission in Nicaragua', p. 250.
46 Sheffield to Kellogg, 5 April 1926, quoted in Smith, *US and revolutionary nationalism*, p. 233.
47 Memorandum dated 19 May 1928, quoted in N. Stephen Kane, 'Corporate power and foreign policy: efforts of American oil companies to influence United States relations with Mexico, 1921–1928', *Diplomatic History* 1 (1977), pp. 189–90. An informative study of the oil dispute is Lorenzo Meyer, *Mexico and the United States in the oil controversy, 1917–1942* (Austin, TX: University of Texas Press, 1972).
48 Kellogg to Fletcher, 26 July 1927, Record Group 59, Havana Conference, Entry 144, Box 425.
49 Quoted in J. Lloyd Mecham, *A survey of United States–Latin American relations* (Boston, MA: Houghton Mifflin, 1965), p. 107.
50 Quoted in Grieb, *Latin American policy of Warren G. Harding*, p. 3.
51 For an interesting contemporary view see João F. Normano, *The struggle for South America: economy and ideology* (London: Allen & Unwin, 1931).
52 A term used by the journalist, Isaac F. Marcosson. See *Saturday Evening Post*, 24 October 1925.
53 Samuel Guy Inman, 'Imperialistic America', *The Atlantic Monthly*, 134 (July 1924), p. 107. See Kenneth F. Woods, '"Imperialistic America": a landmark in the development of US policy toward Latin America', *Inter-American Economic Affairs* 21 (1967–8), pp. 55–72.

5 THE GOOD NEIGHBOR (1928–45)

1 Hoover to Root, 16 November 1928, Hoover Presidential Library, West Branch Iowa, Hoover Papers, Box 59.
2 In a speech delivered in Honduras, Hoover stated his desire that inter-American relations should be those of 'good neighbors'. Quoted in Alexander DeConde, *Herbert Hoover's Latin American policy* (New York: Octagon Books, 1970), pp. 17–18.
3 Press Meeting dated 20 November 1928, Hoover Papers, Box 170.
4 Silvino Gurgel do Amaral to Pacheco, no. 97, 19 November 1925, Arquivo Histórico Itamaraty 234/4/5.
5 Clark Memorandum quoted in Robert H. Holden and Eric Zolov, *Latin America and the United States: a documentary history* (New York: Oxford University Press, 2000), p. 136.
6 *New York Times*, 25 October 1930.
7 On account of his past dealings with Latin America, Franklin D. Roosevelt had something of a reputation to live down. He had served as assistant secretary of the navy under Woodrow Wilson and had been actively involved in the policy of armed intervention. In fact, he boasted in 1920 that he had personally written the constitution of Haiti.
8 Roosevelt's First Inaugural Address, 4 March 1933, quoted in Henry Steele Commager, *Documents of American history* (2 vols) (New York: Crofts, 1944, 3rd edition), II, p. 421.
9 On the formulation of the 'Good Neighbor Policy' see Alexander DeConde, *Herbert Hoover's Latin American policy* (New York: Octagon Books, 1970) and

Bryce Wood, *The making of the good neighbor policy* (New York: Columbia University Press, 1961).

10 Cordell Hull, *The memoirs of Cordell Hull* (2 vols) (New York: Macmillan, 1948), I, p. 313.

11 Letter dated 6 September 1933, quoted in Wood, *Making of the good neighbor policy*, p. 81.

12 Hull, *Memoirs*, I, p. 319.

13 See J. Lloyd Mecham, *A survey of United States–Latin American relations* (Boston, MA: Houghton Mifflin, 1965), pp. 115–16.

14 Quoted in Gordon Connell-Smith, *The Inter-American system* (Oxford: Oxford University Press, 1966), p. 90.

15 Welles to Hull, 4 October 1933, quoted in Louis A. Pérez, Jr., *Cuba and the United States: ties of singular intimacy* (Athens, GA: University of Georgia Press, 1990), p. 200.

16 Hull, *Memoirs*, I, p. 347. For a perceptive analysis of US economic policies see Dick Steward, *Trade and hemisphere: the good neighbor policy and reciprocal trade* (Columbia, MO: University of Missouri Press, 1975). Another important study is David Green, *The containment of Latin America: a history of the myths and realities of the good neighbor policy* (Chicago, IL: Quadrangle, 1971).

17 It was significant that Mexico, Argentina and Chile did not sign reciprocal agreements prior to the outbreak of the Second World War. This reflected their desire to stress policies of national economic development and import substitution rather than the reliance on exports that had made their economies so vulnerable to changes in the pattern of world trade.

18 Osborne to Foreign Office, no. 982, 30 August 1934, FO 371/17519.

19 Quoted in Hull, *Memoirs*, I, 344.

20 Aranha to Vargas, 30 July 1937, quoted in Stanley E. Hilton, *Brazil and the great powers, 1930–1939: the politics of trade rivalry* (Austin, TX: University of Texas Press, 1975), p. 162.

21 Letter dated 21 July 1938, quoted in Cole Blasier, *The hovering giant: US responses to revolutionary change in Latin America* (Pittsburgh, PA: University of Pittsburgh Press, 1976).

22 Daniels to Hull, 27 March 1938, quoted in Wood, *Good neighbor policy*, p. 211.

23 Memorandum by Baruch, 29 March 1938, quoted in Green, *Containment of Latin America*, p. 33.

24 In addition, in 1941 the Export–Import Bank loaned Mexico $30 million for construction of the Mexican section of the Pan-American Highway designed to link Alaska with Tierra del Fuego.

25 *New York Times*, 22 April 1942, quoted in Wood, *Good neighbor policy*, p. 259.

26 Roosevelt to Augustin Justo, 30 January 1936 in *Roosevelt's foreign policy, 1933–1941: Franklin D. Roosevelt's unedited speeches and messages* (New York: Wilfred Funk, 1942), p. 92.

27 Speech dated 5 December 1936, quoted in James W. Gantenbein (ed.), *The evolution or our Latin American policy: a documentary record* (New York: Octagon, 1950), p. 79.

28 Hull, *Memoirs*, I, p. 500.

29 Quoted in Connell-Smith, *Inter-American system*, p. 97.

30 Sumner Welles, *The time for decision* (London: Hamish Hamilton, 1944), p. 162.

31 Hull, *Memoirs*, I, p. 690.

32 *El Día* (Montevideo), 24 December 1939, quoted in R. A. Humphreys, *Latin America and the Second World War* (2 vols) (London: Athlone Press, 1981–2), p. 48.

33 Hull, *Memoirs*, II, p. 1145. For the general diplomatic background see Humphreys, *Latin America and the Second World War*. Informative accounts of US wartime diplomatic relations with individual countries are Frank D. McCann, *The Brazilian-American alliance, 1937–1945* (Princeton, NJ: Princeton University Press, 1973) and Michael L. Francis, *The limits of hegemony: United States relations with Argentina and Chile during World War II* (Notre Dame, IN: University of Notre Dame Press, 1977).
34 Quoted in Francis, *Limits of hegemony*, p. 82.
35 Memorandum dated 30 January 1942, quoted in C. A. MacDonald, 'The politics of intervention: the United States and Argentina, 1941–1946', *Journal of Latin American Studies* 12 (1980), p. 369.
36 Quoted in William F. Sater, *Chile and the United States: empires in conflict* (Athens, GA: University of Georgia Press, 1990), p. 114.
37 Brazil did not formally declare war on Japan until June 1945.
38 The title of chapter 99 in Hull, *Memoirs*, II, pp. 1377–89.
39 Letter dated 29 February 1944, quoted in Humphreys, *Latin America and the Second World War*, II, p. 165.
40 OSS Report dated 4 September 1943, quoted in MacDonald, 'Politics of intervention,' p. 377.
41 Hull, *Memoirs*, II, p. 1402.
42 Quoted in Humphreys, *Latin America and the Second World War*, II, p. 193.
43 Quoted in Humphreys, *Latin America and the Second World War*, II, p. 203.
44 In order to boost Brazil's hemispheric and international prestige and thereby its potential for influence in the post-war world, President Vargas ordered the creation of an expeditionary force known as the Força Expedicionária Brasileira (FEB) that would be sent to participate in the Allied invasion of Italy. The FEB was equipped, transported and supplied by the US government and served under American military commanders. In July 1944 the first contingent left Rio de Janeiro for Italy where they joined the United States Fifth Army commanded by General Mark Clark. Around 25,000 Brazilian troops were sent to Italy and were in action from 6 September 1944 to 2 May 1945. The exploits of the FEB, notably their contribution to the hard-fought Allied victory at Monte Castello in March 1945, evoked great pride and patriotism in Brazil.
45 Brazil's decision to enter the war was influenced as much by the German submarine threat than American pressure or blandishment. Even though Brazil was ostensibly neutral, just as in the First World War, the increase in trade between Brazil and the Allies and the granting to the United States of the use of military bases on Brazilian territory, signified to the German government that Brazil was effectively on the side of the Allies. From February 1942 onwards, Brazilian merchant ships experienced attacks from German U-boats operating in Atlantic waters. A major German submarine offensive was launched in August 1942 that resulted in the sinking of six Brazilian ships within a period of less than a week. Four were passenger ships so the loss of life was heavy. Mass demonstrations erupted throughout the country demanding retaliation. German and Italian-owned businesses were attacked. President Vargas responded by issuing a declaration of war against Germany and Italy on 22 August 1942.
46 Welles, *Time for decision*, p. 169.
47 *La Hora* (Santiago de Chile), 21 August 1940, quoted in Green, *Containment of Latin America*, p. 93.
48 Quoted in Green, *Containment of Latin America*, pp. 111–12.
49 Roosevelt to Claude Bowers, quoted in Max Paul Friedman, *Nazis and good neighbors: the United States campaign against the Germans of Latin America in World War II* (Cambridge: Cambridge University Press, 2003), p. 54.

50 Rockefeller to Marshall, 28 August 1942, quoted in Elizabeth Anne Cobbs, *The rich neighbor policy: Rockefeller and Kaiser in Brazil* (New Haven, CT: Yale University Press, 1992), p. 40.

51 Bonsal to Welles, 2 January 1942, quoted in Friedman, *Nazis and good neighbors*, p. 93.

52 Quoted in Friedman, *Nazis and good neighbors*, p. 190.

6 COLD WAR POLITICS (1945–74)

1 Sumner Welles, *Time for decision* (London: Hamish Hamilton, 1944), p. 188. During the war Welles had frequently clashed with Hull over Latin American policy. Welles resigned from his office as under secretary of state in August 1943.

2 Another reason for American reluctance to agree to the holding of an inter-American meeting was the difficulty of preventing the attendance of Argentina whose pro-fascist government insisted on maintaining a policy of neutrality during much of the war.

3 Resolution XXX of the Inter-American Conference on War and Peace, 1945, quoted in Gordon Connell-Smith, *The Inter-American system* (London: Oxford University Press, 1966), p. 132.

4 Argentina under Juan Perón notably challenged American economic thinking by proposing a 'third position' between capitalism and Communism. See Glenn J. Dorn, 'Perón's gambit: the United States and the Argentine challenge to the inter-American order, 1946–1948', *Diplomatic History* 26 (2002), pp. 1–20.

5 Statement by the Office of Financial Development in Norman Ness to Willard Thorp, 19 February 1948, Department of State, *Foreign relations of the United States* (1948), IX, p. 5.

6 Vargas to Lourival Fontes, July 1951, quoted in Stanley E. Hilton, 'The United States, Brazil, and the Cold War, 1945–1960: end of the special relationship', *Journal of American History* 68 (1981), p. 611. Disillusion with the United States led to the establishment by the UN in 1948 of the Economic Commission for Latin America (ECLA) that formulated an alternative economic policy stressing economic cooperation and integration among the Latin American countries. A prominent influence upon ECLA was the Argentine economist, Raúl Prébisch, who argued that the structure of the world economy and its domination by the United States was fundamentally disadvantageous to Latin America.

7 Address by Marshall, 1 April 1948, quoted in Arthur M. Schlesinger, Jr. (ed.), *The dynamics of world power: a documentary history of United States foreign policy, 1945–1973* (5 vols) (New York: Chelsea House, 1983), III, pp. 45–6. The importance of private US investment in Latin America, especially the examples of Nelson Rockefeller and Henry Kaiser, are examined in Elizabeth Anne Cobbs, *The rich neighbor policy: Rockefeller and Kaiser in Brazil* (New Haven, CT: Yale University Press, 1992). For further reading on post-war US policy towards Latin America see Bryce Wood, *The dismantling of the good neighbor policy* (Austin, TX: University of Texas Press, 1985).

8 George F. Kennan, *Memoirs, 1925–1950* (London: Hutchinson, 1968), p. 481.

9 Dean Acheson, *Present at the creation* (London: Hamish Hamilton, 1970), p. 257.

10 The Rio Treaty, 1947, quoted in Robert H. Holden and Eric Zolov, *Latin America and the United States: a documentary history* (New York: Oxford University Press, 2000), p. 188.

11 Lovett to Truman, 1 December 1947, Department of State, *Foreign relations of the United States* (1947), VIII, p. 93.

12 Charter of the Organization of American States, 1948, quoted in Holden and Zolov, *Latin America and the United States*, p. 192. On the Rio Pact and the OAS see J. Lloyd Mecham, *The United States and inter-American security, 1889–1960* (Austin, TX: University of Texas Press, 1961) and Connell-Smith, *Inter-American system.*
13 Letter dated 17 July 1945, quoted in Gaddis Smith, *The last years of the Monroe doctrine, 1945–1993* (New York: Hill and Wang, 1994), p. 55.
14 Truman's Message to Congress, 12 March 1947, quoted in Schlesinger, *Dynamics of world power*, I, p. 113.
15 Address by Truman, 26 March 1952, quoted in Schlesinger, *Dynamics of world power*, III, pp. 140–1.
16 Fontoura to Vargas, February 1951, quoted in Hilton, 'US, Brazil and the Cold War', p. 609.
17 Memorandum dated 29 March 1950, Department of State, *Foreign relations of the United States* (1950), II, p. 603.
18 Quoted in Kyle Longley, 'Resistance and accommodation: the United States and the nationalism of José Figueres, 1953–1957', *Diplomatic History* 18 (1994), p. 5, n. 14.
19 Harry Kantor quoted in Longley, 'Resistance and accommodation', p. 13.
20 National Intelligence Estimate, 6 December 1955, Department of State, *Foreign relations of the United States* (1955–7), VI, p. 36.
21 Quoted in Louis A. Pérez, Jr., 'International dimensions of inter-American relations, 1944–1960', *Inter-American Economic Affairs* 27 (1973), p. 48.
22 Annex to NSC/144, 6 March 1953, quoted in Stephen G. Rabe, *Eisenhower and Latin America: the foreign policy of anti-communism* (Chapel Hill, NC: University of North Carolina Press, 1988), p. 32. The NSC study concluded that 'overriding security interests' would justify unilateral intervention by the United States even if this action was in violation of existing treaty arrangements.
23 Quoted in Stephen M. Streeter, 'The myth of Pan Americanism: US policy toward Latin America during the Cold War, 1954–1963', in David Sheinin, *Beyond the ideal: Pan Americanism in inter-American affairs* (Westport, CT: Praeger, 2000), p. 177.
24 UFCO was also known in Guatemala as '*la frutera*' (the fruit-bowl).
25 Paper on 'Current Relations with Guatemala', 12 June 1951, Department of State, *Foreign relations of the United States* (1951), II, pp. 1437–8. The influence of big business on US policy towards Guatemala is highlighted in Stephen C. Schlesinger and Stephen Kinzer, *Bitter fruit: the untold story of the American coup in Guatemala* (Garden City, NY: Doubleday, 1982). Richard H. Immerman, *The CIA in Guatemala: the foreign policy of intervention* (Austin, TX: University of Texas Press, 1982) is a scholarly examination of the policy of the Eisenhower Administration, while Piero Gleijeses, *Shattered hope: the Guatemalan revolution and the United States, 1944–1954* (Princeton, NJ: Princeton University Press, 1991) provides a comprehensive study that includes copious evidence from Guatemalan sources.
26 Quoted in Immerman, *CIA in Guatemala*, p. 115.
27 Peurifoy to Department of State, 17 December 1953, Department of State, *Foreign relations of the United States*, 1952–4, IV, p. 1093.
28 Quoted in Connell-Smith, *Inter-American system*, p. 162.
29 Tenth Inter-American Conference Declaration of Solidarity, 28 March 1954, quoted in Schlesinger, *Dynamics of world power*, III, p. 260.
30 Quoted in Immerman, *CIA in Guatemala*, p. 157.
31 *Washington Post*, 21 May 1954, quoted in Piero Gleijeses, *Shattered hope*, p. 298.

32 Quoted in Nick Cullather, *Secret history: the CIA's classified account of its operations in Guatemala, 1952–1954* (Stanford, CA: Stanford University Press, 1999), p. 97.
33 Radio Address dated 30 June, 1954, quoted in Schlesinger, *Dynamics of world power*, III, p. 285.
34 *New York Times*, 1 July 1954, quoted in Gleijeses, *Shattered hope*, p. 368.
35 Memorandum of NSC meeting, 10 March 1955, Department of State, *Foreign relations of the United States*, 1955–7, VI, p. 616.
36 Dwight D. Eisenhower, *The White House years* (2 vols) (Garden City, NY: Doubleday, 1963–5), I, p. 427.
37 Quoted in Walter LaFeber, *Inevitable revolutions: the United States in Central America* (New York: Norton, 1993), p. 109.
38 Statement by Robert D. Murphy, 19 May 1958, quoted in Schlesinger, *Dynamics of world power*, III, p. 375.
39 Memorandum by Allen Dulles to Foster Dulles, 27 May 1958, Department of State, *Foreign relations of the United States*, 1958–60, V, p. 253.
40 *Washington Post*, 15 May 1958, quoted in Marvin R. Zahniser and W. Michael Weis, 'A diplomatic Pearl Harbor? Richard Nixon's goodwill mission to Latin America in 1958', *Diplomatic History* 13 (1989), p. 163.
41 Instruction from the Department of State to All Diplomatic Posts in Latin America, 4 February 1960, Department of State, *Foreign relations of the United States*, 1958–60, V, p. 275. An excellent study of Eisenhower's policies towards Latin America is Rabe, *Eisenhower and Latin America*.
42 In 1958 President Juscelino Kubitschek of Brazil took a major initiative and proposed 'Operation Pan America', an aid programme designed to stimulate the economic development of the whole of Latin America. The plan was not acted upon principally because no support was forthcoming from the Eisenhower Administration. The idea, however, influenced both Eisenhower and especially Kennedy in formulating and implementing their own schemes of financial aid for the hemisphere.
43 Report from the Task Force on Immediate Latin American Problems, 4 January 1961, Department of State, *Foreign relations of the United States* (1961–3), XII, p. 3.
44 Quoted in Stephen G. Rabe, *The most dangerous area in the world: John F. Kennedy confronts communist revolution in Latin America* (Chapel Hill, NC: University of North Carolina Press, 1999), p. 19.
45 Address dated 13 March 1961, quoted in Schlesinger, *Dynamics of world power*, III, p. 502.
46 Charter of Punta del Este, 1961, quoted in Holden and Zolov, *Latin America and the United States*, p. 232.
47 *New York Times*, 15 March 1961, quoted in James William Park, *Latin American underdevelopment: a history of perspectives in the United States, 1870–1965* (Baton Rouge, LA: Louisiana State University Press, 1995), p. 214.
48 Leonard Gross, *Look*, 28 August 1962, quoted in Michael E. Latham, 'Ideology, social science and destiny: modernization and the Kennedy-era Alliance for Progress', *Diplomatic History* 22 (1988), p. 223.
49 Quoted in Rabe, *Most dangerous area in the world*, p. 153. American officials often made a more fitting analogy with Puerto Rico where 'Operation Bootstrap' was launched during the 1950s and was regarded as an example of successful political and economic modernization. See Henry Wells, *The Modernization of Puerto Rico* (Cambridge, MA: Harvard University Press, 1969).
50 Memorandum by Deputy Assistant Secretary of State for Inter-American Affairs Arturo Morales-Carrion, 9 April 1962, Department of State, *Foreign relations of the United States* (1961–3), XII, p. 101.

51 See Eduardo Frei Montalva, 'The alliance that lost its way', *Foreign Affairs*, 45 (1967), pp. 437–48. An early assessment of the performance of the alliance is Jerome Levinson and Juan de Onís, *The alliance that lost its way: a critical report on the Alliance for Progress* (Chicago, IL: Quadrangle, 1970).
52 Quoted in Park, *Latin American underdevelopment*, p. 225.
53 Quoted in Kent M. Beck, 'Necessary lies, hidden truths: Cuba in the 1960 campaign', *Diplomatic History* 8 (1984), pp. 45, 47.
54 Quoted in Robert E. Quirk, *Fidel Castro* (New York: Norton, 1993), p. 132.
55 Quoted in Jeffrey J. Safford, 'The Nixon–Castro meeting of 19 April 1959', *Diplomatic History* 4 (1980), p. 431.
56 Special National Intelligence Estimate, 30 June 1959, Department of State, *Foreign relations of the United States* 1958–60, V, p. 393.
57 June 1959, quoted in Jules R. Benjamin, *The United States and the origins of the Cuban revolution* (Princeton, NJ: Princeton University Press, 1990), p. 182.
58 See Stephen E. Ambrose, *Eisenhower: the president* (London: Allen & Unwin, 1984), p. 556. For critical accounts of US policy towards Fidel Castro see Thomas G. Paterson, *Contesting Castro: the United States and the triumph of the Cuban revolution* (New York: Oxford University Press, 1994) and Jules R. Benjamin, *The United States and the origins of the Cuban revolution: an empire of liberty in an age of national liberation* (Princeton, NJ: Princeton University Press, 1990). A competent study of the formulation and implementation of Operation Zapata is Trumbull Higgins, *The perfect failure: Kennedy, Eisenhower, and the CIA at the Bay of Pigs* (New York: Norton, 1987).
59 Quirk, *Fidel Castro*, p. 371.
60 After protracted negotiations between the US and Cuban governments the prisoners were eventually released in December 1962. Cuba received $60 million in food and medical supplies from the US government.
61 Arthur M. Schlesinger, Jr., *A thousand days: John F. Kennedy in the White House* (London: Andre Deutsch, 1965), p. 251.
62 Quoted in Theodore Sorensen, *Kennedy* (London: Pan, 1966), p. 344.
63 Stevenson to Kennedy, 19 April 1961, Department of State, *Foreign relations of the United States* (1961–3), X, p. 296.
64 Statement by the Government of the Soviet Union dated 18 April 1961, quoted in Schlesinger, *Dynamics of world power*, III, p. 536.
65 Quoted in Piero Gleijeses, *Conflicting missions: Havana, Washington, and Africa, 1959–1976* (Chapel Hill, NC: University of North Carolina Press, 2002), p. 22.
66 Quoted in Philip Brenner, *From confrontation to negotiation: US relations with Cuba* (Boulder, CO: Westview Press, 1988), p. 15.
67 Quoted in Morris H. Morley, *Imperial state: the United States and revolution and Cuba, 1952–1986* (Cambridge: Cambridge University Press, 1987), p. 157.
68 TV Address by Kennedy, 22 October 1962, quoted in Schlesinger, *Dynamics of world power*, III, p. 590.
69 Fidel Castro would not admit UN officials into Cuba for the purpose of supervising the withdrawal. Consequently, US reconnaissance aircraft carried out the task of verifying that the withdrawal was carried out.
70 Quoted in Morley, *Imperial state*, p. 151. At the same time as Operation Mongoose, the CIA had conducted a less well-known covert operation that successfully destabilized the government of Cheddi Jagan in Guyana. See Rabe, *Most dangerous area in the world*.
71 Quoted in Lars Schoultz, *Human rights and United States policy toward Latin America* (Princeton, NJ: Princeton University Press, 1981), p. 179. Kennedy was referring to the creation of the Office of Public Safety, part of the Agency of International Development within the state department.

72 Quoted in *Washington Post*, 8 March 1977.
73 Report from the Inter-Departmental Survey Team on Brazil, 3 November 1962, Department of State, *Foreign relations of the United States* (1961–3), XII, p. 475.
74 Quoted in John W. F. Dulles, *Unrest in Brazil: political-military crises, 1955–1964* (Austin, TX: University of Texas Press, 1970), p. 307.
75 Quoted in Phyllis R. Parker, *Brazil and the quiet intervention, 1964* (Austin, TX: University of Texas Press, 1979), p. 85. An informative study of US diplomatic relations with Brazil is W. Michael Weis, *Cold warriors and coups d'état: Brazilian-American relations, 1945–1964* (Albuquerque, NM: University of New Mexico Press, 1993).
76 Lyndon B. Johnson, *The vantage point: perspectives on the presidency, 1963–1969* (London: Weidenfeld & Nicolson, 1972), p. 180.
77 Serious anti-American demonstrations had also occurred during the Eisenhower Administration on Panamanian Independence Day, 3 November 1959.
78 Johnson, *Vantage point*, p. 183.
79 Johnson, *Vantage Point*, p. 198.
80 John B. Martin, *Overtaken by events: the Dominican crisis from the fall of Trujillo to the civil war* (Garden City, NY: Doubleday, 1966), p. 716.
81 Quoted in Holden and Zolov, *Latin America and the United States*, p. 249. Scholarly studies of the intervention are Abraham Lowenthal, *The Dominican intervention* (Cambridge, MA: Harvard University Press, 1972) and Piero Gleijeses, *The Dominican crisis: the 1965 constitutionalist revolt and American intervention* (Baltimore, MD: Johns Hopkins University Press, 1979).
82 Telegram from Kennedy to Department of State, 16 December 1961, Department of State, *Foreign relations of the United States* (1961–3), XII, p. 683.
83 Quoted in Seymour M. Hersh, *Kissinger: the price of power. Henry Kissinger in the Nixon White House* (London: Faber & Faber, 1983), p. 263. Hersh is severely critical of US policy towards Allende. For a balanced approach see Paul Sigmund, *The overthrow of Allende and the politics of Chile, 1964–1976* (Pittsburgh, PA: University of Pittsburgh Press, 1977).
84 Kissinger, *The White House years* (Boston, MA: Little, Brown, 1979), p. 564.
85 Although the amounts were far less than those given to his opponents, Allende also received funds from overseas. For example, it was estimated that Cuba contributed $300,000 to his campaign in 1970.
86 See Paul E. Sigmund, 'Crisis management: Chile and marxism,' in John D. Martz (ed.), *United States policy in Latin America: a quarter century of crisis and challenge, 1961–1986* (Lincoln, NE: University of Nebraska Press, 1988), p. 161.
87 Quoted in William F. Sater, *Chile and the United States: empires in conflict* (Athens, GA: University of Georgia Press, 1990), p. 171.
88 Quoted in Nathaniel Davis, *The last two years of Salvador Allende* (London: I.B. Tauris, 1985), p. 124.
89 Kissinger, *Years of upheaval* (Boston, MA: Little, Brown, 1982), p. 395.
90 Quoted in Sigmund, 'Crisis management', p. 161.
91 Quoted in Davis, *Last two years*, p. 348. The debate has continued recently with the publication of declassified US diplomatic documents on the internet. See the website of National Security Archive, maintained by George Washington University, Washington DC, http://www.gwu/edu/~nsarchiv.
92 Quoted in Sater, *Chile and United States*, p. 124.
93 Kissinger, *Years of upheaval*, p. 412.
94 Quoted in Sigmund, 'Crisis management', p. 164.

7 END OF THE TWENTIETH CENTURY (1974–2000)

1 Address at the Conference of Tlatelolco, 21 February 1974, News Release, Department of State, Bureau of Public Affairs. On becoming president, Nixon had indicated an interest in the Western Hemisphere when he instructed Nelson Rockefeller to tour and make a report on Latin America. The 'Rockefeller Report' was published in 1969, but its recommendation to direct more attention and resources to Latin American affairs was ignored by the Nixon Administration.
2 Quoted in William J. Jorden, *Panama odyssey* (Austin, TX: University of Texas Press, 1984), p. 191. Jorden served as US ambassador to Panama and gives a valuable insider's account of events. For a thorough study of diplomatic events see John Major, *Prize possession: the United States and the Panama Canal, 1903–1979* (Cambridge: Cambridge University Press, 1993). Another informative work is Walter LaFeber, *The Panama canal: the crisis in historical perspective* (New York: Oxford University Press, 1989).
3 Quoted in Jorden, *Panama odyssey*, p. 316.
4 See Linowitz Commission, *The United States and Latin America: next steps* (New York: Center for Inter-American Relations, 1976). This was the second report published by the Commission. For the first report see Linowitz Commission, *The Americas in a changing world* (New York: Quadrangle, 1975).
5 Zbigniew Brzezinski, *Power and principle: memoirs of the national security adviser, 1977–1981* (New York: Farrar, Straus, Girou, 1983), p. 134.
6 Cyrus Vance, *Hard choices: critical years in America's foreign policy* (New York: Simon and Schuster, 1983), p. 140.
7 Quoted in Jorden, *Panama odyssey*, p. 514.
8 Quoted in Jorden, *Panama odyssey*, p. 621.
9 Quoted in Robert A. Pastor, 'The Carter administration and Latin America: a test of principle', in John D. Martz (ed.), *United States policy in Latin America: a quarter century of crisis and challenge, 1961–1986* (Lincoln, NE: University of Nebraska Press, 1988), p. 79.
10 Brzezinski, *Power and principle*, p. 178.
11 Quoted in Lars Schoultz, *Human rights and United States policy toward Latin America* (Princeton, NJ: Princeton University Press, 1981), p. 113.
12 Quoted in Schoultz, *Human rights*, p. 116.
13 Quoted in Anthony Lake, *Somoza falling: a case study of Washington at work* (Amherst, MA: University of Massachusetts Press, 1989). A perceptive insider's view of Carter's policies towards Nicaragua is Robert A. Pastor, *Condemned to repetition: the United States and Nicaragua* (Princeton, NJ: Princeton University Press, 1987). A readable and detailed account of US diplomacy towards Central America that includes the policies of both the Carter and Reagan Administrations is William M. LeoGrande, *Our own backyard: the United States in Central America, 1977–1992* (Chapel Hill, NC: University of North Carolina Press, 1998). For a critical view of Reagan's policies see Thomas W. Walker (ed.), *Reagan versus the Sandinistas: the undeclared war in Nicaragua* (Boulder, CO: Westview Press, 1987).
14 Quoted in Lake, *Somoza falling*, p. 232.
15 After a brief spell in Miami, Somoza chose to go into exile in Paraguay where he was assassinated in 1980.
16 Jeane Kirkpatrick, 'US security & Latin America', *Commentary* 71 (January 1981), p. 29.
17 Jeane Kirkpatrick served in the Reagan Administration as American ambassador to the UN. Her most influential article was 'Dictatorships and double standards', *Commentary* 69 (November, 1979), pp. 35–45.

18 Quoted in Robert A. Pastor, 'The Reagan administration: on its own petard', in John D. Martz (ed.), *United States policy in Latin America: a decade of crisis and challenge* (Lincoln, NE: University of Nebraska Press, 1995), p. 5. See Committee of Santa Fe, *A new Inter-American policy for the eighties* (Washington DC: Council for Inter-American Security, 1980).
19 Quoted in LeoGrande, *Our own backyard*, pp. 55–6.
20 Speech dated 10 March 1983, quoted in Pastor, 'The Reagan administration: on its own petard' in Martz , *US policy in Latin America: a decade of crisis and challenge*, p. 9. For further reading on Reagan's policy see Thomas Carothers, *In the name of democracy: US policy toward Latin America in the Reagan years* (Berkeley, CA: University of California Press, 1991).
21 Alexander M. Haig, Jr., *Caveat: realism, Reagan, and foreign policy* (London: Weidenfeld and Nicolson, 1964), p. 122.
22 Haig, *Caveat*, p. 126.
23 Quoted in Peter Kornbluh, 'The covert war', in Walker, *Reagan versus the Sandinistas*, p. 23.
24 Radio Address dated 16 February 1985, quoted in LeoGrande, *Our own backyard*, p. 410.
25 Quoted in George P. Shultz, *Turmoil and triumph: my years as secretary of state* (New York: Charles Scribner's Sons, 1993), p. 422.
26 Statement dated 8 December 1982, quoted in LeoGrande, *Our own backyard*, p. 303.
27 The Court ruled in favour of Nicaragua in June 1986 and ordered the US government to pay damages.
28 The first Esquipulas Peace Accord had been signed in May 1986 at Esquipulas in Guatemala.
29 See Haig, *Caveat*, p. 266.
30 See Haig, *Caveat*, pp. 297–8.
31 Statement dated 13 April 1979, quoted in Gary Williams, 'Prelude to intervention: Grenada 1983', *Journal of Latin American Studies* 29 (1997), p. 133.
32 Shultz, *Turmoil and triumph*, p. 329.
33 Shultz, *Turmoil and triumph*, p. 344.
34 Speech dated 7 June 1984, quoted in Riordan Roett, 'The debt crisis: economics and politics', in Martz, *US policy in Latin America*, p. 250.
35 Speech dated 23 September 1985, quoted in Roett, 'Debt crisis', p. 254.
36 Quoted in Sue Branford and Bernardo Kucinski, *The debt squads: the US, the banks, and Latin America* (London: Zed, 1987), p. 1.
37 James A. Baker, III, *The politics of diplomacy: revolution, war and peace, 1989–1992* (New York: G. P. Putnam's Sons, 1995), p. 607.
38 Speech dated 16 September 1992, quoted in George W. Grayson, 'US–Mexican relations: the challenge of NAFTA', in Martz, *US policy in Latin America*, p. 129. For an account of the complex diplomatic negotiations see Maxwell Cameron and Brian Tomlin, *The making of NAFTA: how the deal was done* (Ithaca, NY: Cornell University Press, 2000).
39 Statement dated 2 April 1992, quoted in Morris Morley and Chris McGillion, *Unfinished business: America and Cuba after the cold war, 1989–2001* (Cambridge: Cambridge University Press 2002), p. 25.
40 Statement dated 8 January 2001, quoted in Morley and McGillion, *Unfinished business*, p. 186.
41 An excellent study of US policy is William O. Walker, *Drug control in the Americas* (Albuquerque, NM: University of New Mexico Press, 1989).
42 Statement dated 12 September 1985, quoted in Walker, *Drug control*, p. 206.
43 Quoted in Walker, *Drug control*, p. 217.

44 Quoted in Margaret E. Scranton, *The Noriega years: US-Panamanian relations, 1981–1990* (Boulder, CO: Lynne Rienner. 1991), p. 203. To justify intervention President Bush cited article 51 of the UN Charter that allowed nations to exercise the inherent right of self-defence in response to armed attacks. Only a few days earlier an American officer, Lieutenant Robert Paz, had been shot and killed in Panama by Noriega's police forces. Noriega had argued earlier that American provocation had created a state of war between Panama and the United States.

45 Baker, *Politics of diplomacy*, pp. 193–4.

SELECTED BIBLIOGRAPHY

Documents and documentary collections

Commager, Henry Steele (ed.), *Documents of American history* (2 vols) (New York: Crofts, 1944, 3rd edition).
Department of State, *Papers relating to the foreign relations of the United States* (Washington DC: US Government Printing Office, 1862–).
Gantenbein, James W. (ed.), *The evolution of our Latin-American policy: a documentary record* (New York: Octagon, 1950).
Holden, Robert H. and Eric Zolov (eds), *Latin America and the United States: a documentary history* (New York: Oxford University Press, 2000).
Manning, William R., *Diplomatic correspondence of the United States concerning the independence of the Latin-American nations* (3 vols) (New York: Oxford UP, 1925).
Richardson, James D. (ed.), *A compilation of the messages and papers of the presidents, 1789–1897* (10 vols) (Washington, DC: Government Printing Office, 1896–9).
Schlesinger, Arthur M. Jr. (ed.), *The dynamics of world power: a documentary history of United States foreign policy, 1945–1973* (5 vols) (New York: Chelsea House, 1983).
Webster, Charles K. (ed.), *Britain and the independence of Latin America, 1812–1830. Select documents from the Foreign Office archives* (2 vols) (London: Oxford University Press, 1938).

Textbooks/surveys

Bemis, Samuel Flagg, *The Latin American policy of the United States: an historical interpretation* (New York: Norton, 1971).
Coerver, Don M. and Linda B. Hall, *Tangled destinies: Latin America and the United States* (Albuquerque, NM: University of New Mexico Press, 1999).
Connell-Smith, Gordon, *The United States and Latin America: an historical analysis of inter-American relations* (London: Heinemann, 1974).
Gilderhus, Mark, *The second century: US–Latin American relations since 1889* (Wilmington, DE: Scholarly Resources, 2000).
Langley, Lester D., *America and the Americas: the United States in the western hemisphere* (Athens, GA: University of Georgia Press, 1989).
Longley, Kyle, *In the eagle's shadow: the United States and Latin America* (Wheeling, IL: Harlan Davidson, 2002).
Mecham, J. Lloyd, *A survey of United States–Latin American relations* (Boston, MA: Houghton Mifflin, 1965).

Molineu, Harold, *US policy toward Latin America: from regionalism to globalism* (Boulder, CO: Westview, 1986).
Niess, Frank, *Hemisphere to itself: a history of US–Latin American relations* (London: Zed, 1990).
Schoultz, Lars, *Beneath the United States: a history of US policy toward Latin America* (Cambridge, MA: Harvard University Press, 1998).
Smith, Peter H., *Talons of the eagle: dynamics of US–Latin American relations* (New York: Oxford University Press, 1996).

Bilateral relations

Coatsworth, John H., *Central America and the United States: the clients and the colossus* (New York: Twayne, 1994).
Conniff, Michael L., *Panama and the United States: the forced alliance* (Athens, GA: University of Georgia Press, 2001, 2nd edn).
Findling, John E., *Close neighbors, distant friends: United States-Central American relations* (New York: Greenwood, 1987).
LaFeber, Walter, *Inevitable revolutions: the United States in Central America* (New York: Norton, 1993).
Leonard, Thomas M., *Central America and the United States: the search for stability* (Athens, GA: University of Georgia Press, 1991).
Pérez, Louis A., Jr., *Cuba and the United States: ties of singular intimacy* (Athens, GA: University of Georgia Press, 1990).
Plummer, Brenda Gayle, *Haiti and the United States: the psychological moment* (Athens, GA: University of Georgia Press, 1992).
Randall, Stephen J., *Colombia and the United States: hegemony and independence* (Athens, GA: University of Georgia Press, 1992).
Sater, William F., *Chile and the United States: empires in conflict* (Athens, GA: University of Georgia Press, 1990).
Schmitt, Karl M., *Mexico and the United States, 1821–1973: conflict and coexistence* (New York: Wiley, 1974).
Tulchin, Joseph S., *Argentina and the United States: a conflictual relationship* (Boston, MA: Twayne, 1990).
Vázquez, Josefina Zoraida and Lorenzo Meyer, *The United States and Mexico* (Chicago, IL: University of Chicago Press, 1985).

Special studies

Bulmer-Thomas, Victor, *The economic history of Latin America since independence* (Cambridge: Cambridge University Press, 1994).
Connell-Smith, Gordon, *The Inter-American system* (Oxford: Oxford University Press, 1966).
Dozer, Donald Marquand, *The Monroe doctrine: its modern significance* (New York: Knopf, 1965).
Hunt, Michael H., *Ideology and US foreign policy* (New Haven, CT: Yale University Press, 1987).
Johnson, John J., *Latin America in caricature* (Austin, TX: University of Texas Press, 1980).
Joseph, Gilbert M., Catherine C. LeGrand and Ricardo D. Salvatore (eds), *Close encounters of empire: writing the cultural history of US–Latin American relations* (Durham, NC: Duke University Press, 1998).

LaFeber, Walter, *The Panama canal: the crisis in historical perspective* (New York: Oxford University Press, 1989).
Mecham, J. Lloyd, *The United States and inter-American security, 1889–1960* (Austin, TX: University of Texas Press, 1961).
Park, James William, *Latin American underdevelopment: a history of perspectives in the United States, 1870–1965* (Baton Rouge, LA: Louisiana State University Press, 1995).
Pike, Fredrick B. *The United States and Latin America: myths and stereotypes of civilization and nature* (Austin, TX: University of Texas Press, 1992).
Sheinin, David (ed.), *Beyond the ideal: Pan Americanism in inter-American affairs* (Westport, CT: Praeger, 2000).

Independence

Brooks, Philip C., *Diplomacy and the borderlands: The Adams–Onís treaty of 1819* (Berkeley, CA: University of California Press, 1939).
Chávez, Thomas E., *Spain and the independence of the United States: an intrinsic gift* (Albuquerque, NM: University of New Mexico Press, 2002).
Hilton, Stanley E., 'The United States and Brazilian Independence', in A. J. R. Russell-Wood (ed.), *From colony to nation* (Baltimore, MD: Johns Hopkins University Press, 1975), pp. 109–29.
Horsman, Reginald, *The diplomacy of the new republic, 1776–1815* (Arlington Heights, IL: Harlan Davidson, 1985).
Johnson, John J., *A hemisphere apart: the foundations of United States policy toward Latin America* (Baltimore, MD: Johns Hopkins University Press, 1990).
Langley, Lester D., *The Americas in the age of revolution, 1750–1850* (New Haven, CT: Yale University Press, 1996).
Liss, Peggy K., *Atlantic empires: the network of trade and revolution, 1713–1826* (Baltimore, MD: Johns Hopkins University Press, 1983).
Lynch, John, *The Spanish-American revolutions, 1808–1826* (London: Norton, 1973).
Perkins, Dexter, *The Monroe doctrine, 1823–1826* (Cambridge, MA: Harvard University Press, 1927).
Shurbutt, T. Ray (ed.), *United States–Latin American relations, 1800–1850* (Tuscaloosa, AL: University of Alabama Press, 1991).
Waddell, D. A. G., 'International politics and Latin American independence', in Leslie Bethell (ed.), *The Independence of Latin America* (Cambridge: Cambridge University Press, 1987), pp. 195–226.
Weeks, William Earl, *John Quincy Adams and American global empire* (Lexington, KY: University Press of Kentucky, 1992).
Whitaker, Arthur P., *The United States and the independence of Latin America, 1800–1830* (Baltimore, MD: Johns Hopkins Press, 1941).

Territorial expansionism

Bauer, K. Jack, *The Mexican war, 1846–1848* (Lincoln, NE: University of Nebraska Press, 1974).
Brown, Charles H., *Agents of manifest destiny: the lives and times of the filibusters* (Chapel Hill, NC: University of North Carolina Press, 1980).
Horsman, Reginald, *Race and manifest destiny: the origins of American racial anglo-saxonism* (Cambridge, MA: Harvard University Press, 1981).

May, Robert E., *Manifest destiny's underworld: filibustering in antebellum America* (Chapel Hill, NC: University of North Carolina Press, 2002).

Merk, Frederick, *Manifest destiny and mission in American history: a reinterpretation* (New York, Vintage, 1966).

Paolino, Ernest N., *The foundations of the American empire: William Henry Seward and US foreign policy* (Ithaca, NY: Cornell University Press, 1973).

Perkins, Dexter, *The Monroe doctrine, 1826–1867* (Baltimore, MD: Johns Hopkins Press, 1933).

Pletcher, David M., *The diplomacy of annexation: Texas, Oregon, and the Mexican War* (Columbia, MO: University of Missouri Press, 1973).

Seckinger, Ron, *The Brazilian monarchy and the South American republics, 1822–1831: diplomacy and state building* (Baton Rouge, LA: Louisiana State University Press, 1984).

Weber, David J., *The Mexican frontier, 1821–1846: the American southwest under Mexico* (Albuquerque, NM: University of New Mexico Press, 1982).

Pan-Americanism

Beisner, Robert L., *From the old diplomacy to the new, 1865–1900* (Arlington Heights, IL: Harlan Davidson, 1986).

Campbell, Charles S., *The transformation of American foreign relations, 1865–1900* (New York: Harper & Row, 1976).

Foner, Philip S., *The Spanish–Cuban–American war and the birth of American imperialism* (2 vols) (New York: Monthly Review Press, 1972).

Grenville, J. A. S. and George B. Young, *Politics, strategy, and American diplomacy: studies in foreign policy, 1873–1917 (*New Haven, CT: Yale University Press, 1966).

Healy, David F., *The United States in Cuba 1898–1902: generals, politicians, and the search for policy* (Madison, WI: University of Wisconsin Press, 1963).

Healy, David, *James G. Blaine and Latin America* (Columbia, MO: University of Missouri Press, 2001).

LaFeber, Walter, *The new empire: an interpretation of American expansion, 1860–1898* (Ithaca, NY: Cornell University Press, 1963).

Leonard, Thomas M. (ed.), *United States–Latin American relations, 1850–1903: establishing a relationship* (Tuscaloosa, AL: University of Alabama Press, 1999).

McGann, Thomas F., *Argentina, the United States, and the inter-American system, 1880–1914* (Cambridge, MA: Harvard University Press, 1957).

May Ernest R., *Imperial democracy: the emergence of America as a great power* (New York: Harcourt, Brace and World, 1961).

Offner, John L., *An unwanted war: the diplomacy of the United States and Spain over Cuba, 1895–1898* (Chapel Hill, NC: University of North Carolina Press, 1992).

Parks, E. Taylor, *Colombia and the United States, 1765–1934* (Durham, NC: Duke University Press, 1935).

Pérez, Louis A., Jr., *Cuba between empires, 1878–1902* (Pittsburgh, PA: University of Pittsburgh Press, 1983).

——, *The war of 1898: the United States and Cuba in history and historiography* (Chapel Hill, NC: University of North Carolina Press, 1998).

Perkins, Dexter, *The Monroe doctrine, 1867–1907* (Baltimore, MD: Johns Hopkins Press, 1937).

Pletcher, David M., *The awkward years: American foreign relations under Garfield and Arthur* (Columbia, MO: University of Missouri Press, 1962).

——, *The diplomacy of trade and investment: American economic expansion in the hemisphere, 1865–1900* (Columbia, MO: University of Missouri Press, 1998).
Smith, Joseph, *Illusions of conflict: Anglo-American diplomacy toward Latin America, 1865–1896* (Pittsburgh, PA: University of Pittsburgh Press, 1979).
——, *The Spanish–American War: conflict in the Caribbean and the Pacific, 1895–1902* (New York: Longman, 1994).
Trask, David F., *The war with Spain in 1898* (New York: Macmillan, 1981).

Dollar diplomacy

Albert, Bill, *South America and the First World War: the impact of the war on Brazil, Argentina, Peru, and Chile* (Cambridge: Cambridge University Press, 1988).
Benjamin, Jules R., *The United States and Cuba: hegemony and dependent development, 1880–1934* (Pittsburgh, PA: University of Pittsburgh Press, 1977).
Calder, Bruce J., *The impact of intervention: the Dominican republic during the US occupation of 1916–1924* (Austin, TX: University of Texas Press, 1984).
Collin, Richard H., *Theodore Roosevelt's Caribbean: the Panama canal, the Monroe doctrine, and the Latin American context* (Baton Rouge, LA: Louisiana State University Press, 1990).
Drake, Paul W. (ed.), *Money doctors, foreign debts, and economic reforms in Latin America from the 1890s to the present* (Wilmington, DE: Scholarly Resources, 1994).
Gilderhus, Mark T., *Pan American visions: Woodrow Wilson in the western hemisphere, 1913–1921* (Tuscon, AZ: University of Arizona Press, 1986).
Grieb, Kenneth J., *The United States and Huerta* (Lincoln, NE: University of Nebraska Press, 1969).
——, *The Latin American policy of Warren G. Harding* (Fort Worth, TX: Texas Christian University Press, 1976).
Hall, Linda B. and Don M. Coerver, *Revolution on the border: the United States and Mexico, 1910–1920* (Albuquerque, NM: University of New Mexico Press, 1988).
Healy, David, *Drive to hegemony: the United States in the Caribbean, 1898–1917* (Madison, WI: University of Wisconsin Press, 1988).
Katz, Friedrich, *The secret war in Mexico: Europe, the United States, and the Mexican revolution* (Chicago, IL: University of Chicago Press, 1981).
Lael, Richard L., *Arrogant diplomacy: US policy toward Colombia, 1903–1922* (Wilmington, DE: Scholarly Resources, 1987).
Langley, Lester D., *The banana wars: United States intervention in the Caribbean, 1898–1934* (Lexington, KY: University of Kentucky Press, 1985).
—— and Thomas D. Schoonover, *The banana men: American mercenaries and entrepreneurs in Central America, 1880–1930* (Lexington, KY: University Press of Kentucky, 1995).
Major, John, *Prize possession: the United States and the Panama canal, 1903–1979* (Cambridge: Cambridge University Press, 1993).
Martin, Percy A., *Latin America and the war* (Baltimore, MD: Johns Hopkins Press, 1925).
Meyer, Lorenzo, *Mexico and the United States in the oil controversy, 1917–1942* (Austin, TX: University of Texas Press, 1972).
Munro, Dana G., *Intervention and dollar diplomacy in the Caribbean, 1900–1921* (Princeton, NJ: Princeton University Press, 1964).
Nearing, Scott and Joseph Freeman, *Dollar diplomacy: a study in American imperialism* (New York: Viking, 1925).

Pérez, Louis A., Jr., *Cuba under the Platt amendment, 1902–1934* (Pittsburgh, PA: University of Pittsburgh Press, 1986).
Quirk, Robert E., *An affair of honor: Woodrow Wilson and the occupation of Veracruz* (New York: Norton, 1967).
Renda, Mary, *Taking Haiti: military occupation and the culture of US imperialism, 1915–1940* (Chapel Hill: University of North Carolina Press, 2001).
Rosenberg, Emily S., *Financial missionaries to the world: the politics and culture of dollar diplomacy, 1900–1930* (Durham, NC: Duke University Press, 2003).
——, 'Revisiting dollar diplomacy: narratives of money and manliness', *Diplomatic History* 22 (1998), pp. 155–76.
Scholes, Walter V. and Marie V., *The foreign policies of the Taft administration* (Columbia, MO: University of Missouri Press, 1970).
Smith, Joseph, *Unequal giants: diplomatic relations between the United States and Brazil, 1889–1930* (Pittsburgh, PA: Pittsburgh University Press, 1991).
Smith, Robert Freeman, *The United States and revolutionary nationalism in Mexico, 1916–1932* (Chicago, IL: University of Chicago Press, 1972).
Tulchin, Joseph S., *The aftermath of war: World War I and US policy toward Latin America* (New York: New York University Press, 1971).
Woods, Kenneth F., '"Imperialistic America": a landmark in the development of US policy toward Latin America', *Inter-American Economic Affairs* 21 (1967), pp. 55–72.

Good neighbours

DeConde, Alexander, *Herbert Hoover's Latin-American policy* (Stanford, CA: Stanford University Press, 1951).
Francis, Michael J., *The limits of hegemony: United States relations with Argentina and Chile during World War II* ((Notre Dame, IN: University of Notre Dame Press, 1977).
Friedman, Max Paul, *Nazis and good neighbors: the United States campaign against the Germans of Latin America in World War II* (Cambridge: Cambridge University Press, 2003).
Gardner, Lloyd C., *Economic aspects of new deal diplomacy* (Madison, WI: University of Wisconsin Press, 1964).
Gellman, Irwin F., *Good neighbor diplomacy: United States policies in Latin America, 1933–1945* (Baltimore, MD: Johns Hopkins University Press, 1979).
Green, David, *The containment of Latin America: a history of the myths and realities of the good neighbor policy* (Chicago, IL: Quadrangle, 1971).
Hilton, Stanley E., *Brazil and the great powers, 1930–1939: the politics of trade rivalry* (Austin, TX: University of Texas Press, 1975).
Humphreys, R.A., *Latin America and the Second World War* (2 vols) (London: Athlone Press, 1981–2).
MacDonald, Callum A., 'The politics of intervention: the United States and Argentina, 1941–1946', *Journal of Latin America Studies* 12 (1980), pp. 365–96.
McCann, Frank D., Jr., *The Brazilian-American alliance, 1937–1945* (Princeton, NJ: Princeton University Press, 1974).
O'Brien, Thomas F., *The revolutionary mission: American enterprise in Latin America, 1900–1945* (Cambridge: Cambridge University Press, 1996).
Roorda, Eric Paul, *The dictator next door: the good neighbor policy and the Trujillo regime in the Dominican republic, 1930–1945* (Durham, NC: Duke University Press, 1998).

Steward, Dick, *Trade and hemisphere: the good neighbor policy and reciprocal trade* (Columbia, MO: University of Missouri Press, 1975).
Wood, Bryce, *The making of the good neighbor policy* (New York: Norton, 1967).

Cold War politics

Bailey, Samuel L., *The United States and the development of South America, 1945–1975* (New York: New Viewpoints, 1976).
Benjamin, Jules R., *The United States and the origins of the Cuban revolution: an empire of liberty in an age of national liberation* (Princeton, PA: Princeton University Press, 1990).
Blasier, Cole, *The hovering giant: US responses to revolutionary change in Latin America* (Pittsburgh, PA: University of Pittsburgh Press, 1976).
—*The giant's rival: the USSR and Latin America* (Pittsburgh, PA: University of Pittsburgh Press, 1983).
Child, John, *Unequal alliance: the inter-American military system, 1938–1978* (Boulder, CO: Westview, 1980).
Davis, Nathaniel, *The last two years of Salvador Allende* (London: Tauris, 1985).
Gambone, Michael D., *Eisenhower, Somoza, and the cold war in Nicaragua, 1953–1961* (Westport, CT: Praeger, 1997).
Gleijeses, Piero, *The Dominican crisis: the 1965 constitutionalist revolt and American intervention* (Baltimore, MD: Johns Hopkins University Press, 1978).
——, *Shattered hope: the Guatemalan revolution and the United States, 1944–1954* (Princeton, NJ: Princeton University Press, 1991).
——, 'Ships in the night: the CIA, the White House and the Bay of Pigs', *Journal of Latin American Studies* 27 (1995), pp. 1–42.
Hersh, Seymour M., *Kissinger: the price of power. Henry Kissinger in the White House* (London: Faber & Faber, 1983).
Higgins, Trumbull, *The perfect failure: Kennedy, Eisenhower, and the CIA at the Bay of Pigs* (New York: Norton, 1987).
Immerman, Richard H., *The CIA in Guatemala: the foreign policy of intervention* (Austin, TX: University of Texas Press, 1982).
Levinson, Jerome and Juan de Onís, *The alliance that lost its way: a critical report on the Alliance for Progress* (Chicago, IL: Quadrangle, 1970).
Longley, Kyle, *The sparrow and the hawk: Costa Rica and the United States during the rise of José Figueres* (Tuscaloosa, AL: University of Alabama Press, 1997).
Lowenthal, Abraham F., *The Dominican intervention* (Cambridge, MA: Harvard University Press, 1972).
—— (ed.), *Exporting democracy: the United States and Latin America: themes and issues* (Baltimore, MD: Johns Hopkins University Press, 1991).
McPherson, Alan, *Yankee no! Anti-Americanism in US–Latin American relations* (Cambridge, MA: Harvard University Press, 2003).
Martz, John D. (ed.), *United States policy in Latin America: a quarter century of crisis and challenge, 1961–1986* (Lincoln, NE: University of Nebraska Press, 1988).
Morley, Morris H., *Imperial state and revolution: the United States and Cuba, 1952–1986* (Cambridge: Cambridge University Press, 1987).
Parker, Phyllis R., *Brazil and the quiet intervention, 1964* (Austin, TX: University of Texas Press, 1979).
Paterson, Thomas G., *Contesting Castro: the United States and the triumph of the Cuban revolution* (New York: Oxford University Press, 1994).
Quirk, Robert E., *Fidel Castro* (New York: Norton, 1993).

Rabe, Stephen G., *Eisenhower and Latin America: the foreign policy of anticommunism* (Chapel Hill, NC: University of North Carolina Press, 1988).
Schlesinger, Arthur M., Jr., *A thousand days: John F. Kennedy in the White House* (Boston, MA: Houghton Mifflin, 1965).
Schlesinger, Stephen and Stephen Kinzer, *Bitter fruit: the untold story of the American coup in Guatemala* (Garden City, NY: Doubleday, 1982).
Sigmund, Paul E., *The overthrow of Allende and the politics of Chile, 1964–1976* (Pittsburgh: University of Pittsburgh Press, 1977).
Smith, Gaddis, *The last years of the Monroe doctrine, 1945–1993* (New York: Hill and Wang, 1994).
Weis, W. Michael, *Cold warriors and coups d'état: Brazilian-American relations, 1945–1964* (Albuquerque, NM: University of New Mexico Press, 1993).
Wood, Bryce, *The dismantling of the good neighbor policy* (Austin: TX: University of Texas Press, 1985).

End of the twentieth century

Carothers, Thomas, *In the name of democracy: US policy toward Latin America in the Reagan years* (Berkeley, CA: University of California Press, 1991).
Child, Jack, *The Central American peace process, 1983–1991: sheathing swords, building confidence* (Boulder, CO: Lynne Reinner, 1992).
Grayson, George W., *The North American free trade agreement: regional community and the new world order* (Lanham, MD: University Press of America, 1995).
Haig, Alexander M., Jr., *Caveat: realism, Reagan, and foreign policy* (London: Weidenfeld and Nicolson, 1984).
Jorden, William J., *Panama odyssey* (Austin, TX: University of Texas Press, 1984).
LeoGrande, William M., *Our own backward: the United States in Central America, 1977–1992* (Chapel Hill, NC: University of North Carolina Press, 1998).
Lowenthal, Abraham, *Partners in conflict: the United States and Latin America* (Baltimore, MD: Johns Hopkins University Press, 1987).
Martz, John D. (ed.), *United States policy in Latin America: a decade of crisis and challenge* (Lincoln, NE: University of Nebraska Press, 1995).
Pastor, Robert A., *Whirlpool: US foreign policy toward Latin America and the Caribbean* (Princeton, NJ: Princeton University Press, 1992).
Schoultz, Lars, *Human rights and United States policy toward Latin America* (Princeton, NJ: Princeton University Press, 1981).
Scranton, Margaret E., *The Noriega years: US-Panamanian relations, 1981–1990* (Boulder, CO: Lynne Rienner, 1991).
Walker, Thomas W. (ed.), *Reagan versus the Sandinistas: the undeclared war on Nicaragua* (Boulder, CO: 1987).
Walker, William O., *Drug control in the Americas* (Albuquerque, NM: University of New Mexico Press, 1989).

INDEX